THE FRAGMENTED POLITICS OF URBAN PRESERVATION

Globalization and Community
Susan E. Clarke, Series Editor
Dennis R. Judd, Founding Editor

(continued on page 203)

The Fragmented Politics of Urban Preservation

BEIJING, CHICAGO, AND PARIS

Yue Zhang

Globalization and Community, Volume 22

University of Minnesota Press
Minneapolis
London

Portions of chapter 2 were originally published as "Steering toward Growth: Symbolic Urban Preservation in Beijing, 1990–2005," *Town Planning Review* 79 (2–3): 187–208; reprinted with permission of Liverpool University Press. Portions of chapter 3 were originally published as "Boundaries of Power: Politics of Urban Preservation in Two Chicago Neighborhoods," *Urban Affairs Review* 47 (4): 511–40; reprinted with permission from Sage Publications, Ltd. http://online.sagepub.com.

Maps created by the Urban Data Visualization Lab, University of Illinois at Chicago.

Unless otherwise credited, all photographs were taken by the author.

Published by the University of Minnesota Press
111 Third Avenue South, Suite 290
Minneapolis, MN 55401-2520
http://www.upress.umn.edu

A Cataloging-in-Publication record for this book is available from the Library of Congress.
ISBN 978-0-8166-8368-0 (hc)
ISBN 978-0-8166-8369-7 (pb)

Printed in the United States of America on acid-free paper

The University of Minnesota is an equal-opportunity educator and employer.

20   19   18   17   16   15   14   13   10   9   8   7   6   5   4   3   2   1

For my parents

CONTENTS

ACKNOWLEDGMENTS

My initial interest in the topic of urban preservation was kindled by the drastic urban transformation of my hometown, Beijing. Since the late 1990s, Beijing has gone through rapid urban renewal, and a large proportion of the historic city has vanished under the wrecking ball. I was sad to see that many places from my memory were gone and that the city had become increasingly unfamiliar. So I decided to write this book. By looking at other cities in the world and exploring how they have handled their architectural legacies, I hope to better understand what happened in my city.

In the course of researching and writing this book, I accumulated enormous personal debts of gratitude to many people and institutions.

This book had its origins as a doctoral dissertation in politics at Princeton University, and I would like to express my profound gratitude to my dissertation committee members—Lynn T. White, Stanley N. Katz, Paul J. DiMaggio, Jessica L. Trounstine, and Michael N. Danielson—for their advice, sustained interest in my project, and unflagging academic and personal support throughout the years. Lynn has been an incredible advisor and mentor. He set a high standard for scholarship and provided constant encouragement and guidance during my graduate study at Princeton. Stan has been an inspirational guide during every stage of this project and taught me to embrace a humanistic vision in social science research. Paul was always able to steer my project in a much better direction by raising questions that alerted me to unseen political and social dynamics. Jessica encouraged me to think big and tie urban preservation to larger questions of democracy. Mike walked me into the world of urban politics research and guided me to crystallize my interest in urban preservation into concrete research questions and projects.

In addition to my dissertation committee, I was fortunate to be surrounded by wise and supportive faculty and peers at Princeton. Special thanks go to Ezra N. Suleiman, Gilbert Rozman, Steven J. Tepper, Susan Naquin, and the participants in the Comparative Politics Research Seminar in the Politics Department for their encouragement and helpful feedback at various stages of the project.

I must also thank Princeton University for its institutional support. The generous financial assistance provided by Princeton enabled fieldwork for this project. My preliminary study of the three cities was made possible by a research grant from the Princeton University Center for Arts and Cultural Policy Studies. The center quickly became a home and, under the efficient yet gregarious leadership of Stanley N. Katz and Paul J. DiMaggio, occupies truly cherished place in my heart. The workshops at the center were an invaluable source of inspiration for my research and provided good venues for me to present my work in progress. I also received crucial financial support throughout my dissertation writing from the Princeton University Institute for International and Regional Studies, the Program in East Asian Studies, and the Princeton–Harvard China and the World Program. I thank all these institutions and agencies for their generous support.

This project is based on extensive fieldwork in Beijing, Paris, and Chicago from 2003 to 2010. I am deeply indebted to the many people who generously took the time to share with me their knowledge, stories, and views on cities. In Beijing, Wang Changsheng, Wang Jianping, Ge Xun, and Wang Youquan offered me the rare access to many preservation projects in the field. Wang Jun and Xu Yong inspired me to dig harder and deeper into the spatial transformation in urban China. In Paris, Patrick Terrior connected me to many key figures in French local and national government and took me to see some of the urban gems of Paris. Bernard Franjou allowed me to bother him frequently and showed me how preservation projects were implemented in Paris. Claire Monod, Dominique Masson, and Elsa Martayan helped me draw a better picture of intergovernmental relations in France. Francesco Bandarin, former director of the UNESCO World Heritage Center, lent me a global vision to investigate the issue of cultural heritage preservation. In Chicago, Tim Samuelson offered me the first and best introduction to the city's history of urban preservation. Brian Goeken and Phyllis M. Ellin greatly enhanced my understanding of how local politics works. Blair Kamin told me why architecture matters and kindled my interest in exploring the stories behind every great building in the city. Paula Robinson, Harold Lucas, Johnnie Blair, and Jonathan Fine showed me the strength of local communities. My exploration of the urban world would have been very different without the many people I got to know during my fieldwork. Collectively, their valuable inputs greatly informed the analyses presented here and made my journey in the three cities a much enjoyable one. I am fortunate to be unable to distinguish who helped with research from who brightened my life with friendship. This book was completed in Chicago after I started my first job in the Department of Political Science at the University of Illinois at Chicago (UIC). My colleagues in different departments at UIC provided good vibes and collegial support. I appreciate several long conversations with Dennis Judd, which were crucial in framing some of the key theoretical questions in the final version of the book. Anthony Orum provided sustained support to my research and has been a reliable source of intellectual companionship. Robert Bruegmann's insightful comments and suggestions have challenged me and greatly improved this manuscript. I also received extremely helpful feedback on research design, data analysis, drafts of chapters, and the publishing process from Dick Simpson, Andrew McFarland, Karen Mossberger, Doris A. Graber, Evan McKenzie, Stephen Engelmann, and Yoram Haftel. Patricia Hajek, Armel Yver, Leslie Price, and Abe Singer are excellent research assistants who helped update some of the data used in the book and proofread part of the manuscript. Nina Savar helped make the maps in the book. A fellowship granted from the Great Cities Institute at UIC provided crucial funding to enable concentrated writing in 2009 and 2010.

Many of the ideas in the book were inspired by conversations and e-mail exchanges with colleagues around the world. I would like to thank specially Françoise Choay, Vincent L. Michael, Larry Bennett, Terry N. Clark, D. Carroll Joynes, Roberta Garner, Martin Horak, Liu Jian, Bian Lanchun, Fulong Wu, Xuefei Ren, Shen Zhihua, Li Danhui, Patrick Le Galè, and Yankel Fijalkow. My undergraduate advisor at Peking University, Xu Zhenzhou, was among the first people who nurtured my initial interest in historic cities. Vincent Renard generously kept his office door open for me when I was conducting fieldwork in Paris, and without hesitation he shared with me his research resources, his enthusiasm for academia, and his love for cities. Luca Zan kindly read the whole manuscript at the final revision stage and provided insightful feedback for revision.

I am also grateful to Pieter Martin, my editor at the University of Minnesota Press, who has been exceptionally supportive and patient in guiding me through the production process. Kristian Tvedten provided very helpful and friendly editorial assistance. Susan Clarke and two anonymous reviewers offered perceptive comments and invaluable recommendations. I thank them all.

The journey of making this book would have been unimaginable without friends and family. I will always be grateful to Sida Liu, who read and edited every chapter of this manuscript more than once and offered incredible support to my research with his heart and mind. I am indebted to my friends for their precious presence in moments of need, above all Ying Liu, Dongning Guo, Jing Chen, Jesse Menefee, Wei Zhang, Elaine Yuan, Sergio López-Piñeiro, Quinton Mayne, Alan Lepp, Anthony V. Pulido, and Stephen Stults. Finally, the love and support from my parents over the years made it possible for me to study and travel the world. Their life philosophy always inspires me and gives me strength while I am continuing my urban journey. To you all, I offer my most heartfelt thanks.

The Paradox of Urban Preservation

The city, however, does not tell its past, but contains it like the lines of a hand.
— ITALO CALVINO, *Invisible Cities*

In the summer of 2005, two large preservation projects were taking place in Beijing. The first one was the restoration of Yongdingmen, the central gate of the Outer City located at the southern end of the Central Axis. Originally built in 1553, Yongdingmen was demolished in the 1950s, along with the city walls and thirteen other city gates, in the construction of the socialist capital. The restoration began in 2003 after Beijing was selected as the Host City of the 2008 Olympics Games, and the project was part of the city's "Cultural Heritage Preservation Plan for an Olympiad of Humanity." Experts involved in the project did a thorough examination of the archives to ensure that the new Yongdingmen looked exactly like the old one. The project took two years to complete and cost more than 19 million RMB (3 million USD). The restored Yongdingmen was celebrated by local officials and the news media. They believed it enhanced the cultural significance of Beijing by completing the configuration of the Central Axis, the longest in the world. And because the Olympic Park was located at the northern extension of the Central Axis, the restored Yongdingmen was considered especially meaningful for the status of Beijing as the host city of the Olympics. A local newspaper wrote, "The restored city gate provides a new starting point for Old Beijing to embrace the future."

Further north on the Central Axis, not far from the restored city gate, another preservation project was carried out in a historic district named Qianmen, which was the downtown of imperial Beijing. Qianmen Street, the main thoroughfare of the area, occupies a prominent position in the city, with a large number of established shops and restaurants catering to the demands of a diverse group of customers. Although some of the shops and restaurants were more than a century old and nationally known, the district remained affordable for working-class customers. Using the old photos of Qianmen Street in the early twentieth century as a blueprint, the preservation project remodeled the façade of the buildings along the street, integrating late Qing and early Republican style motifs into the final design. Many old shops and restaurants left Qianmen Street after the preservation project because of the rise in rent. But local officials were not concerned by this loss of tenants, because their goal was to attract outlets of world-renowned luxury brands and "turn Qianmen Street into another Champs-Élysées," to use the words of a local official. A dense residential area made up of centuries-old courtyard houses and surrounding Qianmen Street was demolished in the preservation project. Developers replaced the one-story historic courtyard houses with two- to six-story buildings in antique style for high-end residential and commercial uses. The original residents who lived in the area before were not allowed to move back after the preservation project was completed.

These stories of Beijing provide us a complicated vision of urban preservation at the beginning of the new millennium. Facing the rebuilt city gate, the remodeled shopping street, and the brand new housing stock with historical appearance, all created through preservation projects, we cannot help but wonder, What is preservation?

In any book on the history or theory of urban preservation, the very word *preservation* carries a strict meaning. It is defined as the act or process of applying measures to sustain the existing form, integrity, and material of a building or a site (Murtagh 2006). The basic dictum of the professional preservationist is to keep as much of the original fabric as possible. Furthermore, history shows that urban preservation is by nature a humanistic endeavor. The earliest preservation efforts date back to the days of the Roman Empire, when historic monuments were carefully maintained for future generations, in order to provide them a tangible form of connection to the past (Riegl 1982 [1903]). In the age of industrialization, when the existence of historic cities was threatened by urban renewal, the subject of preservation expanded from individual monuments to urban residences and entire city blocks, the so-called urban fabric. This development in preservation practice protects residents from dislocation and thus mediates the devastating social impact of modernization.

It seems self-evident that urban preservation's essence is to protect the architectural integrity and social sustainability of cities. In reality, however, *preservation* has become an umbrella term encompassing a variety of activities. Some of them are in conflict with the original meaning of *preservation* and present challenges to the humanistic concerns historically associated with the term. Beijing is not alone in creating a picture of urban preservation fraught with controversies. In cities from West to East, the practice of urban preservation has become increasingly problematic. This book seeks to explain the complexities and controversies in the practice of urban preservation in modern cities, investigating the politics of urban preservation by answering two specific sets of questions. First, why do governments in different cities have different understandings of what urban preservation is and make distinct decisions about what to preserve and how to preserve it? Second, how are the various preservation initiatives being implemented by the government, and why are some of them more likely to be carried out than others?

In this book, the politics of urban preservation is explored through a comparison of preservation practices in Beijing, Chicago, and Paris from the 1980s to the present. As three great cities of the world, they have prominent positions in the history of architecture and planning, yet their urban landscapes are under constant challenges of creative destruction. Although urban preservation is considered an important policy issue in all three cities, their preservation practices vary significantly. To explain the various preservation practices in the three cities, the book argues that urban preservation has become a strategic device used by different political and social actors to fulfill their distinct and occasionally contradictory goals. Whereas the content of the preservation initiatives is defined by the interests and preferences of different actors, implementation of the initiatives is constrained by the fragmented power structure in cities. Political fragmentation serves as a filter, facilitating the implementation of preservation initiatives within single jurisdictions while prohibiting the implementation across jurisdictional boundaries. For cross-boundary issues, different types of political fragmentation are associated with predictable patterns of policy processes and settlements, thus creating different patterns of urban preservation.

The experiences of the three cities demonstrate how political institutions are intertwined with interests and inclinations, fundamentally shaping the policy process of urban preservation. In Beijing, urban preservation is a tool for the local government to promote economic growth and create a better image for the city. While many historic monuments were restored as cultural icons in preparation for the Olympics, the functional fragmentation between municipal bureaus prevented historic districts from being effectively protected. With the demolition of old neighborhoods and the construction of historic-looking pastiche, urban preservation has become increasingly symbolic. In Chicago, urban preservation serves the goals of increasing property values and revitalizing neighborhoods, which are often entangled with issues of racial inequality and gentrification. The territorial fragmentation along ward boundaries has turned urban preservation into a privilege of aldermen and blocked the initiatives to preserve neighborhoods across multiple wards. With historic districts largely confined within single wards, urban preservation shows a mosaic pattern. And in Paris, urban preservation provides a channel for national and municipal governments to compete for control over urban space. Whereas the former symbolizes cultural heritage as a source of the French national identity and has long monopolized the power of urban preservation, the latter is empowered by decentralization and has begun to propose a new agenda of balancing preservation and development. The intergovernmental fragmentation has generated a contested yet shared control between the central and local authorities, thus generating a pattern of joint preservation.

Urban preservation is a critical policy issue for cities. The intrinsic historic and artistic value of architectural heritage is a sufficient justification for anyone to devote time and attention to this topic, but urban preservation is a valuable window into much broader issues of economic and social changes in cities, beyond the specific battles to save individual buildings and places. Since the work of Lewis Mumford (1961) and Jane Jacobs (1961), urban scholars have noted that urban preservation has a significant impact on the character of urban development and the quality of life of citizens. Today, when cities are undergoing unprecedented economic restructuring and spatial reorganization in the context of globalization, urban preservation has become increasingly important for shaping a healthier urban environment and strengthening the cultural roots of our society. It deserves greater attention if we have a sincere interest not only in understanding the causes and consequences of changes in cities but also in making our cities better places to live.

The policy process of urban preservation is extremely complex, with various interests and values involved. However, it has received little attention from political scientists. Although a number of urban scholars and preservation practitioners have recognized the significant role of politics in successful or failed preservation efforts, they rarely offer any systematic analysis on how politics influences preservation.[1] By wedding political science theory and method to the study of urban preservation, this book is one of the first efforts to reveal the political underpinnings of urban preservation. It contributes to our understanding of urban preservation in three major ways. First, it challenges many existing conclusions on urban preservation by asking why there are multiple understandings of what urban preservation is, how these understandings are created, and how they are manipulated as part of the political strategy. Answers to those questions reveal the political origins of government efforts. Second, the theory of political fragmentation provides an institutional approach to explain why some preservation initiatives are more likely to be implemented than others. By showing how different types of political fragmentation have affected the policy process of urban preservation in predictable ways, the theory can be applied to other cities beyond the three cases, and it permits comparisons across urban settings. Third, the study is based on extensive fieldwork in three cities on three continents that are embedded in very different cultural and political contexts. The comparative approach not only is critical to test the theoretical framework presented but also depicts a richer picture of the modes of spatial and social governance in cities.

This is a book about urban preservation, but it is also about the interlayered processes by which political actors attempt to transform urban space and govern people's lives through large-scale public policies. The primary theoretical objective of the book is to build the linkages between policy discourse, political institutions, and policy processes. It demonstrates that in order to understand a policy process, we must examine both the substantive aspect and the institutional aspect of the policy initiative. Whereas the former articulates the content of the policy initiative and explains why the policy initiative is proposed as it is, the latter answers how the initiative is processed and why or why not it can be implemented in reality. Any policy analysis is incomplete if either of the two aspects is missing from the discussion. The institutional aspect of the policy initiative of urban preservation is examined in chapter 1 through a detailed analysis of the fragmented power structure in cities. The remainder of this chapter discusses the substantive aspect of preservation initiative by introducing the major motivations behind urban preservation across time and space. It is followed by a brief overview of preservation practices in Beijing, Chicago, and Paris. I also detail the design of the research and provide an overview of the remainder of the book.

Urban Preservation: One Policy, Many Purposes

The essence of any kind of public policy is political reasoning, which offers policymakers a language to form their argument and fulfill their goals (Stone 2002; Rochefort and Cobb 1994; Fischer and Forester 1993). Urban preservation is no exception. It provides a discourse with which political and social actors deliberately and consciously frame their propositions, justify their choices, and promote their favored course of action. The multiple motivations lead to different preservation practices, some of which have challenged the original goals of urban preservation by undermining the architectural integrity and social sustainability of cities. The paradox of urban preservation demonstrates the controversial relationship between history and its instrumental use in human societies. The following section discusses four major purposes that have motivated the practice of urban preservation, through which we can observe the inconsistency between the preservation practice and the original goals of urban preservation.

Preservation for Urban Planning

The relationships between urban preservation and urban development have been the subject of great debates since the post–World War II era. Facing the devastating effects of urban renewal, policymakers began to use urban preservation as a planning device to control development. In 1962, with the passage of the Malraux Act in France and the creation of a master plan for Rome, entire city blocks and streetscapes could be secured behind the fortified boundary lines of historic districts. These preservation ordinances, still in effect today, not only prevent historic structures from being demolished but also regulate any alterations or additions in historic districts. In an attempt to control new development, preservation ordinances are usually associated with zoning policies. In some cities, preservation and zoning ordinances require that new buildings are not taller than historic structures, so that they remove the incentive of the market to demolish and rebuild (Tung 2001).

When used as a strategy to control urban development, urban preservation saves historic cities from the wrecking ball and consequently prevents residents from being displaced by urban renewal. However, it raises the possibility that when little space is allowed for new development, cities might slowly evolve into museums. This type of regulation constrains the space for architectural or economic innovation, thus diminishing the diversity and vigor of urban life—something many European historic centers have already experienced. Some cities have lost between 30 and 90 percent of their residential population, especially those in the lower-income groups, to areas outside the city because living space in the city is scarce and expensive (Choay 2001; Boyer 1994). Besides accommodating a small number of wealthy inhabitants, those cities have increasingly become outdoor museums for tourists, leaving residents to feel that there is no future in their cities.

Preservation for Urban Development

In contrast to its usage as a planning device to control development, urban preservation can be used to attract investment and promote urban revitalization. This goal is achieved by linking urban preservation with tax benefits. In postwar America, the federal government got involved under the nationwide pressure for urban preservation. However, instead of abandoning the agenda of urban renewal, the government tied preservation to urban renewal and changed the latter's bulldozer mentality to one of community rehabilitation through a series of tax ordinances (Boyer 1994). In the Tax Reform Acts of 1976 and 1986, and the Economic Recovery Act of 1981, tax credits are offered to private developers and property owners who rehabilitate and renovate historic structures (Frank 2002; Fitch 1982; Reichl 1997; Newman 2001). These tax ordinances were intended to promote preservation-based urban revitalization in American cities and became a tool for private property owners to obtain tax benefits. It facilitates, rather than inhibits, the government's agenda of urban development.

Although preservation-based redevelopment prevents historic structures from being demolished and gives them a new life through rehabilitation, it largely ignores the welfare of the local residents. As revitalization activity accelerated, real estate values began to rise in inner-city neighborhoods, taxes were reassessed, rents started to climb, and gentrification took place, in which the working class, minorities, and renters were replaced by newcomers who tended to be middle class, white, and property owners (Zukin 1987). Many newcomers were attracted to working-class ethnic neighborhoods by the unique culture and lifestyle, which is ironic, as Sharon Zukin (2010) notes, because it was the newcomers' demands for authenticity that drove out those who first lent the neighborhood its authentic aura. It is evident from the experiences of many cities that when used as a strategy of urban revitalization, urban preservation often caters to the tastes of educated, economically better-off urbanites, reinforcing the entrenched social and economic inequality in cities (Freeman 2006; Smith 1996). Although the concept of social preservation was coined in urban studies literature to emphasize the importance government should assign to protecting the interests of the indigenous, officials have yet to master the actual practice of doing so.

Preservation for International Recognition

The concept of urban preservation is largely an invention of the West, and it was exported and progressively disseminated beyond Europe beginning in the second half of the nineteenth century (Choay 2001). Under the promotion of international organizations, urban preservation has increasingly become a global institution and a way for nation-states to gain international recognition. One of the most influential international initiatives of the kind, the World Heritage Convention, was adopted by the United Nations Educational, Scientific and Cultural Organization in 1972. It proclaimed the universal value of cultural heritage, created a series of obligations for its member countries, and established a World Heritage List as part of the Convention. Assets assigned world heritage status are selected under a complex set of criteria and subject to the purview of an "international system of cooperation and assistance" at the "financial, artistic, scientific and technical" levels. As of September 2012, 190 nations had signed the Convention, and 962 sites had been placed on the World Heritage List.[2]

Many nation-states have launched preservation initiatives as an effort to show their conformity to global standards and gain international recognition. For instance, because the number of monuments inscribed on the World Heritage List tends to be taken as a sign of a country's international prestige, it has become an object of emulation among nation-states, despite the fact that the selection criteria are not always correctly interpreted by public officials (Choay 2001). In some cases, public officials are less interested in protecting cultural heritage than in obtaining heritage status, so that the inscribed heritage sites are short on maintenance and suffer from dilapidation. Major global events, such as the Olympic Games, serve as a stage for nation-states to display their achievement in urban preservation and increase their global prestige. As the two recent host cities of the Olympic Games, Athens and Beijing spent a substantial amount of money renovating and restoring historic monuments after they won the Olympic bid, although both were criticized internationally for their insufficient protection of their cultural heritage beforehand (Long 2003; Wang 2003; Hadoulis 2004).

Preservation for Tourism Economy

Urban preservation has also been used as a strategy for promoting tourism since the late twentieth century. This new function of urban preservation is largely associated with globalization and increased transnational cultural consumption. Historic structures are judged by not only their historic and aesthetic values but also their capacity to attract large crowds of tourists and entice local economic growth. In many cities, historic monuments—even those that vanished long ago—are restored or rebuilt as cultural spectacles to enhance the image of the place. Meanwhile, old neighborhoods are repacked into "historic districts," where buildings are reconstructed in historical styles, pedestrian pathways are paved or cobbled in the old fashion, and stereotypes of urban leisure—open-air cafés, restaurants, craft and souvenir shops, and art galleries—are created to meet the demands of tourists.

Without enough sensitivity to the architectural history or social dimension of cities, those preservation projects usually turn out to be arbitrary and fantastical. They often turn historic urban centers and neighborhoods into Disneyland, undermining rather than increasing the cultural integrity and social sustainability of cities. In Quebec, for example, the entire old city center was reshaped by a vast nationalist and tourist project, where a group of ancient buildings were destroyed, only to be reconstructed in the style of eighteenth-century French architecture (Boyer 1994). In Singapore, the remodeling of the city center as a historic district led to the demolition of massive ancient urban dwellings and the eviction of local residents and older forms of business (Kwok and Low 2002). When used as a strategy to promote tourism, urban preservation has increasingly turned certain segments of cities into tourist bubbles, which are consumption spaces in line with universal tastes (Judd and Fainstein 1999; Clark 2003; While 2006; Trasforini 2002; Zukin 1993). The authentic urban landscape is lost, and quality of life for locals is marginalized in the pursuit of tourism economy.

In sum, individuals, social groups, and government agencies have attached multiple meanings to the concept of urban preservation, which reflect their diverse, sometimes conflicting values and interests. The four categories discussed in this section are examples of the major purposes of modern preservation practice. They are not confined to any particular countries but exist in cross-national urban settings. However, those categories do not cover all actions taking place in the name of urban preservation. There are still many other peculiar purposes that preservation practice serves in different urban contexts. For example, in American cities urban preservation is increasingly used as a strategy for racial minorities to recognize their long neglected history and promote local economic development (Saito 2009a; Boyd 2008). Members of the minority groups may be less interested in preserving the architectural forms in which they live than in protecting minority rights and improving racial equality. It is important to investigate the discourse of urban preservation in specific urban contexts.

A Tale of Three Cities

In an effort to investigate the policy process of urban preservation, this book focuses on the preservation practices in Beijing, Chicago, and Paris. These cities have been chosen because they illustrate a broad range of variation in institutional structures that I believe are critical to the politics of urban preservation. Although they are often considered as places dominated by a strong centralized authority, their political systems are fragmented. More importantly, each of the three cities displays a major type of political fragmentation: Beijing is primarily an example of functional fragmentation, Chicago of territorial fragmentation, and Paris of intergovernmental fragmentation. Thus, they provide fertile conditions for exploring the impact of institutional structures on the policy process. In each city I select preservation projects managed by single jurisdictions and those that are overseen by multiple jurisdictions. This permits me to assess in detail the role of jurisdictional boundaries in the policy process of urban preservation. The cases represent the major preservation debates taking place in each city in recent years, so that they provide the reader with the most up-to-date picture of urban preservation in the three cities.

A reasonable question about the case selection is how one compares three cities that occupy different stages in the historic evolution of preservation practice, with policymakers who have very different priorities, all of which affect the social perceptions of urban preservation in varied ways. Among the three cities, Paris has the longest history of urban preservation and has developed a high extent of public awareness over preservation issues. By contrast, Beijing is in its earliest stage of preservation practice: the public just began to realize the importance of protecting the built environment after its economic boom in the 1990s. Chicago is somewhere in the middle, as the preservation movement began in the city in the turmoil of the postwar urban renewal. Specifically, the fact that urban preservation emerged in Beijing after a drastic economic expansion increases the difficulty of systematically protecting the urban landscape.

This book does not deny the importance of time in explaining the differences in preservation practices across cities and countries. However, to simply reduce the differences to time or history does not tell us much about why some preservation initiatives are more likely to be implemented than others. In other words, although time can shape the social perception and public awareness of urban preservation, it does not determine the policy process through which the preservation initiatives are implemented. All social and political interactions must be understood against the broader background of the historical development of the locality, but as a social scientist I am more interested in revealing *how* those interactions actually play out. As three political systems characterized by distinct patterns of political fragmentation, the three cities provide us an opportunity to answer this question. Furthermore, the dimension of time is not missing in this book but is integrated into the discussion of the discourse of urban preservation in each city, and therefore it enables more general theoretical analyses on the instrumental use of urban preservation in different urban settings.

Another possible problem one might raise with the case selection is that both Beijing and Paris are capital cities, whereas Chicago is not. Indeed, capital status is important for a city, but it should not be treated as something separated from or at odds with other institutional characters of the political system. Rather, it should be woven into the general institutional structure of the city. If the capital status of a city increases the weight of the national government in the local policy process, its impact will be articulated by examining the power relations between the center and the local, so that it will find itself being integrated into the general institutional structure of the city. By contrast, if the capital status of a city proves to be insignificant in the local policy process, we need to investigate other institutional characteristics of the city that play a more significant role. In either situation, the capital status of a city does not dictate the policy process.

As cities from three countries on three continents, these are also different in history, culture, socioeconomic conditions, and property rights. Although the diversity of the cities reflects the complexity of urban life in the world, my selection of cases has retained certain constancy. All three cities have prominent positions in the national and international histories of architecture and urban planning. Their treasured urban landscapes have been under constant challenges in recent decades, so urban preservation is a critical policy issue in all three cities. Despite the fact that urban preservation has an important position on the policy agenda of all three cities, the cities have offered different answers as to how urban preservation should be defined and how preservation initiatives should be implemented.

Data and Methods

The central research agenda of this book is to explain why Beijing, Chicago, and Paris have such different patterns of urban preservation. The three cities all have great architectural heritage that deserves to be preserved, yet government performance varies significantly in their urban arenas and generates distinct patterns of preservation. More importantly,

although all the three cities are often conceived as under centralized political control, their power structures are fragmented in distinct patterns. A
comparison of the three fragmented urban power structures provides us
a chance to develop a more general account of how political institutions
influence the policy process. Using cities as the units of analysis enables us
to observe closely the political dynamics in the decision-making process.
Nonetheless, the theoretical validity of the study can be tested in larger
or smaller political entities more generally.

The book uses multiple qualitative research methods, including comparative historical analysis, case studies, and process tracing. I use comparative historical analysis to explore the history of urban preservation
and the development of political institutions in Beijing, Chicago, and Paris.
These analyses provide bigger pictures on why different meanings of urban
preservation are formed and how different types of political fragmentation evolve in the three cities. Under the larger framework of a three-city
comparison, I conducted case studies and comparative analyses in each
city, which helped me examine in detail the impact of political fragmentation on the policy process of urban preservation. The cases within each
city also add details on how the hypothesized causal mechanism operates.
Process tracing allows me to combine histories, archival documents, interview transcripts, and other sources in order to trace the links between
possible causes and observed outcomes.

The primary data presented in the book were collected from extensive
fieldwork and archival research in Beijing, Chicago, and Paris. From 2003
to 2010, I took nine research trips to the three cities and spent a total of
twenty-four months in the field. An important and enjoyable part of my
fieldwork is to walk around the cities and observe what happened on the
street. From historic urban cores to inner-city neighborhoods to newly developed outskirts, I tried to immerse myself in the richness and complexity of the urban texture and experience the minutiae of urban changes, as
those who live there every day do. This immersion sharpened my intuitions
and provided innumerable clues about the interactions between residents
and the built environment.

A total of 210 personal interviews were conducted in the three cities,
with sixty-five interviews in Beijing, seventy-five interviews in Chicago,
and seventy interviews in Paris. The interviewees include government officials, preservation and planning professionals, developers, activists, and
residents. Most interviews were individual, and some of them were collective. I combined a standardized set of questions with questions writ-
ten for the given interviewee. These interviews were open-ended and did
not follow any particular format. When permitted, I recorded interviews;

this was the norm. These interviews lasted anywhere from thirty minutes to four hours; the average interview ran for sixty to ninety minutes. The interviews provided me a substantial amount of firsthand information on the varied interests and values behind the preservation initiatives and on how political institutions work in shaping preservation practice. By meeting and speaking with some interviewees repeatedly over the years, I was able to obtain the most up-to-date information and construct a moving picture of urban preservation in the three cities.

Besides conducting personal interviews, I regularly attended public meetings held at the municipal, submunicipal, and community levels in all the three cities. These included public meetings organized by the Beijing Municipal Commission of Urban Planning and Shishahai Scenic Area Administration; regular meetings of Commission du Vieux Paris and public hearings in the 7th and 18th Arrondissements of Paris; public hearings held by the Commission on Chicago Landmarks, community meetings in Pilsen and Bronzeville of Chicago, and regular meetings of Pilsen Alliance and Black Metropolis Convention and Tourism Council. On each of these occasions, I remained a silent observer. However, I talked extensively with the organizers and other participants before and after each meeting. The meetings provided nuanced information about the ongoing policy debates in urban preservation.

Finally, I supplemented fieldwork with extensive archival research. The sources of the archival data include government reports, minutes from community meetings and planning forums, newsletters, city and neighborhood newspapers, professional journals, and the personal archives of neighborhood activists. They provided a rich supply of information that illuminated the changes in preservation practice over decades and the impact of political decisions on cities and urban life.

Plan of the Book

In the chapters that follow, I develop a theory of political fragmentation and apply it to the policy processes of urban preservation in Beijing, Chicago, and Paris. Chapter 1 presents the main theoretical framework of the book. After defining the concept of political fragmentation, I identify three major types of political fragmentation, namely functional fragmentation, territorial fragmentation, and intergovernmental fragmentation, and I specify the effects of each type on the policy process. Using this theory, I detail more specific propositions about the relationship between political institutions and the policy process of urban preservation, which are explored through comparative and historical analyses in chapters 2 to 4. I also highlight alternative explanations of the policy process, and of urban preservation policy more specifically, as the basis for comparison with the propositions I advance here.

Chapter 2 examines how local officials' purposes of pursuing urban growth and enhancing the global image of Beijing are filtered through the structure of functional fragmentation, thus generating a pattern of symbolic preservation in Beijing. I begin the chapter by offering a historical overview of the architectural significance of Beijing and the creative destruction that the city went through. Many historic monuments were torn down in the 1950s and 1960s to make way for a socialist capital, and a large number of old neighborhoods have been destroyed since the early 1990s in the citywide housing renewal program. I then discuss why the municipality's policy agenda changed from demolition to preservation at the turn of the century after Beijing was selected as the Host City of the 2008 Olympics. I argue that new preservation initiatives were proposed to smooth out the function of the growth machine and to create a better image for Beijing in front of the global audience.

Despite the making of preservation plans and the designation of historic districts, the new preservation initiatives did not result in better protection of the historic city. Functional fragmentation between municipal bureaucratic agencies largely constrains the implementation of preservation initiatives and makes urban preservation in Beijing increasingly symbolic. To demonstrate how functional fragmentation works, I provide three case studies. The relatively unified administrative structure facilitates the restoration of the city walls; however, the segmentation between municipal bureaucracies prohibits the implementation of preservation initiatives in the two historic districts, Qianmen and Shishahai. Specifically, I demonstrate that functional fragmentation causes the de facto devolution of authority from the municipality to the district government, and it generates a vacuum of power for the local administration to exercise its discretion. Under the district government's plan to promote local economic growth, Qianmen was demolished and replaced with brand-new buildings in historical style, whereas Shishahai was turned into a bar district to meet the demand of tourists.

Whereas urban preservation in Beijing serves the functions of urban growth and image creation, it is related to the increase of property value and community revitalization in Chicago. Chapter 3 demonstrates how territorial fragmentation along ward boundaries divides local communities and generates a model of mosaic preservation in Chicago. To provide a background for better understanding the meanings of urban preservation in Chicago, the chapter discusses the postwar urban renewal and the new urban revitalization in the city beginning in the 1990s. I emphasize that the new urban revitalization causes spatial and social changes in inner-city ethnic neighborhoods, so urban preservation is used by community members and local officials in those areas as a tool to cope with the challenges.

The remainder of the chapter discusses the structure of local political representation in Chicago and its impact on the policy process of urban preservation. In the long history of machine politics, the tradition of aldermanic prerogative gives aldermen tremendous autonomy to rule the wards as their monopolies. The impact of territorial fragmentation is examined by comparing the landmark designation in two neighborhoods, Pilsen and Bronzeville. Although the two neighborhoods are comparable in many aspects, their different locations on the ward map contribute to their different outcomes of landmark designation. Pilsen is united within one ward, but Bronzeville is split between three wards. In Pilsen, even though the landmark designation was opposed by community members because of its potential for accelerating gentrification, it could generate economic and political benefits for the alderman, so it was quickly made under his direction. In Bronzeville, landmark status does not directly benefit any alderman but has the potential to weaken their local autonomy, so the preservation initiative raised by community members has been blocked by the aldermen before it could be reviewed by federal officials.

In both Beijing and Chicago, local government plays a critical role in urban preservation. In Paris, by contrast, cultural heritage is considered a source of French national identity, and urban preservation has long been the privilege of the national government. Chapter 4 reviews the history of urban transformation in Paris and discusses how the national government implemented a series of strict zoning and preservation policies to limit the impact of postwar urban renewal on the historic city. Specifically, I highlight the role of specialized technocrats in the centralized French urban preservation system. The monopoly of the national government constrains the potential for urban innovation in Paris and challenges the autonomy of the municipality. Empowered by the decentralization reform, the municipality attempts to increase its power over the urban territory. Urban preservation therefore becomes a battlefield between local and central authorities, and the main debate is where to draw the boundaries of their respective jurisdictions.

I explore how intergovernmental fragmentation affects the policy process of urban preservation through three major preservation projects in Paris in recent years. The city's attempt to designate 5,607 Municipal Heritage Buildings was opposed by the state because it challenged the authority of the state in defining and protecting cultural heritage. The dispute was sent to the administrative court and was finally settled by a compromise between the two levels of government. In the redevelopment of Les Halles, a huge transportation hub and shopping complex in the center of Paris, the state was not directly involved, but it influenced the project through a state-owned transportation company. Finally, the state gave the city complete discretion in renovating Château Rouge, a predominantly ethnic community at the north fringe of the city. Together, the three cases reveal the competition, compromise, and collaboration between the city and the state, through which urban preservation in Paris is gradually changed from state monopoly to a joint venture between the city and the state.

I conclude by synthesizing the results of the book and describing the implications of the study for urban preservation, social justice, and broader urban changes. I examine the explanatory power of the theory of political fragmentation by discussing its potential application to the preservation practice in a number of major world cities. Although these cities differ in history, culture, regime type, and economic conditions, political fragmentation provides institutional constraints and shapes their policy processes of urban preservation. I also discuss how urban preservation influences social justice by presenting potential challenges to the human conditions in cities. I conclude with reflections on the impact of the current global institutional changes on cities and urban policymaking.

CHAPTER ONE

The Logic of Political Fragmentation

The empire, long divided, must unite; long united, must divide.
—LUO GUANZHONG, *Romance of the Three Kingdoms*

In this chapter, I develop a general theory of how political fragmentation influences the policy process. I identify three major types of political fragmentation, namely, functional fragmentation, territorial fragmentation, and intergovernmental fragmentation, and I specify the effects of each type on the policy process. Using this theory, I detail more specific propositions about the relationship between political institutions and the policy process of urban preservation, which are explored through comparative and historical analyses in chapters 2 to 4. I also highlight alternative explanations of the policy process, and of urban preservation policy more specifically, as the basis for comparison with the propositions I advance here.

The focus on political fragmentation is rooted in scholarly research investigating the relationships between institutions and patterns of political decision making. Institutions have been an enduring concern of political science since ancient times, but recent studies of historical institutionalism have tackled institutional questions with renewed vigor and creativity. Historical institutionalists attempt to illuminate how political struggles "are mediated by the institutional settings in which [they] take place" (Ikenberry 1988, 222–23). They work with a definition of institutions that includes both formal organizations and informal rules and procedures that structure conduct (Hall 1986). The fundamental point of historical institutionalism is that institutions influence political outcomes because they shape actors' power and strategies and mediate their relations of cooperation and conflict (Steinmo, Thelen, and Longstreth 1992; Steinmo

2001; Shapiro, Skowronek, and Galvin 2006; Lieberman 2009). Despite the focus on how institutions constrain and refract politics, institutional analyses do not deny the role of other variables: the players, their interests and strategies, and the distribution of power between them. Instead, they put these factors in context, showing how they relate to one another by drawing attention to the way political situations are structured (Steinmo, Thelen, and Longstreth 1992; Hall 1986).

The theory of political fragmentation contributes to the studies of historical institutionalism by revealing how and why different types of political fragmentation have affected the patterns of policymaking and implementation in different ways. It demonstrates that what matters for the policy process is not only whether a political system is fragmented but how it is fragmented. In so doing, it provides more general insights on the relationship between political institutions and policy processes that permit comparisons across political systems. In the remainder of the chapter, I develop the logical foundations of the theory of political fragmentation.

Defining Political Fragmentation

Political fragmentation is a frequently used term in political science research. Like a big umbrella covering a variety of things, it is often associated with different meanings in different contexts. In the literature of federalism, *political fragmentation* refers to the tensions and conflicts that exist between the center and territorial authorities (Pierson 1995; Rodden 2004), whereas in studies on state governance, it describes the separation of powers between the legislative, executive, and judicial branches of government (Friedberg 2000). In comparative politics, it implies the disintegration and fragility of nation-states due to class and ethnic cleavages (Lieberman 2003; Kohli 2004); however, in urban politics it refers to the segmentation of municipalities throughout metropolitan areas, paralleled by the spatial division of racial, ethnic, and socioeconomic groups (Danielson 1976; Orfield 1974–75; Teaford 1979; Miller 1981; Weiher 1991; Morgan and Mareschal 1999; Ostrom, Tiebout, and Warren 1961).

Despite the widely existing scholarly interest in the phenomenon of political fragmentation, there is no consensus on an analytical definition of this term. A main reason for the lack of such a definition is that scholars often underestimate the independent function of political fragmentation and tend to conceive it either as something to be explained by other factors or as a background against which political and social interactions take place. Different from previous studies that recognize the importance of political fragmentation, this book treats political fragmentation as an independent variable that puts varied factors in context and shapes political and social realities.

In order to systematically investigate the impact of political fragmentation on the policy process, we need an analytical definition of the concept. In this book, I define political fragmentation as *the dispersed allocation of decision-making authority among multiple jurisdictions.* Jurisdictions are bounded areas to which political agencies apply their right or authority (Abbott 1988; Lamont and Molnár 2002). In David King's (1997) words, jurisdictions are "property rights over issues": they distinguish one political agency from another and set boundaries on what political actors can and cannot do. Reconfiguring jurisdictions usually results in reallocation of resources and power and redefinition of the rules of the game, which explains why battles over jurisdictions are so hard fought (King 1997). Political fragmentation is a critical characteristic of government institutions. This is not only because nearly every modern political system is multijurisdictional but also because political agencies' interests, agendas, and priorities are increasingly diverse across jurisdictional boundaries.

The distinction must be made between political fragmentation and veto players. Veto players are individual or collective actors whose agreement is needed for a change of the status quo. The potential for policy change decreases when there are more veto players and diminishes even more when there is a lack of congruence and cohesion between these players (Tsebelis 1995; McCubbins, Noll, and Weingast 1989; Immergut 1992). Although the existence of veto players increases political fragmentation, the two concepts have substantial differences. First, veto players are political agencies, whereas political fragmentation is an institution that broadly includes agencies, formal organizations, and informal rules and procedures. Second, the role of veto players is more determinative, as their objections kill the policy initiative. By contrast, political fragmentation provides a tendency for blockage, which can be overcome by effective coordination between political actors.

Political fragmentation displays an institutional pattern in which the degree of structural unity is weakened in a significant and largely stable fashion by the configuration of jurisdictional boundaries. However, a fragmented political system is not necessarily without centralized authority. On one hand, upward shifts of authority from governments of the lower level to the higher level take place in some highly fragmented, federalist political systems. They generate a pattern of "fragmented centralization," in which channels of centralized control are created (Meyer and Scott

1983; Meyer, Scott, and Strang 1987). On the other hand, many centralized states face a lack of administrative coherence (Suleiman 1987). In studies on Chinese bureaucracy, for instance, the term *fragmented authoritarianism* is coined to describe the disjointed allocation of authority among the national ministries below the peak of the centralized Chinese state (Lieberthal and Oksenberg 1988; Lieberthal and Lampton 1992). In a word, political fragmentation may exist in both decentralized and centralized systems and function under centralized authority. In fact, the fragmented political structure may well be purposefully created by political leaders at the top, as it increases the power of the leaders over the policy process by giving them chances to step into the jurisdictions of various agencies and solve the problems of collective action (King 1997).

The consequences of political fragmentation have been the topic of immense scholarly and policy debate for decades. Some studies demonstrate that political fragmentation causes troubles within the policy process by increasing the difficulty of coordinating activities between various political agencies, preventing the building of consensus around policy solutions, or slowing down the policy process. For example, King (1997) contends that political fragmentation destroys the effectiveness of the U.S. congressional committees so that the Congress cannot speak with a strong and coherent voice about any national problems at all. Hedrick Smith (1989, 699) describes the costs of political fragmentation plainly: "Fragmentation often leaves our politicians wallowing in deadlock because the government lacks the cohesion to form the durable coalitions needed to resolve the nation's most demanding problems." In the urban politics literature, scholars also note the negative impacts of political fragmentation on metropolitan development, as it increases the difficulty of achieving economies of scale, equitable distribution of public funds, and comprehensive zoning and planning policies at the metropolitan level. Consequently, centralized regional governments are considered the solution to the problems caused by fragmented metropolitan governance (Tiebout 1956; Savitch and Vogel 2000; Feiock 2004, 2007; Vicino 2008).

Despite the costs of political fragmentation, some degree of fragmentation might benefit the policy process. First, some degree of political fragmentation may be informationally efficient because there are "more people at the table when important decisions are being made" (King 1997, 144). The presence of a more heterogeneous group of people reduces bias in the decision-making process. Second, a fragmented political context can facilitate better matching of citizen preferences and government policy through sorting and can lead to smaller, more efficient, less corrupt government and, under some conditions, more secure markets and faster growth (Rodden 2004, 481–82; Friedberg 2000). Specifically, polycentrists in urban politics argue that small, fragmented governments are preferable because competition between local units attracts economic growth (Ostrom, Tiebout, and Warren 1961). Third, political fragmentation dismantles the monopolies of certain political agencies by increasing the points at which various interest groups can access the policy process. The destruction of these issue monopolies makes it more likely that new voices will be heard (King 1997; Baumgartner and Jones 1993).

A Typology of Political Fragmentation

A political system can be fragmented in various dimensions. In order to theorize the impacts of political fragmentation on the policy process, we need to identify the various typologies. This section defines three ideal types of political fragmentation: functional fragmentation, intergovernmental fragmentation, and territorial fragmentation. When ideal types are considered, few political systems are pure cases of any one, and some may reflect a mix of elements of the various types. Nonetheless, the primary goal of specifying this limited number of ideal-type fragmentations is to suggest major qualitative differences in political structure, providing a strong sense of system-level variation.

Functional fragmentation is characterized by the segmentation of authority between bureaucratic agencies at the same administrative level. As one of the main features of the modern bureaucracy, the functional division of responsibility between bureaucratic agencies is supposed to generate greater efficiency for the activities around which each bureaucracy was organized (Weber 1978). However, bureaucratic agencies are constrained by their own professional norms and departmental interests, so that they often function without much reference to one another, and the leadership of each is self-perpetuating and not readily subject to the control of any higher authority. According to Sayre and Kaufman's (1960) and Lowi's (1967, [1969] 1979) studies of New York City, professionally organized, autonomous career bureaucratic agencies have become "islands of functional power," which make the modern city well run but ungoverned.

The political structure of Beijing provides a good example of functional fragmentation. Although Beijing is the capital city of the centralized Chinese state, the roles of both the central government and the municipal mayors are limited to making general principles for urban policies. The real power over specific policy issues belongs to the municipal bureaucracies, a total of forty-seven bureaus, with urban preservation housed in at least five of them. Although so many bureaucratic agencies appear to be involved in urban preservation, each agency has its own slant on different parts of the bill, like a patchwork quilt, so that there is no comprehensive protection of the built environment. This is a particularly serious problem for the preservation of historic neighborhoods, because none of the bureaus considers the issue as within its own jurisdiction. Although the municipal government attempts to facilitate the cooperation between bureaus, its efforts remain fruitless.

Different from function-oriented bureaucratic segmentation, *territorial fragmentation* entails a spatial division between government units at the same tier of the state apparatus. It is usually associated with the uneven distribution of resources or population across territorial boundaries (Brunn 1974; Holmes 1944). Territorial fragmentation exists at different levels of the state apparatus. For example, there is spatial differentiation and disintegration between different regions of the nation-states. Subnational territorial fragmentation provides the basis for exploring the unbalanced economic and political development across regions (Putnam 1993; Lieberman 2003; Kohli 2004). The segmentation between municipalities is another level of territorial fragmentation and as such has become a critical problem facing American metropolitan areas. In many cases, local governments implemented exclusive zoning and economic policies in order to prevent racial minorities from entering their borders. These efforts increased residential segregation and impeded metropolitan development (Danielson 1976; Orfield 1974–75; Teaford 1979; Miller 1981; Weiher 1991; Morgan and Mareschal 1999).

Territorial fragmentation is not limited to metropolitan areas. It also exists within the city limits. Chicago is well known for having a centralized political machine and strong mayoral authority; however, local politics in the city is deeply shaped by the territorial fragmentation between submunicipal units, or wards. The city is divided into fifty wards, each presided over by an alderman. The aldermen respect the mayor's authority on citywide or major development issues, and, in return, the mayor rewards the aldermen with enormous discretion on issues within their wards, including urban preservation. When the city council votes on specific issues within a ward, especially those related to land use, council members usually defer to the local alderman for decisions. This aldermanic privilege turned wards into aldermen's local monopolies and has effectively fragmented the entire city along ward boundaries. However, ward boundaries rarely coincide with those of the city's officially recognized community areas or informally defined neighborhoods. As a result, many local communities are divided by ward boundaries, and their development is jeopardized by territorial fragmentation.

Intergovernmental fragmentation is the segmentation between government units at different tiers of the state apparatus. Whereas functional fragmentation and territorial fragmentation are horizontal, intergovernmental fragmentation is a vertical relationship. There are two major types of government systems: federalist systems and unitary systems. Intergovernmental fragmentation is often considered an inherent feature of the federalist system, because federalism not only creates clear divisions between the central authority and constituent political units but also guarantees the constituent units significant political autonomy (Riker 1964; Pierson 1995). However, it is important to note that intergovernmental fragmentation also exists in the unitary system (Tarrow 1977; Ashford 1982; Gourevitch 1978). In unitary states, local authorities could obtain enormous power and challenge the implementation of national objects, depending on such factors as their wealth, their strategic significance, and the personal connections, ambition, and acumen of their leaders. Meanwhile, decentralization reforms launched in many unitary states have formally increased the power of subnational units and increased the tensions and conflicts between tiers of the state apparatus (Schmidt 1990; Tarrow 1977).

Intergovernmental fragmentation generates the main political discord in Paris. Different from most cities in the modern era, Paris did not have an elected mayor until 1977. Under the tradition of state centralism, the capital city of France was once governed by a prefect directly appointed by the central authority. The national government implemented strict protection of the urban environment through a group of highly specialized civil servants, which created a monopoly by the state and constrained the autonomy of the municipality. This competition between the municipality and the state generated a great deal of political tension, which increased after the election of the first Parisian mayor. The autonomy of the municipality was formally increased by decentralization reforms beginning in the 1980s. As a means of exercising its discretion over the urban territory, the city began to propose its own agenda of urban preservation, and some of the initiatives have challenged the traditional jurisdiction of the state. But even when the city expanded its boundary of power, the state did not withdraw from the decision-making process.

The Effects of Political Fragmentation on the Policy Process

The three ideal types of political fragmentation provide the foundation for exploring how fragmented structures affect decision making. In general, political fragmentation acts as a filtering mechanism that creates a tendency for blockage in the policy process. A policy initiative is more likely to be implemented if it is within the boundary of one jurisdiction and less so if it is situated across jurisdictional boundaries. For policy initiatives across jurisdictional boundaries, different types of political fragmentation are associated with predictable patterns of policy processes and settlements. The following section examines each type of political fragmentation by looking at four indicators: the ambiguity of boundaries, the inequality and interdependence between jurisdictions, and the likelihood of overcoming fragmentation. A comparison of the three types of political fragmentation provides the logical foundations for understanding their discernible settlements of policy initiatives across jurisdictional boundaries.

Functional Fragmentation

An important feature of functional fragmentation is that the jurisdiction of bureaucratic agencies is not immutable (Hooghe and Marks 2003). First, different from the visible geographic boundary between localities, the division between functional bureaus is conceptual and disputable. For instance, it is controversial whether school physicians and nurses should be under the authority of the Department of Health or the Department of Education. Second, because of the changes in political and social realities, the jurisdiction of functional bureaus is undergoing constant transformation. This can take the form of the birth of new bureaucratic agencies, the elimination or absorption of old ones, or major modification of existing ones (Sayre and Kaufman 1960). Despite the large number of state regulations defining the jurisdiction of each agency, these regulations are often ambiguous and sometimes contradictory, leaving blurred and permeable areas for contests in practice (Halliday and Carruthers 2007). Blatter (2004, 534) describes the ambiguities of jurisdiction between functional agencies as "fuzzy scales," which sometimes precipitate turf wars between those actors.

In the situation of functional fragmentation, bureaucratic agencies at the same administrative level appear to be equal. However, they have different statuses because of their various political capacities, and typically those with more resources have more weight in the policy process. Bureaucratic agencies are independent from one another for two main reasons: each agency is designed to handle a specialized issue area and is directed under its own organizational rules and professional norms. Nonetheless, bureaucratic agencies are also interdependent because every one of them is a functional component of a larger political organization. The degree of interdependence between bureaucratic agencies is further increased by the complexity of the modern political world, in which fewer and fewer policy issues can be solved without the mutual accommodation of various agencies (Sayre and Kaufman 1960; Lowi [1969] 1979; Lowi 1967).

In order to handle issues across the boundaries of multiple jurisdictions, bureaucratic agencies need to develop common understandings and build alliances by negotiation and agreement. However, different professional norms and departmental interests of bureaucratic agencies increase the cost of collective action and make it difficult to achieve collaboration across jurisdictions (Olson 1971). To avoid administrative rivalry and protect the interests of their organizations, bureaucrats often choose to ignore issues that are across or near the jurisdictional boundaries (Sayre and Kaufman 1960). In other words, suspension is one of the most common treatments for cross-boundary issues in functional fragmentation. Although many bureaucratic agencies appear to be involved in the policy area, none of them takes responsibility for cross-boundary issues, so that those issues eventually fall into no-man's land.

Aside from suspension, there are two other possible settlements for issues being ignored in the context of functional fragmentation. First, political authorities at the higher levels may create interagency task forces to mobilize and integrate the resources of different bureaucratic agencies and to handle the cross-boundary issues (Sayre and Kaufman 1960). Usually temporary, interagency task forces may not become stakeholders themselves, meaning that they do not necessarily increase fragmentation. However, it is questionable whether they could effectively facilitate multijurisdictional cooperation. Without a strong mandate, those agencies are no more than symbolic entities that provide new battlefields for diverse bureaucratic interests.

The second settlement is de facto devolution of power from bureaucratic agencies to political authorities at a lower level. Such settlement enables political agencies at the lower level to exercise their discretion and make decisions on specific issues or projects affecting their jurisdictions. For example, functional segmentation between the planning and transportation bureaus in the municipal government may inhibit the making and implementation of citywide regulations for road construction. Therefore, when a road is to be built in a local district, the district governor might have the discretion to decide on the details of the project. However, political fragmentation between upper-level bureaucratic agencies may impede the exercise of power at the lower level. According to King (1997), public managers in Washington fear jurisdictional fragmentation between congressional committees because their multiple masters occasionally give conflicting demands. Sometimes these conflicts appear trivial, but they can tie up an agency's decision making for months.

Territorial Fragmentation

Similar to functional fragmentation, jurisdictions in territorial fragmentation are subject to change. The reorganization of territorial boundaries is often dictated by changes in social geography and political goals (Paddison 1983; Brunn 1974). For example, U.S. congressional and state legislative districts are redrawn almost every decade under uniform geographic standards. Similarly, ward boundaries in Chicago are redrawn after each federal census in order to equalize populations in every ward (Suttles 1972; Guterbock 1980). The redistricting process might be manipulated by politicians in order to create special territorial boundaries favorable to their partisan or personal interests, which is called gerrymandering (Bullock 2010).

Although territorial boundaries are constantly subject to change, they are more clearly defined than the boundaries of functional agencies, which Blatter (2004, 534) describes as "clear-cut scales." Because there is less ambiguity about the visible geographic boundaries between localities, the probabilities of turf wars are lower in the situation of territorial fragmentation. However, the incongruence between sets of territorial boundaries provides another source for tensions and conflicts. For instance, the boundaries of school districts and police districts in a city are often mismatched. Similarly, ward boundaries in Chicago rarely coincide with those of the city's officially recognized community areas or informally defined neighborhoods (Suttles 1972; Guterbock 1980). The incongruence of territorial boundaries within certain geographic areas makes the territories more fragmented and increases the conflicts of interests between political agencies.

Among territorial authorities, there is a high degree of equality and mutual exclusion with one another's jurisdictions. Regardless of the uneven distribution of resources and population across territorial boundaries, territorial authorities at the same administrative level have the same legal status and autonomy (Lieberman 2003; Kohli 2004). Meanwhile, territorial authorities enjoy significant independence from one another. First, because of the clarity of territorial boundaries, it is easier for territorial authorities to distinguish issues within their own jurisdictional boundaries from those outside. Second, the territorial authorities usually have complete autonomy over their own jurisdictions, so that they do not need the accommodation of others to manage their local issues. As a result, they make general plans independently and jealously guard their prerogatives around land use and development. Typically, there is neither incentive nor platform for these players to work together (Innes, Booher, and Di Vittorio 2011). This situation is complicated by their need to compete for business, investment, and market opportunities to their territories.

The high levels of equality and independence between jurisdictions make it extremely difficult to overcome the hurdles of territorial fragmentation. Instead, territorial authorities tend to maintain a balance of power in order to preserve their own fiefdoms. Facing policy initiatives across territorial boundaries, any single territorial authority is unlikely to take over those initiatives on its own, because by doing so it risks violating the autonomy of others. Such actions would break the balance of power between territorial jurisdictions and put its own autonomy under the threat from others. Therefore, the optimal choice for territorial authorities is to ignore cross-boundary issues and maintain the balance of power. Using river restoration in the United States as an example, projects within one state's jurisdiction are more likely to be implemented, whereas those across state boundaries are more time consuming and more likely to be suspended (Lowry 2003).

In some circumstances special authorities are created to handle cross-boundary issues in territorially fragmented systems. Although the special authorities may effectively handle the work that no other government institution is legally equipped to do, they might become independent stakeholders and increase fragmentation in the metropolitan area. In the history of urban America, the most powerful special authorities are probably those created by Robert Moses in the 1930s, including the Port of New York Authority and the Triborough Bridge and Tunnel Authority (Caro 1984). To deal with the issues of transportation and recreation, these agencies transcended the tangled network of boundary lines of the 1,400 cities, boroughs, counties, townships, villages, sewer districts, fire districts, police districts, and water districts in the New York metropolitan area. Possessing not only the power of a large private corporation but some of the power of a sovereign state, those special authorities became an independent empire whose operation was out of the control of any officials the people had elected, including the mayor. Although the special authorities were efficiently run under the mandate of Moses, the entire City of New York was ungovernable by the mid–twentieth century (Caro 1984; Sayre and Kaufman 1960).

Intergovernmental Fragmentation

In order to investigate the characteristics of intergovernmental fragmentation, we first need to review how the government systems are organized. There are two major types of government systems: federalist and unitary. In a federalist system, sovereignty and power are shared between the central authority and constituent political units. The constituent units, usually named states or provinces, have significant political autonomy, and their power cannot be unilaterally abrogated by the central government. By contrast, the unitary system is governed as one single unit in which the central government is supreme, and any subnational units exercise only powers that the central government chooses to delegate. Furthermore, the central government can abrogate or curtail the power that it delegated to the subnational units (Le Galès 2006).

Just as governments at the upper tier are superior to those from the lower tier in unitary systems, intergovernmental relations are also unequal in federalist systems. A federalist system is more than a loose alliance of independent agencies. The fact that some political privileges, powers, and resources are exclusively concentrated at the upper tiers gives the upper-tier governments, especially national governments, ultimate dominance and long-run ability to direct the flow of policy decisions (Schattschneider 1960). Meanwhile, many federalist systems also have unitary structures in their lower tiers, in which the power of the local governments is devolved from the state or provincial governments. For instance, although the United States is a federalist system, the states themselves are unitary structures under Dillon's Rule, meaning that counties and municipalities have only the authority granted to them by the state governments.

Although there is substantial inequality across jurisdictional boundaries, there is also a high degree of interdependence between tiers of governments. On one hand, the lower-tier governments depend on the upper tier for political power and resources. In most cases, the power of the lower-tier governments is granted by the upper tier and can be curtailed or abrogated by the upper tier. The upper-tier governments also provide the lower tier with resources, including regular budgets and funds for special purposes. Even in the federalist system of the United States, local governments heavily rely on federal funds for community development and urban renewal (Hyra 2008). On the other hand, the upper-tier governments need the assistance and support of the lower tier in order to successfully intervene in local affairs (Webman 1981). Resistance from the lower tier may jeopardize the implementation of policies made by the upper tier. In other words, neither upper-tier nor lower-tier governments can fulfill their complete function or operate successfully without the agreement of the other.

Many unitary states launched decentralization reforms in recent decades as an effort to reduce the fiscal burden of central governments and to increase the effectiveness of policies at the local level (Schmidt 1990; Bardhan and Mookherjee 2006). Globalization and continental integration are among the major impetuses for decentralization. For example, it is in the context of European integration that many European Union member states witnessed the decentralization and multiplication of layers of governance, which facilitate the regional cooperation between subnational actors across the borders of nation-states (Blatter 2004; Leibfried and Pierson 1995; Keating 2003).

Although decentralization often leads to a more autonomous level of governance on the subnational level, very rarely do central governments fully cede autonomy to subnational governments. Central governments are still important sources of power and resources for subnational governments. To use France as an example, more than 40 percent of local budgets still come from the central government even after decentralization reforms (Savitch and Kantor 2002). Therefore, rather than increasing the independent authority of state and municipal governments, decentralization entails a move from complete central dominance to joint involvement of the center and one or more subnational tiers (Rodden 2004). It often creates a more complex, intertwined form of governance and increases the interdependence between tiers of government.

The high degree of interdependence between tiers of governments makes it easy to overcome the hurdles of intergovernmental fragmentation. When differences do occur between tiers, the matter might be unresolved at the beginning, but usually a process of political negotiation will ensue, allowing some compromise to emerge, so that all tiers of governments can modestly or partially, if not completely, fulfill their goals. Policy initiatives across jurisdictional boundaries are often settled under the collective action of different tiers of government, in a pattern of overlapping, shared, and contested control, a pattern often colloquially called "marble cake" (Grodzins 1966). Nonetheless, because of the differentiation of interests between tiers of government, the process of negotiation might be lengthy and fraught with contests. Because political agencies at different levels of government could intervene to advance their concerns at any point in the course of a program, projects are subject to change, and minimalist strategies are often adopted (Webman 1981).

We can draw two main conclusions from Figure 1, which summarizes the characteristics of the three types of political fragmentation. First, there is no clear association between the ambiguity of jurisdictional boundaries and the likelihood of overcoming political fragmentation. However, more ambiguity in the jurisdictional boundaries would lead to more uncertainties in the policy process and could precipitate turf wars between political agencies when the issue in dispute is appealing to both. Second, the extent of inequality and interdependence between jurisdictions is positively related to the likelihood of overcoming political fragmentation. The more unequal the power relations between jurisdictions, the more likely it is for the powerful one to take actions to break the stalemate and initiate negotiation. Meanwhile, the interdependence between jurisdictions reduces the chances of confrontation and increases the prospect of coordination. Among the three types of political fragmentation, intergovernmental fragmentation demonstrates the highest degrees of inequality and interdependence between jurisdictions, and therefore it has the highest likelihood of overcoming fragmentation.

In terms of the impacts of political fragmentation on the policy process, the central prediction from the preceding discussion is that different types of political fragmentation are likely to have discernible effects on the implementation of policy initiatives across jurisdictional boundaries (Figure 2). Among the three types of political fragmentation, intergovernmental fragmentation is more likely to implement the cross-boundary initiatives through modest compromise and collaboration across jurisdictions, whereas functional fragmentation and territorial fragmentation are more likely to leave those cross-boundary issues alone. Compromise and collaboration in the context of intergovernmental fragmentation might produce only lowest-common-denominator policies instead of perfect solutions, but they could still mitigate the cost of political fragmentation on the policy process. In systems dominated by functional fragmentation or territorial fragmentation, some special agencies can be created to handle the cross-boundary issues. However, there is the risk that those agencies will grow into independent stakeholders and increase fragmentation or merely become battlefields for different political interests.

. In sum, as an institutional structure of the political system, political fragmentation creates a tendency for blockage in the policy process. Some policy initiatives are more likely to be implemented than others, depending on their relations to the jurisdictional boundaries. Nevertheless, the hurdles of political fragmentation are not insurmountable. They can be overcome by effective coordination, despite the fact that the likelihood of overcoming the hurdles varies between types of political fragmentation. Coordination is often associated with tacit understandings and informal arrangements;

	Functional Fragmentation	Territorial Fragmentation	Intergovernmental Fragmentation
Ambiguity of Boundary	High	Low	Medium
Inequality between Jurisdictions	Medium	Low	High
Interdependence	Medium	Low	High
Likelihood of overcoming fragmentation	Medium	Low	High

FIGURE 1. Comparing the three types of political fragmentation.

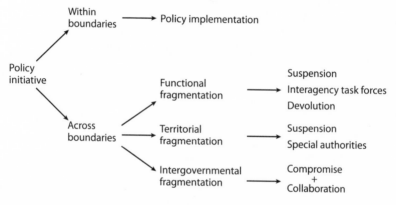

FIGURE 2. How political fragmentation shapes the policy process.

therefore, it is important for us to pay attention to not only the formal structures but also the informal relations in a fragmented political system.

Implications for Urban Preservation

Political fragmentation is likely to shape the policy process of urban preservation in several ways. First, preservation initiatives within the boundaries of single jurisdictions are more likely to be implemented than those across multiple jurisdictions. For the preservation initiatives within single jurisdictions, political actors in charge of those jurisdictions tend to have complete discretion over the policy processes. They can mobilize resources and implement projects in a more coherent, timely manner, without being interrupted or constrained by other agencies. As a result, those initiatives are more likely to be transformed into policy outputs. On the contrary, implementing the cross-boundary initiatives usually requires consensus and collaboration between various jurisdictions. However, the differentiated interests, values, and policy priorities of various political agencies might generate conflicts, struggles, and stalemates in the policy process, which would increase the challenges of coordinating collective action and prohibit the implementation of those cross-boundary preservation initiatives.

Second, in a city dominated by functional fragmentation, the likelihood for preservation initiatives to be implemented depends on the complexity of the initiatives. Less complex initiatives are usually within the jurisdiction of a single bureaucratic agency, so they are more likely to be implemented. Specifically, policy initiatives to preserve historic monuments are more likely to be implemented than those to preserve historic districts. Because the former are concerned primarily with the physical form of individual buildings, they are more likely to be within the jurisdiction of a single bureaucratic agency and thus more likely to be implemented. By contrast, the latter involve varied factors, including housing renovation, urban infrastructure improvement, and resident allocation. Such initiatives are more likely to cross the boundaries of bureaucratic agencies so that they tend to be blocked by the hurdles of functional fragmentation. As chapter 2 shows, functional fragmentation between municipal bureaus in Beijing has generated different policy processes of preserving historic monuments and historic districts. Whereas significant historic monuments are renovated and restored, historic districts are largely marginalized by the bureaucratic anarchy, and urban preservation eventually becomes icon making.

Third, in a city dominated by territorial fragmentation, whether or not the preservation initiatives can be implemented depends on the geographic scale of the initiatives (i.e., size of the geographic area covered by the initiatives). The preservation initiatives concerning smaller geographic areas tend to be within the boundary of a single territorial authority and are more likely to be implemented by their home authorities. In contrast, the initiatives concerning larger geographic areas are often across the jurisdictional boundaries of multiple territorial authorities and are more likely to be ignored or suspended by those authorities. Consequently, a citywide preservation agenda is not likely to develop in the context of territorial fragmentation. Instead, the preservation areas might look like mosaics

scattered in the urban landscape, each of them confined within the jurisdictional boundary of a single territorial authority. Chapter 3 demonstrates
how territorial fragmentation along ward boundaries transformed urban
preservation in Chicago into a ward-based business, which facilitates the
implementation of preservation initiatives within single wards but prohibits the implementation of those across multiple wards.

Fourth, in a city dominated by intergovernmental fragmentation, how
easily the preservation initiatives can be implemented depends on the
political significance of the initiatives. If the preservation initiatives are
politically more significant, they might induce more involvement of the
higher-tier governments, and thus they constrain the autonomy of local
authorities and create more conflicts and struggles across jurisdictional
boundaries. These conflicts and struggles can interrupt or slow down the
policy process of urban preservation. In contrast, if the preservation initiatives are politically less significant, they are more likely to be left to the
discretion of the local authorities. When fewer tiers of governments are
involved, there is less political contest, and the preservation initiatives are
more likely to be implemented. As we will see in chapter 4, intergovernmental fragmentation between the central and local authorities in Paris
turned the protection of cultural heritage into a political debate, which
eventually transformed the policy process of urban preservation from state
monopoly to a joint venture between the city and the state.

Fifth, among the three types of political fragmentation, intergovernmental fragmentation is most likely to implement cross-boundary preservation initiatives through modest compromise and collaboration between
jurisdictions. Because of the differentiation of interests between tiers of
government, there might be lengthy negotiations until agreements are
reached, and the compromise and collaboration might only partially fulfill
the goals of various political agencies. Nonetheless, the collective action
between tiers of the state apparatus could mitigate the negative effects
of political fragmentation on the policy process of urban preservation.

Alternative Explanations

It is my central thesis that the theory of political fragmentation helps explain the policy process of urban preservation, but this does not mean
that other factors are inconsequential. Indeed, many other factors influence policymaking in predictable ways, such as elite interests, political
resources, regime types, and government budgets. Therefore, it is important to assess the explanatory power of my argument relative to others.

Moreover, if the types of political fragmentation have observable effects on political processes, we need to know whether the effects are independent or whether they are washed away when we control for other factors. Here I critically review three alternative explanations and examine their relations to the theory of political fragmentation.

Elite Interests

One prominent alternative account of variations in the policy process of urban preservation focuses on the interests and preferences of elites. One could hypothesize that some preservation initiatives are more likely to be implemented than others because they are in the best interests of political and economic elites. This argument builds on the elitism assumption that society is hierarchically constructed between the powerful and the powerless. The policymaking process is considered to work to the advantage of the most powerful and the detriment of the least powerful (Hunter 1953; Mills 1956; Domhoff 1967). To explain how elites make decisions, the rational choice model contends that the decisions of elites are often based on calculations of cost and benefit (Gilboa 2010). Among a wide range of policy initiatives they might implement, elites will choose the ones that are most likely to be popular and easily implemented and to provoke little resistance, because those initiatives would help them maximize political and economic returns at the lowest costs. In the area of land use, the growth machine theory argues that it is in the best interest of elites to intensify land use in order to maximize economic returns, so that they often prioritize demolition and redevelopment over preservation (Logan and Molotch 1987).

The key problem with the elitism arguments is that they assume elites are a unitary, cohesive group of people who share the same interests. This proposition ignores the fact that the interests of elites are largely differentiated; a policy initiative that works to the advantage of some elites may impose costs on others. The rational choice model falls short in dealing with elite preferences at the level of assumption, without much concern about how elites define their self-interest. The growth machine theory neglects the fact that the practice of urban preservation is extremely diverse and can be used by elites as a strategy to promote their economic and political interests. In an effort to fill in the gaps in elitism arguments, the theory of political fragmentation demonstrates that elite members' different positions in political and social institutions may provide structural constraints on their understandings and calculations of costs and benefits, so that elite groups and individuals may develop different opinions on the same policy initiative. It does not deny the importance of elite interests and preferences but complements elitism arguments by showing how the interests and preferences of elites are shaped by calculations relevant to boundary politics.

Political Resources

Pluralism provides a different understanding of the policy process of urban preservation by focusing on the allocation and mobilization of political resources. According to pluralism, various kinds of political resources are distributed unequally between different groups so that political leaders cannot entirely dominate all decision-making processes without the involvement of other actors (Dahl 1961; Polsby 1963). In order to fulfill their policy goals, political actors must mobilize the political resources in the hands of stratified citizens. Therefore, the policy process is considered to be open to any groups that are active, organized, and willing to use their resources (Dahl 1961; Truman 1960; Sayre and Kaufman 1960). To apply the pluralism theory to the policy process of urban preservation, one could hypothesize that some preservation initiatives are more likely to be implemented because the political actors can mobilize sufficient political resources to support their action.

Whether or not political actors can mobilize sufficient political resources is an important factor in the success or failure of policy processes of urban preservation. However, the argument falls short if we try to understand why political resources can be more easily mobilized in some contexts than in others. In other words, we gain more analytical leverage if we consider the mobilization of political resources as part of the puzzle that needs to be explained rather than as an exogenous determinant of the policy process. Taking a historical institutionalist approach, the theory of political fragmentation recognizes the importance of political resources but places those resources in context. It demonstrates how political structure constrains the choices of political and social actors and conditions the distribution and mobilization of resources by the actors.

Regime Types

A central task for students of comparative politics is to characterize the relationship between the nature of political regimes and the action of states. For this study, an obvious question is whether the policy initiatives of urban preservation are more likely to be implemented in democratic states than in other political regimes. It is easy to advance conflicting theoretical propositions to explain the relations between regime type and the policy process of urban preservation. One can imagine that democracies provide fertile conditions for public participation, so that preservationists have more chances to influence decision making and promote implementation of preservation initiatives (MacPherson 1977; Pateman 1970; Harrop and Miller 1987). Alternatively, one can also argue that authoritarian governments might be more effective in implementing preservation initiatives because they may be better at limiting the number of dissenting opinions and they may be more willing to use coercive and invasive tactics in policy implementation (Collier 1979; Walzer 1981). Thus, there are reasons to believe that the likelihood that a preservation initiative will be implemented may be either positively or negatively associated with democratic regimes. And of course, it is possible that the effects are mixed. The conflicting propositions suggest that regime types probably have no independent effect on the policy process.

Other Factors

Besides the three prevailing alternative explanations, other factors are critically important for the policy process of urban preservation. For example, culture often shapes attitudes toward urban preservation and influences the implementation of preservation projects. The Western tradition is to revere the marks of time on their monuments, so that people attempt to retain as much as possible of the original fabric and material of old buildings. By contrast, some East Asian cultures are inspired by the will to escape the action of time and by the desire to perfect. People in those countries periodically renovate or rebuild historic structures so that they continue to look the way they did when first constructed (Tung 2001). In Japan, people sometimes construct exact replicas of an original temple and then destroy their earlier copies (Choay 2001). The ritual reconstruction of historic monuments is culturally bound and relevant to the fact that most buildings in Japan have wood frames that do not last as long as stones.

Besides the culture of preservation, technical proficiency, the financial capacity of government, types of property rights, and the overall quality of historic architecture all influence the implementation of preservation projects (Fitch 1982; Frank 2002; Datel and Dingemans 1988). Individual personalities and accidental historical circumstances also shape the policy process of urban preservation (Tung 2001). This book does not deny the impacts of those factors; rather, it illustrates the impacts of those factors in each city in the chapters that follow. However, I approach the analysis of urban preservation as a social scientist, in the sense that I am more concerned to identify general patterns and relationships that go beyond the particularities of any individual country's circumstances. In this regard, political fragmentation is a vital, yet not well explained, influence that conditions the impacts of other factors and helps us better understand the politics of urban preservation in a cross-national context.

Conclusion

In this chapter, I provided theoretical accounts of how political fragmentation might affect the policy process. With the greater structural complexity of government institutions and the greater differentiation of interests between political agencies, political fragmentation has become pervasive in the modern political world. It serves as a filtering mechanism for the policy initiatives of urban preservation, and it sometimes creates a tendency for blockage in the policy process. A policy initiative is more likely to be implemented if it is within the boundary of one jurisdiction and less so if it is situated across jurisdictional boundaries. The chapter discusses three major types of political fragmentation, each associated with predictable patterns of policy processes and settlements when the policy initiatives are handled across jurisdictional boundaries. It demonstrates that what matters for the policy process is not only whether the political system is fragmented but how it is fragmented.

Although the theory of political fragmentation puts a spotlight on the institutional structure of the political system, it does not deny the impacts of various other factors. Instead, it puts these factors in context, showing how they relate to one another by drawing attention to the way political situations are structured. Theories that focus on the characteristics and preferences of political actors themselves could not account for why actors with similar organizational characteristics and similar preferences could not always influence policy in the same way or to the same extent in different political contexts. The theory of political fragmentation approaches the problem by revealing that the strategies and relative power of those actors, as well as their choices of coalition and coercion, are defined by the institutional context in which the political game is played. Such ideas lay the groundwork for an explanation of why the policy processes of urban preservation vary in different cities.

CHAPTER TWO

Beijing

Bureaucratic Anarchy and Symbolic Preservation

When a man has traversed the streets of a city for fifty years,
certain buildings become familiar landmarks. He first saw
them perhaps on trudging to school with his books, and has
seen them nearly every day since. He experiences a slight shock
whenever such buildings are destroyed. There appears something
wrong in the general aspect of the town. Of late years these
shocks have followed one another so continuously that he
may well wonder whether he is living in the same place.
—EDWARD HAGAMAN HALL, *Old Buildings of New York City*

On a hot summer day in 2010, I went to interview an official in a district
government of Beijing who is in charge of cultural heritage preservation
in the district. Our interview place was chosen in a temple, located in the
center of the city but no longer open to the public, where he and his assistants were doing some work. As soon as I entered the temple, I was
surprised by the piles of stone tablets and gate piers, in complete forms or
just segments, scattered on the grass of the temple (Figure 3). Both unique
components of traditional Chinese architecture, the former are usually
located in imperial mansions or palaces, whereas the latter are found
outside almost every courtyard house, used for supporting and fixing the
gate and indicating the social status of the owner. The official told me he
had collected everything from the demolition sites within the district in
the past a few months, and he had no idea what to do with those relics.
Despite his position as cultural heritage chief of the district, he could not
prevent those centuries-old courtyard houses and historic buildings from
being demolished. All he could do is to pick up those small segments from
the vanished buildings and leave them in the temple.

FIGURE 3. Stone tablets and gate piers collected by a district official from the demolition sites are temporarily placed in a temple in Beijing.

Since the early 1990s, when the Beijing Municipal Government launched the citywide housing renewal project, a large number of old neighborhoods and historic buildings have been demolished. The scale of destruction has prompted widespread criticism, and in response, the government has passed preservation laws, designated preservation districts, and increased funds to renovate historic structures. But even in the face of these preservation initiatives, the pace of demolition has yet to slow down. This chapter explains the controversial picture of urban preservation in Beijing. It shows how the pursuit of urban growth and the hurdle of functional fragmentation create a pattern of symbolic urban preservation. Despite the changes in the municipal agenda from demolition to preservation, urban preservation serves primarily as a tool to smooth the functioning of the growth machine and to create a better global image for the city. Meanwhile, the processing of the preservation initiatives is significantly constrained by the segmentation between different bureaucratic agencies, which facilitates the preservation of historic monuments but prohibits the preservation of historic districts.

The chapter begins with a historical overview of urban transformation in Beijing, which provides a background for better understanding the strategic role of urban preservation in the city. It then describes how the institutional structure shapes the policy process of urban preservation in Beijing. It offers a brief institutional history of the emergence and evolution of functional fragmentation in the Chinese state, followed by an investigation of the fragmented political structure of urban preservation in the Beijing Municipality. To demonstrate the impacts of the progrowth regime and functional fragmentation on the policy process of urban preservation, the chapter provides three case studies: the restoration of the city walls and the preservation of two historic districts, Qianmen and Shishahai.

Remaking Beijing: From an Imperial Capital to a Socialist Beacon

Beijing has a long history that dates back more than 3,000 years. It has served as the capital of five imperial dynasties: Liao (938–1122), Jin (1122–1215), Yuan (1267–1367), Ming (1368–1643), and Qing (1644–1911). The spatial layout of most ancient cities in the world evolved over centuries; however, Beijing was designed to be a giant artistic whole under a complex set of Chinese design philosophies, and most of the city was constructed by the Ming emperor Yongle from 1406 to 1420 (Naquin 2000).[1] Based on the Chinese design philosophy of hierarchy, symmetry, and unity, Beijing is divided into four roughly concentric encirclements, each surrounded by a city wall (Figure 4). The Forbidden City, the residence of the imperial family, was located in the geographic center. It is surrounded by the Imperial City, which enclosed private gardens, lakes, and workspace reserved exclusively for the ruling family and high-ranking bureaucrats. The Inner City in the north contains more residences, mostly of noble families and high-ranking bureaucrats, and the Outer City in the south hosts more commerce. A central axis of 7.9 kilometers runs south to north, with the most significant monuments situated along it.

The traditional residential compound typical of Beijing is the *siheyuan*, or courtyard house. It is a one-story residence with an inner courtyard surrounded by four buildings. *Hutong* is the narrow lane lined by the houses (Figure 5). Because nearly all courtyard houses had their main buildings and gates facing south to get the maximum amount of sunshine, a majority of *hutong* run from west to east. Between the main *hutong*, many tiny lanes run north and south for convenient passage, thus creating a street pattern that looks like a chessboard. The residential fabric provided an ideal background for the monuments: layers of thick brick walls concealed the yellow-roofed palaces, surrounded by a sea of gray courtyard houses

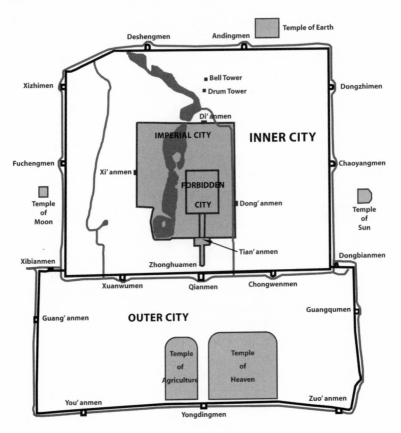

FIGURE 4. Map of Old Beijing.

built along narrow lanes. It was the aesthetic integrity of its urban design that prompted noted American urban planner Edmund Bacon (1967, 244) to describe Beijing as "possibly the greatest single work of man on the face of the earth."

Beijing has experienced numerous human and natural calamities throughout its history and waves of modernization campaigns since the nineteenth century; however, its architectural character and splendor remained largely intact until the Communist regime came to power in 1949. The socialist transformation of Beijing must be understood in the context of the antiurban bias of the Chinese communist leadership. Although the Chinese Communist Party (CCP) was active in the cities in its early days, after 1927 it was driven into the countryside by the Nationalist Party and developed an overwhelmingly rural-based party membership. The experience induced Chinese communist leaders to form strong animosities toward the conspicuous consumption and urban lifestyle of the previous republican period. They saw cities as places of vice, corruption, and class exploitation. After the CCP came to power in 1949, the government initiated a series of reforms to purge urban evils and to transform the pre-1949 consumption cities into socialist production centers (Whyte and Parish 1984).

The antiurban bias of the communist leadership had a devastating impact on the architectural legacy of Beijing. A critical decision that sealed the fate of the historic city was the location of the new administrative center for the Communist regime. Despite the proposal by renowned architects Liang Sicheng and Chen Zhanxiang to preserve the entire historic city and build an administrative center west of Old Beijing, Chinese leaders decided to locate the government and industrial expansion in the old city. The decision made the destruction of Old Beijing inevitable as the historic city became the site of new development. Historic buildings were stigmatized as symbols of the backward, imperial political order, and many of them were destroyed between the 1950s and 1970s. One of the most striking cases was the demolition of the city walls. The government launched a large political campaign to destroy the city walls and mobilized almost all residents of Beijing to participate. The city walls, together with fourteen city gates, were largely demolished and replaced by a ring of highways and a subway (Shen 2002; Wang 2003). With the demolition of its architectural heritage, Chinese leaders began to transform Beijing into a shining beacon of socialism. The entire urban space of Beijing was reorganized following the Soviet model of urban planning: Tiananmen Square became the symbol of New China and a politically charged space, government complexes and heavy industrial facilities were constructed in the city center, and urban amenities and service sectors were significantly reduced (Wu 2005; Whyte and Parish 1984).

While numerous historic monuments were dismantled to make way for a socialist capital, old neighborhoods were suffering from dilapidation. Because of the rapid population growth and the influx of people from the countryside, there was a serious housing shortage in the early days of the new regime. To alleviate the housing shortage, the government settled a large number of families into existing homes that were already occupied. Such an arrangement made most courtyard houses extremely overcrowded and eventually turned them into "courtyard-less compounds" (Wu 1999; Fang 2000). It also violated the rights of property owners and created confusion as to who actually owned the home and the property. Therefore,

FIGURE 5. The urban texture of Old Beijing: *(above left)* Birdseye view of a court-yard house. Beijing gu jianzhu (Beijing: Wenwu chuban she, 1959), plate 139. *(below left)* Exterior of a courtyard house. *(above)* A typical *hutong* in Beijing.

no one wanted to spend money to repair or maintain the houses, so the condition of the courtyard houses further deteriorated, prompting the citywide housing renewal in the decades that followed.

Housing Renewal and the Call for Urban Preservation

The government's effort to transform Beijing into a socialist capital severely damaged the architectural profile of the historic city. While a large number of historic monuments were demolished and replaced by new construction, the old neighborhoods were suffering from dilapidation. To improve living conditions, the municipality initiated the Old and Dilapidated Housing Renewal (ODHR) program in the early 1990s. Started as a social welfare project, the ODHR program soon turned into an engine of real estate development prompted by land market reform and political decentralization. The selling of land had been an ideological taboo in socialist China for decades; however, the central government introduced a land lease system in 1987, and Beijing adopted it in 1992 (Gaubatz 1999; Xie, Parsa, and Redding 2002). Under the new statutory policy land is still publicly owned, but local government can contract land use rights to private agents. Meanwhile, decentralization reform placed huge pressure on both the municipality and the district government to raise revenue locally (Ma and Wu 2005). Under such circumstances, leasing land to developers and carrying out real estate development seemed to be the most logical choice for local officials to increase local revenue, achieve a sort of visible growth, and enrich themselves.

Housing renewal nurtures a land-based elite composed of local officials and private developers. The former controls the land, whereas the latter mobilizes capital. The collaboration between the two turns the city into a growth machine whose priority is to maximize profit from land speculation (Logan and Molotch 1987). In the last few years of the 1990s, a large share of local government revenues was drawn from real estate development (Fang 2000; Wang 2003). Each of the four inner-city districts[2] has a large commercial development project that is funded by either foreign or Hong Kong real estate investors.[3] Although these projects all were implemented in the name of housing renewal, none of them has provided affordable housing to local residents, so that the majority of them have been relocated to cheaper land in the suburbs after their neighborhoods were demolished. Increasingly, the choice of areas to be demolished is based on their location and latent land value rather than the degree of dilapidation (Fang 2000).

Urban renewal has fundamentally changed the urban landscape of Beijing. The construction of shopping centers, office towers, and luxury apartment buildings has largely improved the local economy, modernized the urban infrastructure, and created a global space in the service of international business and consumption demands. However, it has also caused the demolition of a substantial proportion of the urban fabric and the removal of hundreds of thousands of inhabitants. According to the data collected by the Beijing Academy of Urban Planning, the number of *hutong*—which exceeded 7,000 in the early 1950s—was reduced to around 2,000 in 1990 and 1,500 in 2003 (Wang 2003). In other words, more than two-thirds of these homes disappeared within fifty years. In 2006, the total acreage of courtyard houses shrank to 15 square kilometers, accounting for only 24 percent of the Old City. A *Washington Post* article commented, "For centuries, the architecture of Old Beijing has withstood rebels and invaders, warlords and imperialist powers, Communist central planners and Red Guards," but during the last decade of the twentieth century the city was leveled by real estate development (Mufson 1997).

Profit-driven housing renewal and massive urban demolition in Beijing have been widely criticized. Besides the complaints from residents and preservationists, the growth regime has faced increased global media exposure and international pressure since the late 1990s. The voice of criticism became even stronger when Beijing started its bid for the 2008 Olympic Games. This is demonstrated in an anecdote about Beijing's Olympic slogan. According to some municipal officials, officials of the International Olympic Committee (IOC) expressed concerns about their Olympic bid slogan, "New Beijing, Great Olympics." Given the widely reported urban demolition and redevelopment in Beijing, IOC officials were worried that the slogan revealed the intent of the Chinese government to destroy Old Beijing and build a new one for the Olympics (B0801,[4] B0803). In an attempt to partially address the concern, the Beijing 2008 Olympic Organizing Committee changed the slogan into "One World, One Dream" after Beijing won the bid. It also articulated the goals of making the Beijing Olympics "an Olympiad of Science and Technology, an Olympiad of Humanity, and a green Olympiad," with the second part specifically emphasizing the importance of protecting the cultural heritage of Old Beijing.

Against the background of increasing domestic and international pressure the municipality initiated a series of new policies of urban preservation. In 2001, it made the Conservation Plan for the Historic City of Beijing and the Conservation Plan for the Imperial City of Beijing. Meanwhile, more historic monuments were designated, so by 2004 their numbers increased from 1,063 to 3,550. From 2000 to 2008, under the auspices of the "Cultural Heritage Preservation Plan for an Olympiad of Humanity," the municipality spent more than 900 million RMB to restore and renovate historic monuments (Long 2003; Wang 2003). In 2007, 250 million RMB was distributed to each of the four inner-city districts to renovate courtyard houses (B0801, B0803). Given that the annual budget for urban preservation was less than 9 million RMB per year in the 1980s and 1990s,[5] the tremendous increase in government support shows that urban preservation was considered an important issue on the government's agenda.

One of the most significant policy changes since their original Olympic bid has been the designation of historic preservation districts. The municipality designated twenty-five historic preservation districts in 2000, and two years later, it added another five. The total acreage of the thirty preservation districts represents roughly one-fifth of the Old City (Figure 6). Under the authorization of the municipality, the Beijing Municipal Commission of Urban Planning (BMCUP) made preservation plans for those districts with the assistance of several major research institutes in Beijing, including the Architecture School of Tsinghua University, Beijing Institute of Architecture Design and Research, and China Architectural Design and Research Group (BMCUP 2002).

Because previous preservation policies dealt only with individual buildings, the municipality considers the designation of entire districts as a great step forward in Beijing's urban preservation history. However, the designation serves more sophisticated goals than just stopping demolition. An urban planner at BMCUP who participated in the designation process reveals (B0619),

> The city government faced lots of critiques in the late 1990s
> when Beijing was in the age of massive demolition and massive
> construction (*da chai da jian*). The municipal leaders and
> developers got very frustrated, so they urged us to designate the
> preservation districts as soon as possible. Some municipal leaders
> told us, "Draw the boundaries of the preservation districts right
> away, so that we know where we can demolish and where we
> cannot."

This example is important, because it conveys that the designation of historic preservation districts is a policy tool for reconciling the contradictory preferences between preservation and redevelopment. The designation placates domestic and international protest about demolition by showing that the land-based elite is attempting to protect the cultural heritage. And,

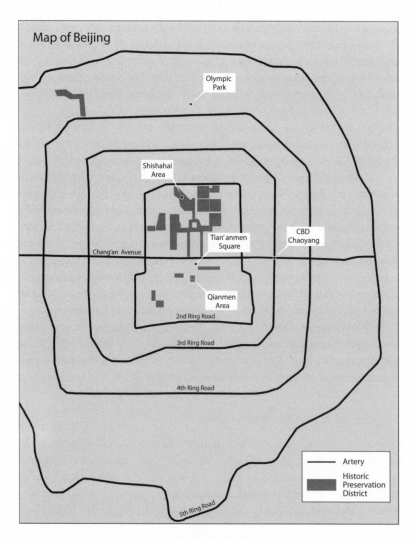

Map of Beijing

Olympic Park

Shishahai Area

Tian'anmen Square

CBD Chaoyang

Chang'an Avenue

Qianmen Area

2nd Ring Road

3rd Ring Road

4th Ring Road

5th Ring Road

— Artery

Historic Preservation District

FIGURE 6. Historic preservation districts in Beijing.

ironically, it gives local officials and developers a green light for redevelopment outside the designated areas. Indeed, the speed of demolition was accelerated after the designation of historic preservation districts. A total of 9.34 million square meters of old houses were bulldozed between 2000 and 2005, nearly twice the number that were demolished between 1990 and 1999 (Deng 2003).

The changes in the municipal agenda demonstrate how the political regime reacts to exogenous forces and adopts urban preservation to fulfill its goals. Urban preservation is no longer the opposite process of urban renewal but a strategic device to smooth the functioning of the growth machine and create a better image for the city. After preservation initiatives are proposed, however, they have to go through complex government institutions in order to be implemented. In order to achieve a complete picture of the policy process of urban preservation, we need to further examine how government institutions influence the processing of preservation initiatives. As the rest of the chapter demonstrates, functional fragmentation between municipal bureaus serves as a filter, facilitating the processing of preservation initiatives for historic monuments but prohibiting the processing of those for historic districts. The following section discusses how functional fragmentation emerged and evolved in the Chinese state while providing an institutional background for examining the fragmented political structure of urban preservation in Beijing.

Fragmented Authoritarianism in China

China is a unitary state, with formal authority constitutionally held by the central government. Yet in reality, as the theory of fragmented authoritarianism suggests, the authority below the very peak of the centralized Chinese state is allocated in a disjointed fashion (Lieberthal and Oksenberg 1988; Lieberthal and Lampton 1992). Specifically, the state apparatus is divided into two dimensions. First, there are vertical cleavages between functional bureaucracies, the so-called *tiao* (line). The second dimension, *kuai* (piece), is based on the geographic separation of local governments at the same administrative level (Schurmann 1966; Barnett 1967; Harding 1981; Mertha 2005a).

Tiao and *kuai* coexist and are woven into each other, but recent scholarly work on Chinese politics focuses primarily on *kuai*. Issues including central–local relations, local autonomy, and the competition between local governments have received the most attention (Oksenberg and Tong 1991; Shirk 1993; Huang 1996; Yang 1997). By contrast, there are far fewer empirical studies of political fragmentation in its functional dimension. A notable analysis conducted by Andrew Mertha (2005b) argues that China's enforcement of intellectual property is deeply constrained by the complex network of bureaucracies. To understand the policy process in the Chinese state, focusing only on territory-based autonomy is not enough. It is important to uncover the configuration of line administration and the rules of the game between bureaucratic agencies. Taking a historical perspective, this section explains how line administration was formed in the Chinese regime and how the situation of functional fragmentation was created.

When the new communist regime was established in 1949, the top leaders attempted to build a highly unified, centralized structure of authority (Schurmann 1966; Lieberthal and Oksenberg 1988). Their efforts resulted in an era of hypercentralization during the First Five-Year Plan, from 1953 to 1957 (Mertha 2005a, 804). With the development of the government structure, however, state bureaucracies rapidly expanded and specialized. They soon began to erode the central control of top leaders (Schurmann 1966; Lieberthal and Oksenberg 1988).

The organizational framework of the Chinese government was substantially influenced by the model of the Soviet Union (Lieberthal and Oksenberg 1988). On one hand, Soviet-type regimes typically expand the function of the state and undermine the role of society by taking over all loci of administrative and political power formerly outside the formal political structure (Jowitt 1971). On the other hand, under the command of Lenin and Stalin, the Soviet system accepted the specialization of labor as a necessary and main criterion in government organization and personnel assignments (Azrael 1970). Following the Soviet model, top Chinese leaders radically enlarged the size of the state through active control over the entire economy, educational system, and other areas that are autonomous or semiautonomous in other societies. Meanwhile, they adopted the core organizing principle of division of labor and rapidly increased the number of functional bureaucracies (Lieberthal and Oksenberg 1988).

With the enlargement of the state and the proliferation of bureaucratic agencies, functional fragmentation occurs in the Chinese state and poses inevitable risks to the leaders' centralized control. First, individuals in specialized bureaucracies tend to prioritize the goals and interests of their departments over national needs. This can lead to conflict of interests between agencies and thereby undermine the general interest of the state (Barnett 1967; Wong 1976). Second, some bureaucratic units may acquire and exercise control over certain resources that are not accessible to others. As a result, they can potentially act as "veto players" and obstruct the process of policy formation and implementation (Pryor 1973; Lieberthal and Oksenberg 1988; Mertha 2005b). To facilitate cross-jurisdiction cooperation and to maintain the formal system, an informal bargaining system emerged. However, it is usually not effective enough to eliminate the jurisdictional barriers and to solve the problems of adequate monitoring and coordination (Lieberthal and Oksenberg 1988; Lieberthal and Lampton 1992).

China launched its economic reform in 1979 to develop a market economy and open its door to the outside world. Functional fragmentation grew increasingly pronounced under the economic reform (Lieberthal and Lampton 1992). Although the reform created a private sector that follows the logic of a market economy, the resources that this nascent private sector desperately needs are still firmly controlled by the public authority. This transitional situation gives bureaucratic agencies abundant opportunities to gain economic profit. They either create their own companies to make money from resources at their disposal or seek rents from private actors by allocating resources to them (Duckett 1998; Yang 2004). Given the conflict of interests between different market actors, the interests of various bureaucratic agencies that regulate the market are also redefined and further differentiated, which has led to the remaking of the Chinese leviathan (Yang 2004). Consequently, the potential for conflict of bureaucratic interests is significantly increased, as is the degree of jurisdictional segmentation.

Although the government implemented several rounds of institutional reforms to reduce the number of central ministries and the number of personnel in line administration, the intense conflict of interests between bureaucratic agencies still exists. When making decisions, officials tend to prioritize their departmental interests and limit their concern to their own jurisdiction instead of seeing the whole picture of the state. The existing jurisdictional boundaries were legalized and strengthened by new legislation in the reform era. The 2003 Administrative License Law requires that functional bureaucracies must administrate based on their departmental laws and cannot exceed their reach beyond their jurisdictions.[6] Because administrating outside one's jurisdiction is considered to violate the authority of other agencies, the law encourages bureaucrats to shy away from problems across jurisdictions or at the edge of jurisdictional boundaries. It enlarges the gray areas between different functional organs and increases the number of issues that are unattended by the government (B0601, B0602, B0613).

It is important to note that top leaders are not powerless in the face of fragmented bureaucracies. In the pre-reform era, Mao checked the authority of central ministries through different means, including ministerial amalgamation and redifferentiation (Schurmann 1966; Townsend 1974). During the reform, the leaders retained substantial capacity to create new bureaucratic organizations and to control principal issues in decision making (Lieberthal and Oksenberg 1988). Nonetheless, as long as the behaviors of individual bureaucrats or bureaus are not in conflict with the general principles set up by the leaders, they have significant discretion in day-to-day administration. The complexity of the reforms makes it even more difficult for the leaders to monitor every action of the functional agencies effectively. External influences and domestic demands are increasingly filtered through specialized bureaucracies. The fragmented bureaucracies, the staffs, and the coordinating bodies exert a growing influence on policy outputs (Lieberthal and Oksenberg 1988).

Urban Preservation in Beijing: Falling into No Man's Land

Functional fragmentation not only exists among central bureaucracies but also prevails at the local level. As the capital city of the centralized state, Beijing is often conceived as being under the firm control of the national government. In reality, the role of the state is limited to setting the general directions for municipal policies. Similarly, top leaders at the municipal level, such as the mayor and the Municipal Party Committee of Beijing, focus mainly on the principles instead of the specifics of the policies. The real power of decision making belongs to the municipal bureaucracies and is dispersed among forty-six bureaus. In other words, similar to the situation in any local government in China, functional fragmentation provides the general context for the policy process in Beijing.

Urban preservation is one of the issues that best illustrates the dynamics of functional fragmentation in the municipality. Although there are unitary municipal agencies in charge of urban preservation in both Paris and Chicago (Commission du Vieux Paris and Commission on Chicago Landmarks), there is no similar agency in Beijing. In practice, urban preservation is primarily within the province of five functional bureaucracies, which are responsible for different aspects of the issue (Figure 7). The Beijing Municipal Administration of Cultural Heritage (BMACH) is in charge of municipal historic monuments and heritage sites. The BMCUP is responsible for designating preservation districts and making preservation plans. The Beijing Municipal Bureau of Landscape and Forestry (BMBLF) takes care of the green space and natural scenes in heritage sites

BMACH: Beijing Municipal Administration of Cultural Heritage
BMCUP: Beijing Municipal Commission of Urban Planning
BMCC: Beijing Municipal Construction Committee
BMBLF: Beijing Municipal Bureau of Landscape and Forestry
BMCDR: Beijing Municipal Commission of Development and Reform

FIGURE 7. Functional fragmentation in Beijing.

or preservation areas. The Beijing Municipal Construction Committee (BMCC) has the authority to issue demolition certificates and construction permits. And, lastly, the Beijing Municipal Commission of Development and Reform (BMCDR) supervises the allocation of land and funds in urban plans (B0503).

The functional division of municipal bureaus is supposed to generate greater efficiency for the activities around which each bureaucracy is organized. Yet in reality, too many bureaucratic agencies and the political boundaries between them may jeopardize the solution of urban problems. First, the boundaries between bureaucratic agencies are often transferable and disputable rather than fixed. Such ambiguity of jurisdiction creates many gray areas in policymaking. Those gray areas are likely to induce turf wars between functional agencies (Sayre and Kaufman 1960; Halliday and Carruthers 2007; King 1997). Second, the specialties of bureaucratic agencies cannot cover every aspect of political and social reality, especially new issues emerging in a changing society. Activities around which bureaucracies are not organized or issues that fall between jurisdictional boundaries are largely neglected in the policy process (Lowi [1969] 1979).

Beijing is not alone in facing the challenges associated with functional fragmentation. These problems are all too common in many American cities that have modernized their governments and management systems in successive reform movements during the first half of the twentieth century. In New York City, for instance, issues such as welfare, the control of environmental pollution, land use, and transportation are all in the hands of a number of bureaucratic agencies. Committed to their own professional norms and departmental interests, bureaucrats from different agencies are reluctant to act collaboratively so that many policy issues have to suffer from stalemate (Sayre and Kaufman 1960). Similar situations existed in Los Angeles, Oakland, St. Louis, and Boston (Lowi [1969] 1979). Such urban experiences prompted Sayre and Kaufman to describe modern bureaucracies as "islands of functional power" and compelled Lowi to name them "new machines," both revealing that functional fragmentation impoverishes the centralized control of mayors and leaves cities ungoverned.

Functional fragmentation has significantly constrained the interaction of actors and shaped the policy process of urban preservation in Beijing. To protect the interests of their agencies and to avoid violating the authority of others, bureaucrats need to distinguish what is within and what is outside their jurisdictions and take care to avoid doing things beyond the boundaries. When problems arise, they tend to run away and blame other agencies. Therefore, although many municipal bureaus are in charge of urban preservation, no one is responsible for comprehensive protection of the Old City. Specifically, historic monuments and urban texture are treated as two separate objects under the framework of functional fragmentation. The former is within the jurisdiction of the single line administration of cultural heritage, whereas the latter is within the domains of different functional bureaus. The relatively unitary political structure makes it easier for public officials to mobilize resources and to carry out preservation projects on historic monuments. By contrast, the dispersed power arrangement turns any given historic district into no-man's land.

After the designation of the thirty historic districts and the creation of preservation plans in those areas, it is not clear which agency should take action to preserve the designated areas. When interviewing a BMCUP official in charge of making the plans, I asked him why the commission did not take further steps to implement the preservation plans in designated areas. He answered, "The duty of our agency is just to make the plans, no more than that" (B0605). Similarly, officials from BMCC contend that their task is to issue demolition, whereas BMCDR officials maintain that their role is to supervise the citywide allocation of land and funds. Neither of them considers the implementation of the preservation plans within their respective jurisdiction. Largely because of their educational background in history or archeology, many officials from the BMACH show strong concerns about the conditions of old neighborhoods. However, they are powerless because their authority is limited to historic monuments. In other words, if there are no monument buildings in an area, they are unable to engage in the preservation practice (B0603). Without specific procedures for preserving historic districts, the designation is largely in vain. Most preservation districts are still suffering from dilapidation or different kinds of destruction.

Collaboration between municipal bureaus is needed for effective preservation of historic districts. However, bureaucrats' loyalty to the professional norms and interests of their own agencies largely prohibits them
from acting collectively. To facilitate the collaboration between bureaucratic agencies, the municipality established a special committee, named
the Leading Group for Social Housing Construction, Old and Dilapidated
Housing Renewal, and Urban Preservation. The special committee is headed
by a vice-mayor and composed of top officials from all relevant municipal
bureaus. A special office is created under the administration of BMCC to
handle the daily affairs of the committee. The goal of the Leading Group
is to provide a stage for different municipal bureaus to coordinate with
each other; thus, it provides better resolutions to the conflict between urban preservation and redevelopment in the Old City and effectively protects the designated areas (B0613).

Although the central leadership decided it was important to preserve
the old districts of Beijing and took actions to facilitate the collaboration
between bureaucratic agencies, the effort is largely in vain. The Leading
Group is designed as an engine for overcoming the hurdle of functional
fragmentation, but officials still prioritize the agendas and demands of their
own agencies so that the Leading Group becomes a battlefield for different
departmental interests (B0613, B0615). Specifically, because the special office is staffed by BMCC, BMCC becomes the most powerful stakeholder in
the Leading Group, and its preferences often outweigh those of other agencies. Officials from both BMCUP and BMACH complain that although
the Leading Group is supposed to complete a wide range of tasks, as its
name indicates, the only thing it has done effectively is construct social
housing, because it is in the interest of BMCC (B0613, B0615).

Besides the conflict of interests between agencies, functional fragmentation generates ambiguity and disputes over the procedures of urban
preservation, substantially slowing down the processing of preservation
initiatives in historic districts. To guide the practice of urban preservation
in designated areas, the special office implemented the Procedure of Housing Protection and Renovation in Historic Preservation Areas. According
to the procedure, a project is eligible to receive funds from BMCDR and
a Letter of Planning Opinions from BMCUP after it is permitted by the
special office. However, BMCDR contends that it will not release funds
to a project unless it passes its financial reviews and receives its permission first; meanwhile, BMCUP maintains that it will not issue a Letter of
Planning Opinions until BMCDR agrees to provide funds for the project.

A similar debate is over when to conduct a survey of residents' opinions
about the preservation projects to be carried out in their neighborhoods.

BMCUP argues that the rules of the Ministry of Construction require the survey to be conducted before it provides the Letter of Planning Opinions. According to the procedure made by the special office, BMCUP should provide the Letter of Planning Opinions and the permit of demolition and removal first, and then the survey can be conducted in the neighborhoods (Beijing Municipal Policy Research Bureau 2004). Because of buck passing between bureaucratic agencies, such a survey was never carried out. This example clearly shows that functional fragmentation increases the difficulty of urban preservation by creating ambiguity in the procedure and leaving space for disputes between bureaucratic agencies.

Despite changes in the municipal agenda from demolition to preservation, the implementation of preservation projects is not smooth. Functional fragmentation at the municipal level serves as the main impediment to preservation projects in historic districts. Without specific guidelines from the municipality on how to preserve historic districts, the authority of managing those areas is devolved to district governments. Regardless of the discretion district officials have over the preservation projects, these projects are not free from the impact of functional fragmentation. On one hand, the fragmented municipal structure serves as a filter through which district officials often have to go in order to turn their policy initiatives into policy outputs. On the other hand, there is functional fragmentation in the district or subdistrict agencies that constrains the implementation of the preservation initiatives at the local level. The following sections provide three case studies to illustrate in detail the policy process of urban preservation in Beijing.

Restoring the Old City Walls

The old city walls with their fourteen city gates were demolished from the early 1950s to the late 1970s, despite the proposal made by renowned architect and urban planner Liang Sicheng to preserve the city walls and convert them into an elevated City Walls Park (Shen 2002; Wang 2003). Similar to many historic monuments torn down in that era, the city walls were seen as the legacy of the imperial political order that deserved to be destroyed in the building of a socialist capital. The demolition was also justified by the need to develop new transportation systems, as the city walls and gates were considered obstacles to the traffic. The government launched a large political campaign to destroy the city walls and mobilized almost all residents of Beijing to participate. With the demolition of the city walls, a ring of highways and a subway were constructed on the site. Nearly fifty years after the demolition, however, the government launched

FIGURE 8. Restoring the Inner City Walls.

preservation projects to restore the city walls. As part of the "Cultural Heritage Preservation Plan for an Olympiad of Humanity," the projects led to the restoration of the southeastern corner of the Inner City Walls, the base of the Eastern Imperial City Walls, and the City Gate Yongdingmen of the Outer City. Two city walls parks were also constructed surrounding the restored city walls.

The restoration of the Inner City Walls was initiated by BMACH. It took place between 2000 and 2002 and cost more than 700 million RMB (Figure 8). Recent fieldwork discovered 16 kilometers of city walls at the southeastern corner of the Inner City (Kong 2002). They survived the demolition because many temporary shelters were built within them in the 1960s. However, this also meant that the remaining walls were in very bad shape (Zheng 2003). After removing the residents and clearing up the environment, the city government encouraged citizens to donate the city wall bricks that many of them had used in building their own houses. Local newspapers publicized a slogan: "In the past, to demolish the city walls was to love Beijing; today, to restore the city walls is also to love Beijing" (Zheng 2003). This slogan shows how the same historic monument is interpreted differently in different time periods, driven by the different goals of the political leaders. The contrasting interpretations reflect

FIGURE 9. Ming City Walls Relics Park.

the fundamental change in political decisions about cultural heritage and urban preservation. As two different yet related social movements, the demolition and restoration of the city walls demonstrate the government's mobilization of citizens that borders on ideological coercion and the imposition of collective interest determined by the central leadership. Given that Beijing is the capital city of the centralized Chinese state, the call for loving Beijing in both movements has the effect of boosting nationalism.

Using the old bricks donated by citizens and some new ones, the municipality renovated the remaining walls and built several new segments. In 2002, the area was finally turned into Ming City Walls Relics Park (Figure 9). The total size of the park is 154,000 square kilometers, including gardens and walking paths (Kong 2002; Zheng 2003). As the first major restoration effort in Beijing's urban preservation history, the project is considered a great success by the municipality. It helped the city rediscover a part of its memory that was forcefully erased decades ago. More importantly, the restored city walls serve as a showcase for the cultural and historical significance of the city.

Following the example of the Ming City Walls Relics Park, Dongcheng District initiated the construction of the East Imperial City Walls Site Park in 2001, and it spent 800 million RMB on the project. Because no relic

of the wall remained above ground, two underground plazas were constructed to display the bases of the wall, as well as a 2.8-kilometer-long,
29-meter-wide pedestrian path to symbolize the eastern wall (Kong 2001).
According to local officials, the project is not only a milestone in reviving
the traditional culture of Beijing but also a great step toward the Imperial City's designation as a UNESCO World Heritage Site (Kong 2001).

Despite the cultural significance of the project, a municipal official at
BMACH revealed that the goal of the East Imperial City Walls Site Park
is not just to capture the historic value of the place (B0615):

> It's very cunning of the district governor to build the park.
> You know the district constructed the New Oriental Plaza[7] in
> 2000. The project was very controversial because it caused the
> demolition of a large amount of well-maintained courtyard
> houses. Many people criticized this project. A major goal
> for Dongcheng District in building the wall park is actually
> to shift people's focus. If they blame the District for the
> demolition caused by the project of the New Oriental Plaza,
> the governor can point to the park and say, "Look, we have
> preservation." So the construction of the park is basically a
> strategy to shut people's mouths. Actually, to make space for the
> heritage park, they demolished several historic neighborhoods
> nearby. But the District never mentions this to the public.

The story of the East Imperial City Walls Site Park clearly shows how
urban preservation is manipulated by the local government to facilitate
the operation of the growth machine. The restoration project helps the
district government placate discontentment about urban demolition and
create a better image for the district. Urban preservation is no longer for
the sake of historic structures but becomes a strategic device for political
actors to achieve political and economic goals.

Another project implemented by BMACH is the restoration of Yongdingmen, the central city gate of the Outer City. The project took two years
(2003–2005) to complete and cost more than 19 million RMB.[8] Whereas
the original Yongdingmen consisted of a gate tower, an embrasure tower,
and a barbican, the restored version has only the gate tower (Figure 10).
However, experts involved in the project did a thorough examination of
the archives to ensure that the new gate tower looked exactly like the old
one. Situated at the southern end of the Central Axis, the rebuilt city gate is
considered by both local officials and news media to have a unique value,

FIGURE 10. *(top)* Original Yongdingmen in the early twentieth century, consisting of the embrasure tower (front), the gate tower (behind), and the barbican. *The Old City Gates of Beijing* (Beijing: Beijing Arts and Photography Publishing House, 2001), figure 164. *(bottom)* Restored Yongdingmen in 2005, with only the gate tower.

because it completes the configuration of the Central Axis of Beijing, the longest central axis in the world (Gao 2003). Furthermore, because the Olympic Park is located at the northern extension of the Central Axis, the city gate is considered especially meaningful for the status of Beijing as the host city of the Olympic Games (Wang et al. 2003).

The rebuilding of Yongdingmen is a typical example of how cultural heritage is selected and reinterpreted to promote urban growth. The city gate is no longer thought of as the politically incorrect relic of the Imperial era, nor is it an obstacle to the construction of a socialist capital. Instead, it is repackaged as a symbol of Beijing's superiority in urban design history and its prosperity as a global city. Despite the significant role of the project in creating a better image for the city, it poses many questions for urban preservation. First, does the rebuilt city gate have any cultural or historical value? Or is it simply a fake antique, without any authenticity? Secondly, even if the rebuilt city gate has certain value, is it wise for the government to invest so much money in this project, given that many existing monuments and centuries-old courtyard houses are suffering from dilapidation? And, finally, does the restoration project stress or deny the importance of urban preservation? If any demolished buildings can be restored, why should we preserve?

From Qianmen to "Champs-Élysées"

Urban preservation in historic districts is a completely different story from the restoration of the city walls. Although renovating or restoring historic monuments is mainly about the physical structure of the buildings, urban preservation in historic districts faces a series of challenges including reducing the population density, improving living conditions in old neighborhoods, and revitalizing the local economy. Solving those problems entails collaboration between municipal agencies, but functional fragmentation largely prohibits them from acting collectively. Despite the policy initiative of the municipality to preserve the residential fabric, the city fails to provide specific guidelines on how to carry out preservation projects in designated areas. In reality, the authority of managing the preservation districts is passed to local political agencies at the district and subdistrict levels. This section examines the policy process of urban preservation in the Qianmen Historic Preservation District. It shows how local officials use urban preservation as a tool to increase the property values of the area and attract outlets of world-renowned luxury brands, in the hope of turning the historical core of the district into another Champs-Élysées.

Qianmen is originally the name of the central city gate that connects the Inner and Outer City, and it also refers to the area surrounding the central city gate. It is a densely populated neighborhood in the Outer City, less than half a mile south of the Forbidden City. In the Qing dynasty, as the ruling Manchu elites ordered all Han Chinese residents and commercial activities to be relocated to the Outer City, the Qianmen area became the downtown of imperial Beijing. Here developed a great congestion of shops, restaurants, tea houses, and operas. With the rapid development of commercial and entertainment activities, residential neighborhoods multiplied. As part of the Central Axis, Qianmen Street is the heart of this area. It occupies a prominent position, with its large number of permanent shops and restaurants catering to the demands of a diverse group of customers, from privileged officials and aristocrats to ordinary citizens. The buildings along Qianmen Street were constructed or renovated in different epochs, from the Qing dynasty to the Republican era, to the socialist regime, and to the most recent economic reform. They represent the architectural styles of different eras and thus turn the street into a panorama of contemporary Chinese history.

Today, as one of the thirty historic preservation districts, the Qianmen area is in Chongwen District. There was no action to preserve or renovate this area until the district government initiated a project to redevelop the area in 2005. To emphasize the importance of the project, the district government named it "No. 1 Project" (B0603). The project has three parts. The first part is to turn Qianmen Street into a pedestrian-only street for shopping and entertainment. Because automobiles are not allowed to enter the street, the second part is to build two new roads—East Side Road and West Side Road—cutting through the preservation district, parallel to Qianmen Street at the east and the west sides (B0615). Surrounding Qianmen Street is a densely populated residential area of 105 hectares, containing about 20,000 families, or more than 60,000 inhabitants (B0620). The last part of the project is to redevelop the residential area.

Although there was no consensus on how to transform Qianmen Street into a pedestrian street, the district government closed the entire street and began to demolish the shops at the end of 2005. During the demolition, many boards were erected along the street, which read "Preserve the character of the Old Beijing." As the demolition went on, there were heated debates at the BMCUP on how to renovate Qianmen Street. One proposal was to preserve and repair existing structures so as to maintain the architectural profile of the street as a panorama of contemporary Chinese history. An urban planner pointed out that because most buildings are in good shape, what the government should do to Qianmen Street is "wash its face" rather than "conducting plastic surgery" (B0615). By contrast, another proposal questioned the historic value of the buildings constructed after the Republican era. It recommended that the government demolish everything built after the Republican era and build new structures in historic style (B0615).

Almost a year after the demolition of the street, the BMCUP made the final decision to adopt the second proposal and to reconstruct Qianmen Street in the late Qing and early Republican styles. The district government strongly favored this approach (B0603, B0615). First, tearing down old buildings and constructing new ones in a uniform style was thought to be easier and quicker to do than evaluating the conditions of existing buildings and repairing them one by one. Because the district government had to finish the project before the opening ceremony of the Olympic Games in August 2008, the reconstruction approach was considered more feasible. Second, by replacing buildings from recent eras with new structures in a more historical style, the reconstruction was supposed to enhance the historical significance of Qianmen Street. It makes visible the district officials' effort to preserve cultural heritage, enhancing the image of the district government. Third, the reconstruction gave the district government a chance to upgrade the physical conditions of the shops and to attract well-known luxury brands to open their stores on the street. One district official said that the district government's goal was to turn Qianmen Street from a working-class shopping area to another Champs-Élysées (B0801). Such a change would significantly increase the rent and generate more revenue for the district government.

The reconstruction of Qianmen Street was rapidly carried out, at a cost of 10 billion RMB from the district government's budget. All but 20 percent of the buildings along the street were demolished. The old photos of Qianmen Street in the early twentieth century were used as a blueprint for constructing the façade of new buildings (B0801) (Figure 11). To highlight the traditional taste of the street, the lamps are made to resemble bird cages and hand drums, which are considered symbols of Beijing folk culture. Although the project has been implemented in the name of urban preservation, many preservationists criticize that it destroys rather than maintains the historic character of the street. They argue that the old Qianmen Street is a good example of how cities grow naturally over time, whereas the new one is simply pastiche made overnight without any authenticity (B0802, B0805).

The preservation project also led to commercial gentrification and fundamentally changed the nature of business activities in the area. The Qianmen area was one of the most popular spots for shopping and dining in

FIGURE 11. The vision for new Qianmen Street.

FIGURE 12. Qianmen Street after the preservation project. Outlets of world-renowned luxury brands have moved in, and street lamps are made to resemble bird cages, a symbol of Beijing's traditional folk culture.

Beijing. Some of the shops and restaurants were more than a century old and nationally known, and the district remained affordable for working-class customers. However, many old shops and restaurants left Qianmen Street after the preservation project because of the rise in rent. But local officials were not concerned by this loss of tenants, because their plan was to attract international brands to Qianmen Street in order to increase revenue and enhance the image of the area. Nevertheless, the road to attracting ideal tenants was not smooth. Because there are already several upscale megamalls nearby, Qianmen Street had difficulty attracting business at first (B0801; B0809). Although construction of the shops was completed in May 2008, most shops remained empty for a year. Today, Qianmen Street is full of international vendors, from more luxury ones such as Rolex and Cartier to more popular ones such as Zara and Swatch (Figure 12). Local restaurants and snack shops have been replaced by international chains, including Starbucks, Häagen-Dazs, and McDonald's. With the process of commercial gentrification, Qianmen Street has gradually disappeared from the locals' shopping map and become a place of entertainment catering to the taste of tourists.

Similar to the reconstruction of Qianmen Street, the redevelopment of the residential area was pushed forward by the district government without a solid plan in place. The demolition was partly legitimized by the construction of the East Side Road and the West Side Road. In the rest of the area, demolition was justified by the proposal to improve the deteriorated conditions of the courtyard houses. The district government designated many houses as "dilapidated and dangerous" *(wei fang)* without a careful examination of their real conditions (B0611, B0616). With the old neighborhood being rapidly bulldozed, the district government made a plan to replace the historic courtyard houses with two- to six-story, historic-looking buildings. Those buildings will not accommodate the current residents of the area. Instead, they will be constructed as high-end residences and sold at market price (B0603, B0615).

The redevelopment plan for the residential area is considered problematic by some municipal officials; however, it was still quickly approved by the municipality. In fact, the functional fragmentation between municipal bureaus creates small niches through which the district government could exercise its discretion in decision making. Officials from the BMACH generally oppose the demolition of old courtyard houses because of their educational background in history and archeology. But there is nothing they can do about the demolition because their authority is limited to historic monuments. Alternately, officials from the BMCUP cannot prevent the plan from being implemented either, because they are in charge of zoning, yet the height of the proposed new buildings does not break the zoning code (B0615). Some well-known experts in urban planning and historic preservation from the China Academy of Urban Planning and Design were invited to participate in the decision-making process. However, they were given very little time to review the plan before the final meeting, so they were unable to provide any constructive suggestions. In other words, the participation of experts is mainly window dressing to lend legitimacy to the project.

After the plan was approved by the municipality, the district government quickly took real steps to carry out the project. Because the law does not allow government agencies to participate in real estate development, the district government established two real estate companies—Tianjie Real Estate Development Company and Da Qianmen Real Estate Development Company—to manage the project. Although both of them are registered as independent companies, they are staffed by district officials and work under the command of the district governor (B0604, B0801). The strategy is called "one team, two titles" *(yi tao ren ma, liang kuai pai zi)*. It is widely used by local governments in China, allowing public officials to manipulate resources and market opportunities and to obtain economic benefits from redevelopment projects. Because the local government exercises its monopoly under the cover of the companies, many people describe the situation as "hanging out a sheep's head but selling dog meat" *(gua yang tou, mai gou rou)*.

Besides creating real estate companies, the district government reorganized its personnel to facilitate the redevelopment project. Specifically, it divided the personnel into four teams responsible for different aspects of the project, including engineering, propaganda, demolition and removal, and coordination. Leaders of the four teams meet every week to discuss important aspects of the project (B0801). To increase the speed of demolition, the district government divided the whole area into several segments. Each segment is led by ten district officials. A district official describes his work as follows (B0604):

> I'm from the District Bureau of Education. The district government
> assigns me to the Team of Demolition and Removal, responsible
> for the 6th segment of the area. We don't know who works
> in other segments adjacent to ours, nor do we know the total
> number of district officials who are involved in the project. But it
> doesn't matter, because we all have the same goal of finishing the
> demolition as soon as possible.

This quote shows the huge capacity of the local government to mobilize its personnel and reinforce political control. Despite the resistance from inhabitants, demolition was rapidly carried out in the area. During the first half of 2006, more than two-thirds of the courtyard houses were demolished. In turn, this led to the displacement of 12,000 families, which accounts for more than 60 percent of the total population displaced in Beijing in that period (B0604).

The residents were left in a vulnerable and disadvantaged position because of the redevelopment project. First, many residents left the neighborhood unwillingly because of the coercion they faced during demolition. To speed up demolition, the district government demolished each house as soon as the residents moved out so that houses still inhabited became small islands in the midst of ruins. Residents who refused to move out faced problems of security and sanitation, along with the inconvenience of purchasing daily supplies as shopping facilities in the area closed. Second, to maximize economic return from the redevelopment project, the district government decided not to build affordable housing in the area. Given the high housing prices after redevelopment, it is almost impossible for working-class residents to afford apartments there, even though some of them have lived in the neighborhood for generations (B0604). Such a policy not only destroys the local community but also undermines the residents' right of inhabitation.

Third, to reduce the cost of relocation, the district government refused to give residents information about the planned land use after the demolition, so that they could not claim the appropriate subsidy amount. A district official reveals the problematic process of distributing subsidies (B0604):

> According to the Demolition Law, the amount of subsidies given
> to residents is based on the type of land use after demolition.
> Some types of land use subsidize the residents more and some less.
> Theoretically speaking, the government should tell the residents
> clearly what is to be done in their neighborhoods after their houses
> are demolished. But none of the residents in this area knows what
> is going to be built after the demolition. To tell you the truth, even
> we, working in the district government, don't know the answer;
> only the district governor knows.... There is no standard in giving
> out the subsidies. Sometimes if the residents insist not to move,
> we have to bargain with them about the subsidies household by
> household, like bargaining on a flea market.

This quote shows how the interests of residents were severely undermined by manipulative district governors. What matters is not the law or the interests of residents but the will of local political actors.

The mismatch between the relocation subsidy and the market price is a major problem in the redevelopment process. In Qianmen, although redevelopment took place in 2006, the standard relocation subsidy for the project was set in 2001. Given the drastically increased housing prices in Beijing, the subsidy does not allow residents to purchase even a small, second-hand apartment within the 4th Ring Road. As a result, many of them have to buy or rent cheap apartments in the newly developed suburbs (B0604, B0623). Those areas are generally short on public facilities, such as hospitals and schools, so the residents' quality of life is degraded. Many working-class families cannot afford a car, and the public transportation system is not well developed. Therefore, many of them suffer long commutes between their new homes in the suburbs and workplaces in the city. The unfair relocation subsidy has become the major source of conflicts in the redevelopment process; however, there is no channel for residents to express their opinions or influence the policy process. Some of them refuse to relocate and become so-called nail households. Although resistance sometimes helps them obtain higher subsidies, more often than not they are driven out by forced demolition led by local government officials.[9]

In Qianmen, although the demolition of courtyard houses and the displacement of residents have been rapidly pushed forward by the district government, the pace of constructing new buildings in the residential area is slow. The district government plans to replace the old courtyard houses with historic-looking luxury residences, but it has no concrete idea on how to carry out the plan even after the courtyard houses are demolished. A vast piece of devastated land filled with demolition debris appears in the center of Beijing, less than half a mile south of the Forbidden City. Considering the demolition site a stain on Beijing's image, the district government built walls around the demolished residential area so that visitors cannot see it (Figure 13). To highlight the historic flavor of the area, the walls are decorated with gray tiles and traditional paintings. The walls separate two different worlds. On one side is the new Qianmen Street, lined up with brand-new, historic-looking stores selling products with global labels; on the other side is the vast land of vacancy and ruins, where the centuries-old courtyard houses used to stand and memories of Old Beijing used to reside.

FIGURE 13. *(top)* A vast historic residential area surrounding Qianmen Street was demolished to make place for new construction. *(bottom)* A wall designed in historical style has been built to conceal the demolition site.

Shishahai: The Bar District Along the Lake

Qianmen and Shishahai are often considered parallel cases for discussion in the urban history of Beijing. Whereas the former represents the folk culture *(su wen hua)*, the latter is the best demonstration of refined culture *(ya wen hua)*. Shishahai is located at the northwestern part of the Old City. Its name is derived from the ten *(shi)* Buddhist monasteries *(sha)* in the area. Its 301.57-hectare area includes more than forty historic monuments (including temples, royal mansions, and imperial gardens), the largest natural lake in the city, and a large historic residential area with well-maintained courtyard houses. The unique combination of architectural profile and natural landscape makes Shishahai one of the most beautiful urban areas in the city.

Shishahai is the largest historic preservation district in Beijing, designated in 2000. Within the political boundary of Xicheng District, two local administrative agencies—the Shishahai Scenic Area Administration (SSAA) and the Shishahai Street Administrative Office (SSAO)—are in charge of the daily affairs of the district. SSAA is responsible for maintaining and managing the physical conditions of the area. Its duties include making local development plans, renovating the environment, and improving tourism facilities. SSAO, on the other hand, deals exclusively with issues related to the inhabitants and the local communities (B0607).

Although SSAA is the main local actor in charge of urban preservation in Shishahai, in reality a variety of municipal and district agencies are involved in the policy process and make the picture of urban preservation extremely complicated. For instance, all historic monuments are under the control of cultural heritage administrations, including the State Administration of Cultural Heritage, the BMACH, and the District Committee of Culture, depending on the heritage status of the structures. The lake is administered by the Environment Protection Bureau and the Science and Technology Commission at the district and the municipal levels. The repair and renovation of courtyard houses is the responsibility of the District Bureau of Housing Administration (B0602, B0607).

The segmentation between different municipal and district bureaus creates obstacles for the local administration in Shishahai. It is difficult for a local administrative agency to be responsible to a number of superior agencies with different interests and policy agendas. An official from SSAA describes the situation as "one daughter-in-law, too many mothers-in-law" (B0616):

> We need to serve so many different bureaus from both the city and
> the district—planning, cultural heritage, housing, landscape and
> forestry, so on and so forth. They are all our "mothers-in-law." We
> don't dare to offend any of them. But they want really different
> things, so it's very difficult to please them all.

This quote reveals a typical problem of public administration in contemporary China. Constrained by their professional norms and departmental interests, public officials often neglect the big picture and refuse to act
collectively. It creates hurdles for local political actors and slows down
the policy process.

However, this is just one side of the coin. On the other hand, when different bureaucratic agencies are involved in the policy process but their
responsibilities are ill defined, no one takes the responsibility for preserving
the historic district. The situation generates a vacuum of power in which
the local administration can exercise its discretion. An official from the
District Committee of Culture explains how political fragmentation increases the local autonomy of SSAA (B0602):

> The government structure is so much fragmented by *tiao* and
> *kuai*. Shishahai Historic Preservation District becomes an
> independent kingdom. There is no way to implement effective
> and comprehensive preservation in the area. Since no municipal
> or district bureau can really do anything, SSAA has gained lots of
> power in reality. It can do many things in the district, including
> rent-seeking with local business owners.

Political fragmentation clearly has dual effects on the local administration
in Shishahai. On one hand, the institutional complexity brings procedural
obstacles to the local actors and slows down the policy process. On the
other hand, it provides channels for local actors to implement their discretion and enlarge their autonomy. The dual effects of functional fragmentation provide an institutional background to understanding the policy
process of urban preservation in Shishahai.

For a long time, there was no specific plan made by the municipality
to preserve Shishahai. From 2002 to 2005, experts from UNESCO and
the European Union (EU)[10] conducted research in Shishahai on how to
protect the residential fabric and maintain social stability in the preservation district, but their suggestions had no substantial impact on the policy
(B0522, B0523, B0612). Under the lead of the district government and the

local administration, however, part of Shishahai has been transformed into a bar district, whereas the vast residential area has been ignored.

Bars first emerged in Shishahai in 2003; at first there were only about ten. In the heart of the historic district, these bars provide a combination of traditional Chinese culture and Western-style entertainment. The unique juxtaposition of the old and the new as well as the Chinese and the foreign has generated a hybrid diversity that makes the area increasingly popular among foreign visitors and young urban professionals. However, commercial activities in historic districts are a completely new phenomenon in Beijing, and the municipality does not have any existing policy to regulate those activities. Worse yet, it is even not clear which government agency should be in charge of the bars. Although the management of bars in Shishahai is a gray area, the local administration has wide discretion in the policy process.

The district government quickly realized the economic potential of the bars and provided strong support for their growth. The vice-governor of Xicheng District commented on the district government's policy toward the bars (B0609):

> We are glad to see the emergence of bars in Shishahai. It shows that history and recreation finds a beautiful junction in the revitalization of the historic district. Small scale and low cost characterize the current managerial mode of the bars, but this stage will be over soon. The district government encourages bar owners to increase their investment and enlarge the scale of their business.... We are not going to forcefully control the number of the bars; we will leave it to the market.

The statement shows that the district government considers commercial activities an important driver in the revitalization of Shishahai. To maximize economic return, the district government encourages the growth of bars without regulations on their number or quality. Under such policies, the number of bars increased to more than 120 by 2005 (B0608). Almost all the houses facing main streets or surrounding the lake have become bars. Many sidewalks have been taken over by bar owners as terraces for their bars, leaving no space for pedestrians to walk around (Figure 14). In an old neighborhood named Yan Dai Xie Jie, a centuries-old Taoist temple is now occupied by a bar that serves drinks and provides entertainment for visitors.

To increase the number of bars, SSAA built a bar street named Lotus

Figure 14. Bars in Shishahai.

Figure 15. Pedicab drivers waiting for customers in Shishahai.

Lane on the bank of the lake in 2003. The construction of Lotus Lane led to the demolition of the old street market, where the locals used to watch the lotus and enjoy seasonal food in summer. At Lotus Lane, high-end bars, cafés, and restaurants are located in new two-story buildings that mimic the historic style. It has become one of the most popular entertainment sites in Beijing among tourists and young professionals, especially at night. More importantly, it enriches the district government and SSAA with rents of more than 5.5 million RMB each year (B0610). Considered a main contributor in revitalizing Shishahai, Lotus Lane was designated as the Bar and Tea House District by the Xicheng District and the Beijing Municipal Bureau of Commerce in 2005.

Besides the boom of bars, various tours and cultural festivals take place in Shishahai. Some tour companies organize *hutong* tours to show tourists around the neighborhood using pedicabs (Figure 15). Others provide boats to visitors so that they can enjoy sightseeing on the lake. In the meantime, many cultural festivals are held in Shishahai. The Tourism and Culture Festival and the Olympic Cultural Festival are two major activities held annually (B0612). The cultural festivals turned the historic district into an outdoor theater.

With the rapid commodification of cultural heritage, a process of Disneyfication is at work in Shishahai. In this process, urban space has increasingly lost its original character and is repackaged under certain themes that appeal to the domestic and international consumerist elite (Zukin 1993, 1996). In Shishahai, although Disneyfication helps improve the local economy by attracting more visitors to the area, it undermines the cultural significance of the historic district. For instance, the renovations made to the old houses by bar owners tend to damage the historic structures; unregulated commercial activities (such as pedicab tours) often destroy the peaceful atmosphere of the old neighborhood.

In addition to the harm caused to the aesthetic unity of the area, Disneyfication has negative social impacts on the neighborhood. First, recreation projects enrich local governments and private business owners, but they provide few economic benefits to the local community. Most inhabitants of Shishahai are working-class people with low or medium incomes. Very few of them can afford to run their own businesses in their rapidly commercializing neighborhood. The only chance for them to obtain an economic benefit is to rent their houses to bar or shop owners from outside the district, and this option is open only to those whose houses face the street or the lake (B0503, B0615). In addition, because most bars and shops like to hire young, cheap migrant workers, the inhabitants are also deprived of job opportunities in the booming local service economy (B0503, B0618).

Second, the creation of urban amenities does not enhance the quality of life for the inhabitants; instead, it generates many inconveniences. Because the majority of residents are working-class people, they generally cannot afford to visit the expensive bars and restaurants in their neighborhood. Nonetheless, they suffer from the associated problems, such as the loss of public space, the noise of the bars at night, and traffic jams caused by pedicab tours (B0415, B0503, B0518). In other words, Disneyfication has drastically changed the urban landscape and human dimension of Shishahai. The creation of urban amenities facilitates urban growth but undermines the cultural significance of old neighborhoods and adversely affects the lifestyle and wellbeing of local communities.

To prepare for the Olympics, SSAA carried out new preservation plans in 2005. However, the plans focused on improving tourist facilities, without much consideration for maintaining historical structures or protecting the welfare of residents in the district (B0613, B0614). An urban planner describes such plans as "speculations" *(tou ji),* which aim at significant events such as the Olympic Games or the 50th Anniversary of the National Day but do not address the long-term interests of the historic district and the local community. Nonetheless, those plans can create visible achievement in a short time, so they help local officials get promotions (B0616).

Facing the prospect of economic returns from recreation, SSAA was no longer satisfied with just being a regulator of entertainment activities and has become a player itself. It established its own investment company and tourism company in 2003, named Beijing San Hai Investment and Management Center and Beijing Shishahai Tourism Development Center, respectively (B0607, B0608). Because of its monopoly on local resources, SSAA can institute many policies that are preferential to its companies. Besides the franchise for organizing the *hutong* tours and lake tours in the most desirable areas, its companies have special permission to organize tours of royal mansions and courtyard houses, which private tourism companies are not allowed to enter (B0610). Manipulation by SSAA leads to illegal commercial activities and vicious competition. An urban planner at Tsinghua University who works with SSAA points out that most of the problems in the local commercial activities are caused by SSAA and its own companies (B0614).

To solve the problems in management and, in particular, to constrain the excessive power of SSAA, the district government took two steps to reorganize the administrative structure of Shishahai in 2008. First, SSAA was relegated from a subdivision of the district government to a subdivision of SSAO. This change is supposed to incorporate the two local agencies so as to find better solutions to problems related to both the physical environment and the residents in the area. However, as the new "boss" of the SSAA, SSAO does not have enough resources or expertise to make decisions in the preservation district. In the process of decision making, SSAA still has to ask for the district government's opinion after consulting with SSAO. The change makes the administrative structure more complicated and further slows down the policy process. Meanwhile, more problems were left unattended in the gaps between the three tiers of local administration (B0804).

Second, the power of SSAA was divided into two parts: regulatory power *(guan li)* and managerial power *(jing ying)*. The former remains in the hands of SSAA, but the latter is given to the District Bureau of Landscape and Forestry (DBLF). In other words, SSAA no longer has the authority to manage public resources (such as lakes and land) for economic return. For instance, if a boat tour company wants to run its business on the lake, it needs to get a permit from DBLF instead of SSAA. Meanwhile, its business is regulated by SSAA, including where the boats can go to and how late they can run on the lake (B0804). The separation between regulatory power and managerial power is meant to establish a mechanism of checks and balances in order to increase fairness and effectiveness in the local administration. However, as an SSAA official points out, SSAA is below the administrative rank of DBLF, so that it cannot effectively exercise its power to regulate DBLF and business owners. Consequently, the commercial activities are still largely out of control.

Genuine steps to preserve the historic district were absent for a long time. Although the courtyard houses have not undergone demolition and reconstruction, as in the Qianmen area, they have suffered from dilapidation for decades. The first initiative to preserve the residential fabric was carried out in 2005 when SSAA launched a pilot project to renovate courtyard houses in Yan Dai Xie Jie. The project is fairly small in scale. It covers a 0.37-hectare area and includes sixteen courtyard houses and forty families. A special office was set up by SSAA to manage the project. Different from the prevailing mode of wholesale demolition and reconstruction, the project adopted a new approach of organic renovation. Because the approach attempts to examine and renovate courtyard houses one by one in order to minimize damage to the houses and protect the interests of residents, it is also called micro-circulation. The first step is to conduct a survey in each courtyard house, with questions that focus on housing quality, the number of residents, and their ownership status. The second step is to reduce population density. Residents make their decisions on whether to stay or to move out though negotiation. Those who agree to move out receive subsidies from the government. And, finally, renovation is implemented house by house. The local government pays for the infrastructure, and the residents who choose to stay pay for the renovation of their own houses (B0614, B0616).

The pilot project in Yan Dai Xie Jie is considered promising because it challenges the old mode of urban redevelopment and offers a new approach for preserving courtyard houses and protecting the welfare of residents. However, carrying out the project is not so easy. In addition to the district government's concern about expenses, functional fragmentation has slowed down the project. For instance, it took the municipality three years, from 2000 to 2003, to approve the project *(li xiang)*. An official in the special office of the Yan Dai Xie Jie project comments (B0614),

> We waited three years for the municipality to approve the
> project. Why? Because the relations between different parts of
> the government are messed up. We have to deal with so many
> government agencies, at both district and municipal levels,
> including urban planning, construction, housing management,
> cultural heritage, finance, and development and reform. The main
> dispute is between BMCC and BMCDR, because neither of them
> can persuade the other to issue our project.... To understand the
> relations between different departments, the most important things
> to keep in mind are responsibility *(ze)*, power *(quan)*, and benefit
> *(li)*. They all want to gain power *(quan)* in order to grab benefit
> *(li)*; meanwhile get rid of responsibility *(ze)*.

This quote shows that beneath the surface of political fragmentation are turf wars over benefits. Policy issues are manipulated by bureaucrats to meet the agendas of their agencies. The hurdles of political fragmentation are not easy to overcome, as they are perpetuated by political actors' enduring pursuit of power and interests.

Political fragmentation still constrained the policy process of the pilot project after it was issued by the municipality. On one hand, there have been endless disputes between the district government and the municipality on how to finance the project. The district government wants the city to provide some funds for the renovation of urban infrastructure, but they have not agreed on how to split the bill (B0614). On the other hand, although officials in the special office blame city officials for their reluctance to take responsibilities, they behave the same way in the implementation of the project. Afraid to take responsibility when decisions are to be made, the best they can do is to "ask for instructions from the superior" *(qing shi shang ji)*. In the worst case scenario, no one knows who the superior is, so that the implementation of the project is slowed down or falls into stalemate (B0616).

The special office has finished surveying the courtyard houses and their residents, but it is not clear when the entire project will be completed. Even if the renovation of the sixteen courtyard houses in the pilot project is completed, the question remains: what to be done to improve housing quality in the rest of the residential area? Without any solid steps being taken, Disneyfication still dominates the agenda of urban preservation in Shishahai. The busy commercial streets and the lakefront receive a lot of attention from the local government, while vast areas of old housing stock sink into dilapidation.

Conclusion

In Beijing, many projects take place in the name of urban preservation. From the restored Yongdingmen Gate Tower to the reconstructed, historic-looking Qianmen Street to the trendy bars in Shishahai Preservation District, urban preservation becomes a tool for local officials to improve the image of Beijing and to increase their revenue. However, if we look beyond the preservation projects and scrutinize the quality of their physical results, we wonder whether the historic city is indeed being preserved or damaged by the "preservation efforts." What policymakers often seem to forget is a basic fact of urban preservation: heritage cannot be saved if it is torn down. When local officials are busy making plans on how to intensify the use of land or how to draw more tourist attention, the maintenance and protection of historic buildings are left out of their agenda. Some historic buildings are simply torn down to make way for historic-looking pastiche. With the marginalization of historic structures, the practice of urban preservation becomes increasingly symbolic.

The essence of symbolic urban preservation is a product of the hybrid pattern of urban growth that reconciles various and often contradictory interests, demands, and goals. Symbolic urban preservation does not stop but facilitates demolition by lending legitimacy to redevelopment efforts outside the preservation zones and by pacifying those who object to urban renewal. Meanwhile, it helps the local government boost the local economy and market the image of the city by transforming cultural heritage into commodities or showcases. To better serve the growth agenda, symbolic urban preservation is highly selective in both the object and the approach of preservation. In terms of object, it prioritizes significant monuments that have obvious appeal but ignores the broader urban texture. In terms of approach, it relies heavily on methods such as restoration and façade protection, which highlight selective elements of the structures but reduce their overall authenticity. As the chapter demonstrates, symbolic urban preservation has substantial negative effects on the cultural integrity of the city and the quality of life of local communities.

Functional fragmentation in municipal bureaucracies plays a critical role in nurturing the emergence of symbolic urban preservation in Beijing. On one hand, it turns the issue of urban preservation, especially preservation in historic districts, into no-man's land. Although many bureaucratic agencies appear to be involved in urban preservation, none of them takes the responsibility of preserving the entire cityscape, so that many preservation decrees and plans merely stay on paper. On the other hand, it generates a vacuum of power for district governments to exercise their discretion in urban preservation, so that they gain opportunities to turn preservation projects into engines of urban growth. Despite the effort made by the municipality to facilitate the coordination between bureaucratic agencies, the hurdles of functional fragmentation are not easy to overcome, because they are deeply rooted in the diverse interests of bureaucratic agencies and are constantly fortified by their struggles for power.

CHAPTER THREE

Chicago

Aldermanic Fiefdoms and Mosaic Preservation

> Put the city up; tear the city down;
>   put it up again; let us find a city.
> Let us remember that little violet-eyed
>   man who gave all, praying, "Dig and
>   dream, dream and hammer, till your
>   city comes."
>   —CARL SANDBURG, "The Windy City"

During my first research trip to Chicago in 2004, I was lucky to meet with and have a long conversation with the deputy commissioner of the Chicago Landmarks Division. After giving me a historical overview of preservation policies in Chicago, he asked me whether I had spoken to any aldermen of the city. My answer was a confused "no"; I had no idea what an alderman was at the time. The deputy commissioner emphasized that I would not be able to fully understand how urban preservation in Chicago works unless I talked to the aldermen. Several weeks later, I had my first chance to speak to an alderman, who was the second-longest-serving alderman in Chicago at the time. After I explained my research topic to him, the alderman threw a question to me: "What is urban preservation?" This simple question caught me off guard. When I was struggling with words in my head to give him an answer, he said, "In Chicago, urban preservation is about neighborhoods." This unexpected answer opened a door for me to see a totally different Chicago.

From its very beginning, Chicago has been a city of neighborhoods (Figure 16). European immigrants arrived in the nineteenth century as the first groups of urban dwellers, followed by new immigrants from all over the world in the twentieth century. As new inhabitants flooded into the city, they found themselves drawn to the neighborhoods where people spoke the same language as them and practiced their brand of religion and where they felt the cultural values reflected their own. Whereas the whole city is racially and ethnically heterogeneous, each neighborhood is largely homogenous. Residents often adopt the architectural styles from their home countries to build new houses in the neighborhoods, creating a city with as many diverse architectural forms as its multiethnic population. When new immigrants came in, old-timers moved farther away from the urban core and built new neighborhoods in the periphery, and thus the city grew (Park and Burgess 1925; Seligman 2005). The change of population in neighborhoods is still happening in Chicago today. An Italian living in Rosemont, a neighborhood in the northwest of the city, told me (C0801),

> Ten years ago, when people heard I was from Rosemont, they
> would say, "That's right, you look Italian!" But now if I tell them I
> am from Rosemont, they would say, "Really? But you do not look
> Mexican!"

Despite the demographic changes, neighborhoods' architectural legacies are inherited by newcomers. It is not unusual in Chicago to see Indian bungalows inhabited by Germans or greystones built by Jews that are now homes to African Americans. With the unique mix of heterogeneity and homogeneity, as well as stability and change, neighborhoods are vibrant elements of the urban life of Chicago. They are the living museums in which we can observe how the city has grown and how different cultures have blossomed within it. If neighborhoods are the living cells of the urban landscape and community life in Chicago, aldermen are the guardians of neighborhoods. The city is subdivided into fifty wards, and each is presided over by an alderman (Figure 17). It is important to note that the boundaries of the wards do not necessarily coincide with those of the neighborhoods. Whereas some neighborhoods are included within single wards, others are divided by different wards. Despite the existence of strong mayoral authority and centralized municipal agencies, aldermen have significant autonomy on local issues in their wards. The longstanding tradition of aldermanic prerogative has turned wards into aldermen's local monopolies and generated a situation of territorial fragmentation.

This chapter examines how territorial fragmentation affects the policy process of urban preservation in neighborhoods. I begin the chapter by

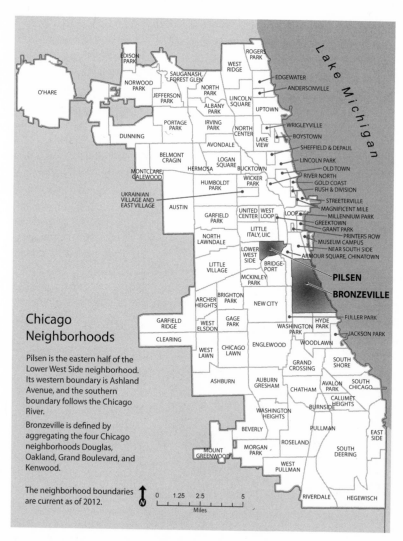

Chicago Neighborhoods

Pilsen is the eastern half of the Lower West Side neighborhood. Its western boundary is Ashland Avenue, and the southern boundary follows the Chicago River.

Bronzeville is defined by aggregating the four Chicago neighborhoods Douglas, Oakland, Grand Boulevard, and Kenwood.

The neighborhood boundaries are current as of 2012.

0   1.25   2.5   5
Miles

FIGURE 16. Chicago neighborhood map.

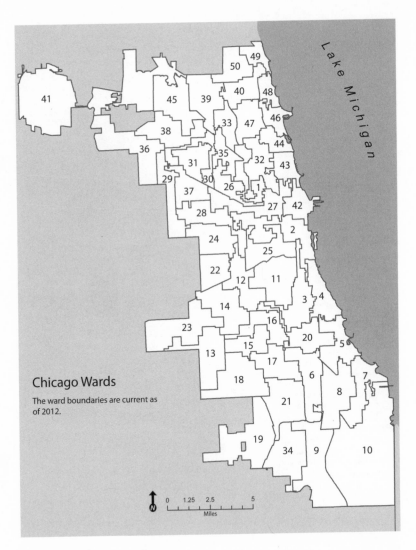

FIGURE 17. Chicago ward map.

reviewing the history of urban transformation and urban preservation in Chicago, with particular emphasis on how urban preservation is used by ethnic neighborhoods as a tool to handle the pressure of urban revitalization. I then provide an institutional history of the ward system and the tradition of aldermanic prerogative in Chicago, which is followed by an investigation of how the structure of local political representation shapes the policy process of urban preservation. In particular, I compare the processes of landmark designation in two Chicago neighborhoods, Pilsen and Bronzeville. The comparison shows that, under the impact of territorial fragmentation, preservation initiatives within single wards are more likely to be implemented than those across multiple wards. Because neighborhoods divided by ward boundaries are hard to preserve as a whole, we observe a pattern of mosaic preservation in Chicago.

"Make No Little Plans": Growth of a Metropolis

Chicago is a quintessential American metropolis. It often assumes the role of the great American exaggeration, the place where common characteristics are stretched to their limits. From its early settlement in the 1830s to the 1890s, Chicago mushroomed from a swampy frontier outpost with barely fifty inhabitants to America's second largest city, with a population of more than 1 million. Railroad tracks, stockyards, lumberyards, and factories appeared at a staggering rate, and measures of industrial output multiplied accordingly. These burgeoning industries drew Irish, German, and Eastern European immigrants into an increasingly crowded city. Chicago became the "City of the Big Shoulders," where rapid commercial and industrial expansion offered people great opportunities for wealth and material growth (Bluestone 1993). The highlight of nineteenth-century Chicago history was the World Columbian Exhibition of 1893. Chicago won the honor of hosting the world event after defeating several major American cities, including New York, Washington, D.C., and St. Louis. The fair significantly boosted Chicago's self-image and earned the city its "Windy City" nickname, which referred to the boastful claims of its leaders, not the weather (Ruble 2001).

The urban landscape of Chicago was completely changed by the Great Fire of 1871.[1] The exact cause and origin of the fire remain uncertain, but the fire incinerated almost a third of the city, including the commercial downtown and most of the North Side. Like a proud phoenix rising from the ashes, Chicago began to rebuild itself immediately after the fire. Postfire Chicago attracted the best of a generation of young architects, such as Henry Hobson Richardson, Dankmar Adler, Daniel Burnham, William LeBaron Jenney, John Wellborn Root, Louis Henry Sullivan, and Frank Lloyd Wright. These innovative young men turned the city into a laboratory of architectural innovation, creating a new commercial architecture, the skyscraper. Soaring to unprecedented heights and monopolizing limited downtown space, the skyscrapers were a bold incorporation of modern technologies, revolutionary design, and an expression of the quest for profit (Bluestone 1993). They cut ties with the aesthetics of the past and set the stage for the next century's architectural paradigms and debates. Outside the gilded downtown, the neighborhoods are living museums of various residential styles of urban residence, from the distinctly American Prairie School to wood-frame Victorian, greystone, and bungalows (Bigott 2001; Seligman 2005).

Besides the remarkable architectural innovation, the quality of public space in the city was improved by Daniel Burnham's 1909 Plan of Chicago. Whereas the urban plans in Beijing and Paris were made under the demand of the government, the Burnham Plan was backed by the Commercial Club of Chicago. In fact, as clearly demonstrated in the postfire rebuilding and the postwar urban renewal, business interest has always been an important force shaping the urban space of Chicago since the founding of the city (Ruble 2001). Envisioning Chicago as a "Paris on the Prairie," the Burnham Plan remade the backdrop of Chicago through French-inspired public works. It reserved the lakefront for recreation and turned most of it into beautiful lakefront parks. It systematically rearranged the streets by widening arterial streets and created new ones, building diagonal streets to facilitate transportation and unifying the street grid (Bruegmann 1997; Zukowsky 1987). The plan was not fully implemented because of the onset of the Great Depression, but aspects of the plan continued to guide planners as they expanded parks, built new bridges, and laid out the city's superhighway network. Chicagoans still make frequent reference to Burnham's vision for the city and to an aphorism posthumously attributed to him, the oft-quoted exhortation to "make no little plans" (Suttles 1990).

From Urban Renewal to Urban Preservation

Like many cities in the United States, Chicago was endeavoring to renew itself in the 1950s. After the stagnation during the Depression and World War II, construction resumed and many old buildings were swept away in order to make way for newer, bigger, and better ones. Although the demolition was spurred by the desire of developers to make profit, it also came from a belief in the future and progress (Bluestone 1994). That is, the glory of the past was not simply erased with the demolition of the old; on the contrary, it is eternalized in the construction of the new. Renowned Chicago School architect Louis Sullivan put it in this way: "Chicago can pull itself down and rebuild itself in a generation" (Logelin 1957, 9). Prevailing among modern architects, business groups, and policymakers, such belief demonstrates a strong local pride and generated rapid economic growth in postwar Chicago. Meanwhile, it caused huge destruction of the urban heritage citywide. From legendary residences and opulent theaters to state-of-the-art office buildings and department stores, a large number of historic structures were recklessly squandered by the wrecking ball of "progress," including the world's first skyscraper (Lowe 2000; Bluestone 1994; Cahan 1994).

The massive demolition made the city aware of the value of its own past and led to the emergence of the modern preservation movement in Chicago. Early preservation practices were initiated by individual preservationists and civic organizations from the bottom up. Photographer Richard Nickel is one of the most famous people who advocated for preserving the city's architectural heritage. Nickel's accidental death in 1972, stemming from salvaging material from Sullivan's Stock Exchange Building, spurred greater vigilance among Chicagoans about their urban heritage (Cahan 1994). The most influential preservation organizations established in the postwar era were the Chicago Heritage Committee and the Landmark Preservation Council. They launched citywide preservation crusades and saved a number of historic buildings, including Frank Lloyd Wright's famous Robie House, located on the campus of the University of Chicago (Hild 2001; Bluestone 1994).

Wide public awareness promoted both the local and the federal government to take more proactive steps in urban preservation. At the local level, the Commission on Chicago Landmarks was established in 1957, which enabled the municipality to formally recognize and protect historic buildings and districts. The first landmark ordinance was passed by the City Council in 1968. Meanwhile, a series of national statutes began to use economic impetus to promote urban preservation. For instance, the 1966 National Historic Preservation Act, the 1976 Tax Reform Act, and the 1981 Economic Recovery Tax Act provided tax incentives for property owners and developers to rehabilitate historic buildings (Frank 2002). Collectively, preservation ordinances have created a unique culture of urban preservation in American cities, where urban preservation becomes a tool to increase land value and manage property taxes (Barthel 1996; Fitch 1982; Reichl 1997).

A new wave of urban renewal took place in Chicago in the 1990s in the context of globalization. After dominating the local economy for decades, manufacturing and industrial activities started to decline. A variety of producer services, such as finance, insurance, and accounting, began to play a pivotal role in economic growth (Abu-Lughod 1999; Sassen 1994, 2001). The economic restructuring has significantly changed the physical form of the city. Chicago has refashioned its downtown space to better cater to the needs of professionals, tourists, and conventioneers in hopes of nurturing the city's ever-growing service sector. Besides the construction of a large number of new buildings, many old buildings in the central part of the city have been converted for residential or commercial use. For instance, Medinah Temple on the Near North Side of Chicago, considered one of the nation's finest examples of a Middle Eastern–style Shrine temple, was turned into Bloomingdale's Home and Furniture Store in 2003 (Figure 18). The acoustics of the temple's auditorium was so good that the Chicago Symphony Orchestra used to record there on occasion. Although some lament that the temple was gutted for business purposes, others applaud it as a good effort to preserve at least the façade of the historic building rather than tearing it down.

The most prominent figure behind the economic and spatial transformation of Chicago is Mayor Richard M. Daley, who finished his sixth and last term as mayor in 2011. Daley widely used tax increment financing as a funding tool to attract public and private investment to Chicago and to promote the physical improvement of the city (Koval et al. 2006). He also strove to beautify Chicago's urban landscape and enhance its image by creating parks and green spaces, preserving historic landmarks, and supporting arts and cultural institutions. The city's most important project since the World's Columbian Exposition of 1893, Millennium Park, opened in downtown Chicago in 2004. It is considered by many as a great gift that Mayor Daley gave to Chicagoans.

The new urban renewal promoted by Mayor Daley has reversed the postwar fashion of suburbanization and brought people back to the city. Chicago's population grew for the first time since the 1950s, rising to nearly 2.9 million in the 1990s (Koval et al. 2006). With the inflow of people, neighborhoods close to the Loop, the central business district of Chicago, have experienced large-scale spatial and social changes (Koval et al. 2006; Hyra 2008; Boyd 2008). The proximity to downtown, relatively low housing prices, and vibrant local culture have made those community areas particularly attractive to middle-class professionals, artists, and students. Therefore, after decades of disinvestment or dilapidation, some areas started to be transformed by the inflow of new urban dwellers.

FIGURE 18. Medinah Temple on the Near North Side of Chicago, occupied by Bloomingdale's Home and Furniture Store.

Working-class cottages have been demolished in order to make room for high-rise condominiums; local mom-and-pop shops have been replaced by big-box chains; and low-income, working-class inhabitants have been displaced by wealthier newcomers.

The new wave of urban renewal changed the agenda of urban preservation in Chicago. Throughout the 1970s and 1980s, urban preservation took place primarily in downtown Chicago or more affluent, predominantly white neighborhoods in the northern part of the city. The neighborhoods of racial and ethnic minorities on the south and west sides were not the main battlefields for urban preservation because of a lack of market interest in those areas (Seligman 2005). In other words, there was little need for preservation without the incentives to redevelop. However, the new urban renewal has brought about drastic spatial and social changes to the ethnic neighborhoods. Urban preservation is no longer the privilege of the rich but has become a possible device for community members and local officials in diverse urban areas to cope with the changes.

Because of these changes, urban preservation has gained new meanings, and its practice has become increasingly complex. Designating a neighborhood as a historic district is not only about protecting historic houses from the wrecking ball; it is also about the future of the community and the livelihood of residents. Although preservation programs are celebrated in some places as a solution for community revitalization, they are deplored in other places as a tool to displace low-income inhabitants. Landmark designation is cheered in some neighborhoods as a way to empower local communities and improve racial equality, but in other neighborhoods, it has been condemned as a means to reinforce the entrenched social and economic disparity. Entangled with issues such as race, class, and the authenticity of local culture, the policy process of urban preservation has become more complicated.

Preservation initiatives have emerged in different neighborhoods in Chicago, but the outcomes vary significantly. Whereas some communities accomplished landmark status in a few months, others are still waiting more than ten years after they launched their preservation campaigns. Multiple factors influence the long and complex designation process for historic preservation districts. Besides much-discussed factors such as voting patterns and political resources, I argue that submunicipal political dynamics is an important factor that must be taken into account. Despite strong mayoral authority in Chicago, local aldermen have substantial discretion over land-related issues in their wards. Therefore, it is important to examine the ward system and the power of aldermen when attempting to understand the different outcomes of landmark designation in Pilsen and Bronzeville.

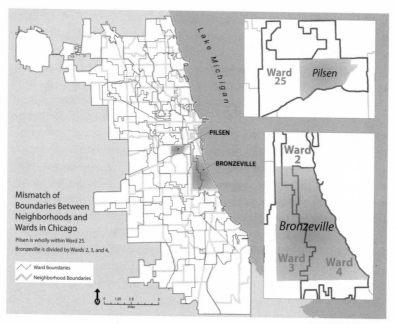

FIGURE 19. Mismatch of the boundaries between neighborhoods and wards in Chicago.

The following section provides a historical overview of the structure of the ward system and the tradition of aldermanic prerogative in Chicago.

Divide and Rule: Territorial Fragmentation in Chicago

Chicago has been divided into municipal legislative districts called wards since its first municipal charter in 1837. With the growth of population and territory, the number of wards increased from six in 1837 to thirty-five in 1889. The current system of fifty wards was adopted in 1923 (Knox 2005). Ward boundaries are redrawn after each federal census to ensure roughly equal representation by population size (Knox 2005). Determined by the requirement for equal numbers of inhabitants but influenced by political gerrymandering, ward boundaries rarely coincide with those of the city's officially recognized community areas or informally defined neighborhoods (Suttles 1972; Guterbock 1980). This mismatch of the two types of boundaries is clearly demonstrated in Figure 19. The nature of ward boundaries led Guterbock (1980, 222) to describe the ward as "a fragmented, arbitrarily defined territory with substantial ethnic and class heterogeneity in each of its neighborhoods."

Each of the fifty wards is represented by an alderman on the City Council, presided over by the mayor (Knox 2005). Directly elected by the voters of their wards, aldermen are motivated to bring particular favors to their constituents. For the same reason, they tend to ignore issues outside their ward boundaries or across multiple wards. Besides introducing ordinances and allocating municipal services to their wards, aldermen have great autonomy in governing their wards. For instance, the current city budget gives each alderman a grant of nearly $2 million per year for "discretionary projects" that are not subject to city council approval.

Among all the privileges, aldermen have a special veto power over their ward issues. If an alderman seeks to initiate or block city council or city government actions in his or her own ward, other city council members would defer to the alderman when they vote. This is called aldermanic prerogative or aldermanic privilege. The tradition is widely recognized by scholars as one of the most significant and constant themes in Chicago local politics (Thale 2005; Rast 1999; Schwieterman and Caspall 2006). The essence of aldermanic prerogative is an informal arrangement between political actors that allows them to exercise power within their own turfs without intervening in others'. Although the arrangement helps political actors maximize their autonomy and avoid conflicts with one another, it also turns the urban arena into divided fiefdoms (Figure 20).

Aldermen have maintained significant discretion in their wards since the early days of Chicago history. From the mid-nineteenth century to the early 1930s, Chicago was run by a strong council, weak mayor form of government. Under the nickname *Grey Wolves,* council members were free from the control of the mayor and fought for their shares of the spoils (Simpson 2001). Despite endless council wars, a tacit understanding of council members' autonomy over their own territories was formed. According to a description of the nineteenth-century Chicago city council, "when an alderman rose in council chambers to speak for a 'courtesy' for his district, he invariably got the support of his fellow political chameleons" (Miller 1996, 452). This tradition enables aldermen to rule their wards like fiefdoms, and some of them were even called "little mayors" (Einhorn 1991).

The political regime in Chicago was drastically transformed during the Great Depression and World War II. A single, all-powerful Democratic Party machine replaced the scattered nineteenth-century political machines and factions and started to rule the city in most of the postwar era (Gosnell 1937; Clifford 1975; Simpson 2001). The Democratic Party machine is a hierarchical pyramid-like structure, with the mayor as the single boss at the top, ward committeemen and precinct captains in the middle, and

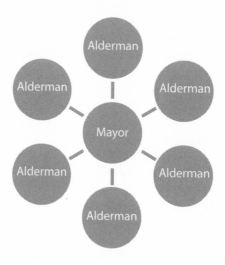

Figure 20. Territorial fragmentation in Chicago.

the voting population at the base. The boss, through a network of ward committeemen and precinct captains, distributes patronage and secures votes. Combining the political resources from both the Democratic Party and the city hall, machine mayors were able to strengthen their control over the city council. Consequently, the governance pattern in Chicago gradually changed from a strong council, weak mayor form of government to a strong mayor, weak council one (Grimshaw 1992).

Although not every alderman is the Democratic Party committeeman of his ward, most of them belong to the regular Democratic majority so that they are still supported by the political resources of the party. Furthermore, their role as the chief broker of municipal services within their wards makes them indispensable in maintaining the machine, so that the local autonomy of aldermen has been preserved in the organization of the centralized Democratic machine (Guterbock 1980). In the reign of Mayor Richard J. Daley (1955–1976), the powerful city boss centralized the decision-making processes on issues affecting the city in general, including the city budget, big public projects, and downtown redevelopment. However, he deferred to aldermanic discretion at the ward level for the purpose of increasing aldermen's loyalty and maintaining the machine (Banfield [1961] 1964; Simpson 2001; Biles 1995). Specifically, Daley gave aldermen power over land-related issues in their wards, from zoning changes to the issuance of building permits. Joel Rast (1999, 41) maintains, "As long as a particular alderman was loyal to the mayor and votes for the machine were being delivered in the ward in question, Daley was unlikely to interfere in something as minor as a zoning variance." In other words, the mayor's effort to maintain the aldermanic prerogative is a political investment. It helps the mayor gain aldermen's support in the city council and win votes in their wards.

The informal political arrangement was threatened when Harold Washington, the first black mayor in Chicago, was in power. As a reformer, Washington proposed many policies to empower community organizations and to weaken Democratic Party ward organizations. These proposals had the potential to weaken the autonomy of aldermen in their wards, so they were strongly opposed by some aldermen from the very beginning (Simpson 2001). To punish those aldermen, Washington delayed or vetoed construction projects in their wards, such as libraries and soccer fields, although these community projects had been considered aldermen's divine right (Fremon 1988, 5). The council wars ended after the special aldermanic elections in 1986, as those elections increased the number of Washington supporters in the city council. However, the brief remaining months in the mayorship of Washington, from 1986 to 1987, were too short to change the tradition of ward-based machine politics (Kleppner 1985).

The political regime in Chicago entered a new phase when Richard M. Daley, the eldest son of Richard J. Daley, was elected mayor in 1989. The hierarchical structure of the Democratic machine under Richard M. Daley closely resembled the organization his father created in the postwar era. However, without holding any official position in the Democratic Party, Richard M. Daley did not control the party or the ward committeemen as his father once did. Instead, he ruled over Chicago by directly influencing the fate of the aldermen.[2] Daley appointed eighteen of the fifty aldermen and maintained a stronghold over thirty of them. As a result, he centralized his authority over the city council during his tenure (Simpson 2001).

The tradition of aldermanic prerogative was largely maintained under the mayoralty of Richard M. Daley. An alderman explained the rules of the game in Chicago politics as follows (C0508):

> It is very hard in the City of Chicago to have initiatives that are not supported by the alderman of the particular ward, because the general view in the city council is we support our colleagues on what they want to do in their wards. It's called aldermanic prerogative. It means simply you respect your colleagues' rights to do things that they want to in their wards, and you could do what you want to in your wards. If the aldermen deny something in their own wards, their colleagues would never bring it up again.

Very few things happen that the aldermen don't want to happen
for their particular wards.

This description shows continuity in the governance norms of Chicago
despite regime changes over time. The tacit understanding between political actors allows aldermen to maintain an effective local monopoly in
their wards so that the entire city is fragmented along ward boundaries.

It is important to note that aldermanic prerogative is not absolute.
The relations between Mayor Daley and the aldermen were intricate. Although the mayor respects the autonomy of aldermen most of the time,
he occasionally supersedes aldermanic ward-specific power over economic
development efforts and citywide issues (Ferman 1996; Fuchs 1992; Hyra
2008). For example, in 2008 the City Council voted 33–16 to approve
Daley's plan to build a $100-million Children's Museum in Grant Park,
despite the opposition of the alderman whose ward includes the proposed
project site. At the time, Daley said that so-called aldermanic prerogative
should not apply on the museum issue because it went far beyond the interests of the residents of that particular ward (Mihalopoulos 2008; Mihalopoulos and Ahmed-Ullah 2008). He also disparaged the local power
of aldermen in an interview, saying that he was unaware of aldermanic
prerogative (Chicago Tribune 2009).

It sounds as if the mayor had sentenced aldermanic prerogative to
death. However, as one of only a few examples in which aldermanic prerogative was violated, the case of the Children's Museum cannot serve as
testimony of the end of the tradition. More importantly, Daley publicly
defended aldermanic prerogative on various occasions. In the same year,
when the *Chicago Tribune* reported that aldermen made zoning changes
for developers and received campaign contributions in exchange, Daley
defended the tradition of aldermanic prerogative that allows aldermen to
dictate the fate of development in their wards. "Zoning is their prerogative," Daley said of the aldermen. "They are elected by local residents in
regards to the quality of life" they provide in each ward (Washburn 2008).

Mayor Daley's apparently conflicting claims of aldermanic prerogative
demonstrate the complex power dynamics between him and the aldermen.
The mayor knew clearly what the aldermen's privileges are and what he
should have done in order to ensure their discretion. Nonetheless, when
facing critical developmental or citywide issues, he exercised his autocratic
power to sweep off aldermanic prerogative and supersede aldermen's decisions. Cases such as the Children's Museum do not indicate the demise of
aldermanic prerogative but reveal the limits of such a tradition.

Urban Preservation in Chicago: Aldermen's Prerogative

Aldermanic prerogative is particularly influential in dealing with land-related issues. A number of studies have demonstrated how aldermen wield power over zoning and redevelopment (Schwieterman and Caspall 2006; Mihalopoulos, Becker, and Little 2008; Rast 1999; Royko 1970), but little attention has been paid to the policy process of urban preservation. Despite the existence of centralized preservation agencies at the municipal level, the aldermen have veto power over preservation efforts in their wards. Although not every preservation initiative is locally generated, aldermen have significant power in shaping preservation efforts, especially those originated in the local communities.

The official protection of historic structures in Chicago started in 1957 with the establishment of the Commission on Chicago Landmarks. As an independent advisory board, the commission consists of nine members appointed by the mayor and is staffed by the Historic Preservation Division of the Department of Zoning and Land Use Planning. Procedurally, all preservation initiatives, whether from local communities or the municipality, must be proposed to the Historic Preservation Division first. The division has the discretion to decide whether or not to prepare research reports for the proposed buildings or areas. The research reports prepared by the division are submitted to the commission for review. After reviewing the reports, the commission holds public hearings and votes on new landmark designations. The designations endorsed by the commission are passed on to the City Council for final vote.

According to the formal procedure of landmark designation, both the Historic Preservation Division and the Commission on Chicago Landmarks play pivotal roles in the policy process. However, aldermen are the real gatekeepers in the urban preservation process. The Deputy Commissioner of the Historic Preservation Division highlights the importance of aldermen in landmark designation (C0506):

> Landmark buildings and districts are shared things. If the City comes to the alderman, important developments will come; if the community comes to the alderman, change will happen too. In any case, things cannot be done without the consent of the alderman....The Historic Preservation Division decides whether to prepare the reports to the Commission. We balance different interests in order to make the decision.

Landmark designation not only is based on the historic and aesthetic value of the district but is built on the balance of interests between players, among whom the alderman is the most important one. Municipal officials' compliance with aldermanic preference results largely from their practical concern over the departmental budget: as legislators, aldermen vote on the annual city budget, so each city office endeavors to cooperate with their wishes to get its budget approved (Guterbock 1980).

A commissioner on the Commission on Chicago Landmarks verified the prominent role of aldermen in the process of landmark designation. The commissioner explains the rules of the game as follows (C0512):

> Aldermen's support is critical to landmark designation. The city staff does not propose buildings or districts to be landmarks if the aldermen do not support, because of how the city government works in Chicago. If the individual alderman does not support the proposal, most of the rest of the aldermen will defer to him or her, and the proposal will not be passed in the City Council.... On the contrary, if the city initiates the designation for new landmarks, the Commission has to vote, yes or no. Generally yes, because the proposals are all very well researched and meet the criteria. The city staff would not do it if there is not enough support from the alderman or the community.

It seems aldermen do not participate in the process of urban preservation until the final City Council vote; however, they have invisible agenda-setting power to influence the landmark designation from the very beginning. Preservation initiatives opposed by the aldermen do not have the chance to enter the formal policy process, whereas those supported by the aldermen are endorsed by the commission. In other words, it is the preference of the local alderman that determines the administrative decision on landmark designation outside the formal decision-making process.

Bureaucratic compliance with the tradition of aldermanic prerogative helps smooth out the relations between the administrative and legislative branches of the municipality. Because the preservation initiatives passed on by the commission are those favored by the local aldermen, the rest of the city council would defer to the aldermen and vote for the initiatives. As a result, the administrative and legislative decisions are in accordance. Even if there are conflicts between the two sides at an early stage, the bureaucrats usually coordinate with the aldermen outside the formal decision-making process. The former commissioner of the Department of Zoning and Land Use Planning commented (C0525), "If there is any disagreement between the City and the aldermen, they would negotiate and work things out, instead of fighting with each other publicly." She emphasized that it is the effective coordination between political actors that explains why Mayor Daley was "so successful" and why the City of Chicago was "so well run."

Under the informal mode of cooperation between political actors, urban preservation has become a ward-based business. An alderman describes the policy process of urban preservation in Chicago (C0527):

> There is no city policy on urban preservation. It is pretty much individual wards. That is the way the whole city is. The way I usually describe it is like Europe in the Middle Ages. There is the King in the court of downtown and those of us in the provinces. We have a great deal of discretion in our provinces as long as we don't challenge the King. What it means is there are very few citywide policies that enforce on everybody. The aldermen just make their own decisions about a lot of things. In terms of urban preservation, it really depends on if the aldermen have commitment to the issue.

The metaphor vividly demonstrates the substantial discretion of aldermen over preservation efforts in their wards. Whereas the tacit understanding among political actors helps them maintain their own turfs, it creates political fragmentation along ward boundaries and inhibits the making and implementation of a citywide preservation agenda.

Yet not every preservation initiative originated in the wards. For instance, Mayor Daley launched the Historic Chicago Bungalow Initiative in 2000 as an effort to encourage the rehabilitation and renovation of the Chicago Bungalows.[3] With more than 80,000 bungalows, the housing style represents nearly one-third of the city's single-family housing stock, so the impact of the preservation initiative spreads all over the city. In 2002, the City Council designated the Michigan Avenue Streetwall as a city landmark, with the strong support of Mayor Daley.[4] Extending approximately one and a half miles from Randolph Street on the north to 11th Street on the south, the streetwall contains some of the city's finest buildings, designed by Chicago's most important architects, such as Louis Sullivan and D. H. Burnham. It forms one of the signature images of Chicago and reflects the development of the metropolis in the late nineteenth and the early twentieth centuries.

Although not all preservation initiatives are locally generated, aldermen's support is crucial if the proposals are raised locally. The Commission on Chicago Landmarks would not endorse a preservation initiative proposed by the local community unless it is backed by the alderman. This is true for both local landmark designation and federal preservation programs. Without the support of local government, there are very few chances for local communities to achieve national landmark status.

It is important to note that, besides landmark designation, zoning is also considered an important tool for urban preservation. Theoretically, if an area is downzoned to such an extent that new buildings cannot be taller than existing ones, the incentives to redevelop are eliminated. This is how the historic urban core of Paris was protected from redevelopment in the postwar era. However, it is a different story in Chicago. Many Chicago aldermen would first downzone their wards, which looks like an effort to limit the scale of redevelopment, but they would not hesitate to make special deals with developers and upzone certain areas if the developers propose to build something exceeding the zoning code (C1002). In other words, aldermen's initial action of downzoning is no more than a trick to increase their bargaining power in local development. It raises the threshold for developers to carry out their projects, and thus it motivates them to make deals with the aldermen. As revealed in a special series in the *Chicago Tribune,* a substantial number of aldermen received campaign donations from developers, enriching themselves through local development. A few of them were even put into jail because of development-related bribery. When the journalists questioned the manipulation of aldermen in local development, however, Mayor Daley defended aldermen's power over zoning as their prerogative (Washburn 2008).

To provide more detailed analysis of urban preservation in Chicago, the following sections investigate the processes of landmark designation in Pilsen and Bronzeville, two Chicago neighborhoods near the downtown Loop. Pilsen proposed to be listed on the National Register of Historic Places (NRHP), and Bronzeville strove for designation as a National Heritage Area (NHA). As two federal preservation programs, the NRHP and NHA are comparable in most aspects. They are both administered by the National Park Service, which is part of the U.S. Department of the Interior. They both rely on economic incentives to promote urban preservation. Specifically, the NRHP offers tax deductions for property owners to renovate their homes, whereas NHA provides federal funds to designated areas for housing renovation and infrastructure improvement. Most importantly, the opinion of the local government plays a crucial role in the two designations: if the property is within a certified local government, the application will be forwarded to the local government for its official comment.[5] In other words, although the final decisions about NRHP and NHA designations are made by federal agencies, neither of them can be approved without local political support.

There are a number of community-level differences between Pilsen and Bronzeville. Pilsen is a Mexican American community, whereas Bronzeville is predominantly African American. Besides the racial difference, Pilsen is a solid working-class community, but Bronzeville is more economically disadvantaged because of long-term disinvestment and the exodus of middle-class blacks. Geographically, Bronzeville is much larger than Pilsen, and therefore unbalanced development is a more serious problem there. Whereas Pilsen has barely any vacant lots, parts of Bronzeville are far more devastated than others, as reflected in vacant land and deteriorated housing conditions.

The racial demographics, economic capacity, and physical conditions of local communities all influence the process of urban preservation, but none of them is a determining factor for landmark designation. Although race may shape the discourse of urban preservation by providing social groups a narrative to reconstruct their collective memory (Saito 2009b; Kaufman 2009), it does not dictate the policy process of urban preservation. As we will see from the rest of the chapter, politics trumps race in both communities. Despite the community-level differences between Pilsen and Bronzeville, both are resource-poor communities with median household incomes below the City of Chicago median. Preservation initiatives have generated conflict of interest in both communities. Therefore, they provide comparable cases to investigate the policy process of urban preservation.

Pilsen: Is the Neighborhood for Sale?

The Near West Side community of Pilsen historically has been known as a port of entry for immigrants. The neighborhood was first settled and developed in the late 1800s by workers from all around Europe, primarily Czech but also Polish, Yugoslavian, and Italian. After the Europeans left, the neighborhood was inherited by Mexican immigrants in the 1950s and is now one of the largest Mexican American communities in the Midwest (Fremon 1988). The history of Pilsen symbolizes the dynamics of ethnic settlement patterns in Chicago and gives the neighborhood unique cultural heritage. Small, single-family cottages with Central European Baroque ornamentation continue to characterize the physical form of the neighborhood (Figure 21). Churches built by different ethnic groups are living

Figure 21. Historic housing in Pilsen.

museums of the neighborhood history. Murals drawn by Mexican artists show the spirit of the Mexican American dwellers and create an artistic atmosphere in the neighborhood.

As downtown Chicago was revitalized under the Daley administration in the early 1990s, many inner-city neighborhoods experienced demographic and spatial changes. Pilsen is one of them. Because of its proximity to the Loop, relatively low rents, and rich local culture, Pilsen is an ideal target for gentrification. As middle-class professionals and artists started to move into the neighborhood, an increasing number of Mexican Americans were displaced. Along with the racial demographic changes, some old houses were torn down to make room for new development (Betancur 2002).

In light of the rapid changes, two different proposals were raised in 2005 to preserve the neighborhood. Some community members suggested nominating Pilsen to the NRHP. The NRHP offers tax incentives for property owners to renovate their homes. Specifically, if an owner spends 25 percent of the property's value on approved rehabilitation within two years, his or her property tax will be frozen for eight years.[6] The proposal was challenged by Preservation Chicago, a nonprofit organization for urban preservation. It argued that the NRHP would not stop real estate speculation from reshaping the neighborhood because the program was totally voluntary. Alternatively, it suggested that the city landmark status was more effective in preserving the neighborhood, because of its mandatory regulations on demolition and new construction. Accordingly, Preservation Chicago raised another proposal to create a City of Chicago Landmark District for 18th Street, the historic heart of Pilsen.

Local government support is crucial for the success of both proposals. Although Pilsen was split between two wards in the early 1980s, it was united into the 25th Ward in the 1986 remapping and remains in the same ward to this day (Fremon 1988). The current alderman of the 25th Ward is a second-generation Mexican American who began his political career as a community organizer in Pilsen in the 1980s. He was appointed by Mayor Daley as alderman of the 25th Ward in 1996, and since then he has been elected and held the position. As a loyal Daley ally, the alderman also serves as president pro tempore of the City Council, overseeing council proceedings in the mayor's absence, and chair of the City Council Zoning Committee.

The alderman had different reactions to the two proposals. He rejected the proposal by Preservation Chicago because he did not want the restrictions imposed by city landmark status to constrain local development. The proposal to nominate Pilsen to the NRHP gained his support. Specifically, the promise of increased property value motivated him to support the NRHP proposal. The alderman contends (C0518),

> The National Register program is based on the residents' self-interest, because they want their property values to go up. If they fix their properties with this program, their property values will go up but they don't need to pay more tax. And if ten or twenty property owners do the same thing, then it's multiplied.

The alderman's ward office is located in Pilsen. Given the strategic location of the neighborhood, an increase in its aggregate property value would contribute to the economic prosperity of the ward and therefore increase the economic and political capacity of the alderman. In addition, as one of the alderman's staff (C0519) reveals, the alderman is often criticized for ruthless redevelopment, and he wanted to use the preservation program to improve his reputation.

In contrast to the enthusiasm of the alderman, a large number of residents, particularly renters, strongly opposed the preservation program. Their main concern was that the increased property values and taxes caused by the preservation program would facilitate the ongoing gentrification. According to the 2000 Census, the socioeconomic characteristics of Pilsen indicate a solid working-class population, with a median household income of $27,763, more than $10,000 below the City of Chicago median of $38,625. Among all housing units in Pilsen, 74 percent are renter occupied. Almost 60 percent of residents have already spent more than 30 percent (the threshold for affordability) of their income on rent. With the increase in property value, rent would go up so that more local residents would be pushed out of the neighborhood.

Besides the large group of renters, working-class homeowners might also find their interests undermined when the property value of Pilsen goes up. An increase in property value goes hand in hand with rising property taxes. Although homeowners are eligible for the tax deduction offered by the preservation program, they have to invest in their property first. Those who do not have enough money to renovate their houses cannot obtain any benefit but have to pay more property tax when the land value of the neighborhood increases, so they may be forced to sell their homes. A preservation professional (C0520), who was hired by the alderman to assess building quality and social conditions in Pilsen, contends that the majority of residents living in Pilsen are not able to take advantage of the tax incentive:

It is reasonable to ask who is likely to use the tax incentives. A
low-income property owner? Or, someone who is coming in and
buying a property there? . . . The vast majority of people living
in Pilsen are not going to end up taking advantage from the tax
freeze associated with the National Register status. Only people
who can afford to invest money on their property can benefit
from it.

His answer shows that the preservation program is not likely to benefit
working-class Mexicans, as the alderman claimed. Instead, it may promote gentrification by encouraging the well-off to buy properties in Pilsen.

Property value has rapidly increased in Pilsen. Whereas rents increased
by an average of 44 percent between 1995 and 2002, house prices rose by
an average of 68 percent between 1990 and 2000. Within the short period of time from 2004 to 2006, Pilsen saw assessed values increase from
$30,000 to more than $200,000. Large numbers of luxury condominiums
were constructed at the east part of the neighborhood, with market values
as high as $699,000 per unit (Betancur 2005; Curran and Hague 2006).
These units are far out of reach in a neighborhood where the median income is $27,000. A local developer who grew up on the Near Southwest
Side and has been working in Pilsen since 2000 (C0530) laments,

> The neighborhood is changing a lot. Some people say the change is
> progress, whereas others ask at whose expense. You feel it is really
> hard when you sit down and talk to people who have been living
> there for 30 years and want to buy a house but cannot afford it
> anymore.

This description reveals that the livelihood of working-class inhabitants
has been threatened by the increased property value. Class stratification
and economic disparity are emerging in this working-class community, as
in other gentrifying neighborhoods (Freeman 2006; Smith 1996).

Here is a personal anecdote that speaks to the complexity of gentrification and community development. When I was conducting fieldwork in
Chicago in 2005, I interviewed the alderman of the 25th Ward in hope of
determining his opinion on gentrification. However, without directly ad-
dressing the issue of gentrification, the alderman told me a story about him
and one of his political opponents. The person used to be a well-known
community activist in Pilsen and former alderman of the Lower West Side
in the late 1980s and early 1990s. Both were running for 25th Ward alderman a few years ago, and one day before the election they had breakfast

together in a restaurant in Pilsen. As soon as the breakfast started, the person said to the alderman in earnest but low voice, "No matter which one of us wins the election, you and I need to make sure that Pilsen is always a working-class neighborhood." At that moment the waitress came to their table. She was a Mexican American living in Pilsen, like everyone else working in the restaurant. Instead of responding to his opponent, the aldermen spoke to the waitress, asking her whether she had any children. The waitress told the alderman she had a son, and the alderman asked her, "What do you want your son to do in the future?" "I want him to go to college and become a doctor," answered the waitress. After the waitress left, the alderman smiled at his opponent and said to him, "You have to face the reality: this is what people in Pilsen want." Of course, the alderman won that election.

Although both the alderman and his opponent were political activists with Mexican origins, they had different views on the future of the community. As this anecdote shows, it is unrealistic for any community activist or politician to dictate the will of the people, especially the will to improve their socioeconomic situation and live a better life. In Chicago and many other American cities, working-class inhabitants move out of the neighborhoods where they originally lived and buy single-family houses in the suburbs when they become better off. Their old neighborhoods are then inhabited by newcomers with different racial or ethnic backgrounds, and those people take the same path. This pattern of residence in central city neighborhoods is a result of disadvantaged people's upward social mobility. It drives the growth of the city and provides a vivid manifestation of the American dream.

However, the upward social mobility of working-class residents should not be confused with displacement of the poor by middle-class newcomers. Although this alderman had the political savvy to defeat his opponents both at the dining table and in the aldermanic election, his ambition of increasing the property value and improving the image of Pilsen may well threaten the livelihood of numerous working-class Mexicans. The wheel of gentrification may kick them out of the community where they have lived for generations before they can afford a home elsewhere. Even the alderman (C0531) himself admits that the Mexican population is shrinking in Pilsen. Many of them have to move out because they cannot afford the rent anymore.

Gentrification has generated heated debate in Pilsen and divided the community. Some homeowners were interested in the preservation program, but many residents considered it a tool to accelerate gentrification, so they opposed the landmark designation. The alderman's office called several community meetings to introduce the economic benefits of the preservation program to the residents and gain their support. At those meetings, however, many Pilsen residents and preservationists from outside Pilsen spoke out to challenge the alderman and his landmark designation plan. Whereas the Pilsen residents were concerned about the potential of the preservation program to increase property value and accelerate gentrification, preservationists argued that the federal program would provide tax credits to homeowners for preservation, but it would not have "teeth," or mandatory regulations, to bar wrecking. Although local residents of Pilsen and preservationists had different concerns, they united to oppose the National Register as their common enemy.

The alderman's gentrification agenda eventually fueled the antipreservation movement in Pilsen. The leader of the movement was Pilsen Alliance, a community-based organization (CBO) created in 1998 that had frequently clashed with the alderman over development issues.[7] Pilsen Alliance organized a series of petitions and protests called "Pilsen Is Not for Sale" both in the neighborhood and outside City Hall. The goal was to raise citywide awareness about the situation in Pilsen. After a community congress in November 2005, the organization collected 550 signatures from local residents and put a referendum on the March 2006 ballot. The referendum asked the alderman of the 25th Ward and the City Council to downzone Pilsen to slow down demolition and gentrification, instead of using the preservation program as a tool to encourage the displacement of local residents. The referendum passed with 75 percent of the vote, a clear indication that the majority of residents were not in favor of the preservation program.

The alderman was upset by the actions of Pilsen Alliance. He claimed that the CBO was always against him, no matter what policies he made, because it was supported by his political opponent, the person whom he defeated in the aldermanic election a few years earlier (C0531). According to the web page of Pilsen Alliance, the executive director of Pilsen Alliance used to work with the political opponent of the alderman. Although the person does not hold any official positions in the organization, he has been actively involved in many protests launched by Pilsen Alliance (Maidenberg 2010). It is inappropriate to conclude that Pilsen Alliance represents the political opponent of the alderman, but the intraward power competition between the two Mexican American political activists gives the alderman an excuse to attack the CBO. It exacerbates the struggle between the alderman and Pilsen Alliance over the development of Pilsen.

The collective action of Pilsen residents did not change the alderman's mind. He emphasized that his goal was to make Pilsen "the best Mexican

American community in the Midwest," and the preservation program was an important tool to help him fulfill the goal. However, as the alderman admitted, such a goal does not benefit everyone (C0531). It is likely that working-class Mexicans, especially renters, will pay for this development. Although renters account for 74 percent of Pilsen's population, their large number does not give them any political clout. A local developer who works closely with the alderman (C0533) explained it in this way:

> Renters are like a moving target, hard to hit. You can try hard
> to help the poor renters, but at the end of the day you don't
> necessarily have the control whether they stay or they leave. Also,
> renters don't vote in the same numbers as homeowners. So the
> question is—do you care as much what they say?

This quote shows that what matters for electoral democracy is not the number of constituents but the political resources the constituents offer to the elected official within his or her jurisdictional boundary. As the developer points out, the nature of renters as a transient population with low socioeconomic status limits their political capacity. Although it is uncertain whether renters are less likely to vote than homeowners, the staff in the alderman's office confirmed that the alderman's support for condominium development and gentrification has generated many grievances in Pilsen, especially among renters, so that he has received fewer votes from Pilsen in recent aldermanic elections. Accordingly, Pilsen has lost its political weight to other neighborhoods in the ward, such as Chinatown, where the alderman received more votes (C0535, C0802, C1001).

Organized Pilsen residents appealed to the city council, but they did not receive support. The city council deferred to the Pilsen alderman on the preservation initiative. With the support of the city council, the application was quickly passed to the state government. The Illinois Historic Preservation Agency (IHPA) provided positive feedback on Pilsen's application and asked for comment from the city. The Commission on Chicago Landmarks voted unanimously to endorse the National Register listing for Pilsen. Upon receiving the municipality's evaluation, the Illinois Historic Sites Advisory Council (IHSAC) voted in favor of Pilsen's nomination.

That move created the Pilsen Historic District, the largest such district in Illinois, stretching from Halsted Street to Western Avenue and from 16th Street to Cermak Road. There are 4,406 buildings in Pilsen that are qualified for the tax incentives. Under the direction of the alderman, a local development company, the 18th Street Development Corporation, set up a special program to guide homeowners through the application process.

According to the program coordinator (C0903), only a small number of homeowners have attempted to pursue the tax benefit, because most of them do not have enough money to renovate their houses. It shows the lack of resident support for the preservation initiative. By the end of 2009, four residents had finished their initial renovation projects and received the tax breaks. At least two beneficiaries, one of whom is non-Mexican, recently moved into Pilsen from other parts of Chicago. About forty other owners are in various stages of the process, and some are having difficulty completing renovation projects because of the economic downturn.

Bronzeville: The Lost Dream of the Black Metropolis

Bronzeville is an African American community located in the Near South Side of Chicago (Travis 2005). Created by two Great Migrations of blacks from the South during the first half of the twentieth century, Bronzeville is historically known as the Black Metropolis, rivaling New York's Harlem as a center of black culture in the United States (Drake and Cayton [1945] 1993). During the days of racial segregation, it provided a home to numerous nationally prominent African American–owned and –operated businesses and cultural institutions, as well as buildings designed and built by black architects.[8] The neighborhood started to decline when racial segregation officially ended in the 1960s. The exodus of wealthy and middle-class African Americans caused disinvestment, and the construction of high-rise public housing apartments led to a concentration of poverty and left the neighborhood with serious social problems (Wilson 1990; Hirsch [1983] 1988).

Like Pilsen, Bronzeville found itself facing the prospect of gentrification in the 1990s. Middle- and upper-income blacks returned to the neighborhood, attracted by the rich cultural legacy and the low cost of housing (Pattillo 2007; Boyd 2008; Hyra 2008). The increase in property value created by "black gentrification" is exacerbated by the pressure of real estate development outside the neighborhood. Developers of the South Loop's upscale condos threaten to build their way down State Street and redevelop Bronzeville from the north, and the University of Chicago campus extends in an ever-encompassing radius from the south (Argentati 2009). The combination of longtime dilapidation and more recent vigorous redevelopment has generated an unruly patchwork in Bronzeville, where vacant lots perch next to antique mansions and dilapidated buildings surround million-dollar new construction (Figure 22).

To prevent urban demolition and displacement, community leaders began to use urban preservation as a tool to influence the process of

FIGURE 22. New townhouses in Bronzeville.

redevelopment. In the late 1980s, several major community organizations in Bronzeville collaborated and formed the Mid-South Planning
and Development Commission (Mid-South), a community-based planning organization. In 1994, the organization developed a land use plan
called "Restoring Bronzeville," which proposed that the foundation of
Bronzeville's economic revitalization should be historic preservation and
heritage tourism (Boyd 2008). Community leaders attempted to recreate
the neighborhood as it existed in the past through combined strategies
of mixed-income housing development, black gentrification, and cultural
heritage tourism.

Another attempt to preserve the cultural heritage of the neighborhood
was made in 2000 when a CBO called Black Metropolis Convention and
Tourism Council (BMCTC) launched a campaign to designate Bronzeville
as an NHA. The NHA program provides financial assistance of up to $1
million annually for ten years and also allows community organizations
to build partnerships with government for local development (C0502).
In other words, it provides a legal channel for community organizers to
influence the policy process.

Similar to members of the Mid-South, community organizers at the
BMCTC emphasize that they are not preserving for preservation's sake.

Instead, their plan is to use the money obtained from the NHA status to develop cultural heritage tourism in Bronzeville. The president of the BMCTC explains the importance of the NHA status as follows (C0502):

> We have to keep in mind that blacks are being pushed out by increasing property values and a lack of jobs. Our agenda is to create an economic opportunity for low-income people and promote community capacity building in Bronzeville.... Black Metropolis National Heritage Area has a regional responsibility to go beyond the local wards and look at the area based on what we perceive historically as the "Black Belt." Once we have our heritage tourism destination established, we can generate as much as 250 million dollars a year—a significant boost to our local economy and a windfall for the city.

Bronzeville has long suffered from poverty and disinvestment. According to the 2000 census, nearly 30 percent of households in Bronzeville have annual income lower than $10,000, whereas the ratio in Pilsen is less than 15 percent. The financial aid provided by the NHA program is extremely important for the community, as it would help Bronzeville create jobs, improve the urban infrastructure, and promote economic growth.

Although both the Mid-South plan and the NHA proposal use urban preservation as a tool for local economic growth and community revitalization, they serve different constituents. The former focuses on the black middle class, but the latter is concerned with low-income and jobless residents. The difference between the two preservation initiatives demonstrates the increasing class stratification and intraracial inequality in the African American community (Boyd 2008; Hyra 2006). However, the idea of preserving the entire community and recreating the Black Metropolis highlighted in both initiatives is built on a common nostalgic vision of black identity, which is widely shared and supported by local residents (Stevenson 1996).

The processing of the preservation initiatives is impossible without aldermanic support. Whereas the implementation of the Mid-South plan needs aldermen's involvement to mobilize local resources, the NHA designation requires local government's endorsement and recognition of the geographic boundary of the designated area. Unlike Pilsen, which is located within one ward, Bronzeville is divided into three wards: the 2nd, the 3rd, and the 4th. The 3rd Ward and the 4th Ward contain the major parts of the community. Despite the aldermen's general interest in urban preservation and community development, none of them supports the preservation initiatives. The combination of intraward power struggles and interward political fragmentation has prevented neighborhood preservation efforts from taking off in Bronzeville.

There is an intricate relationship between CBOs and aldermen, as CBOs are important breeding grounds for potential up-and-coming aldermen. Aldermen in the wards that make up Bronzeville did not support the two preservation initiatives partially because they feared this would reduce their within-ward powerbases. For instance, the former 3rd Ward alderman was reluctant to support the Mid-South plan, because by endorsing it she would have effectively endorsed the executive director of the plan, who eventually defeated her in the 2007 aldermanic election. The current 3rd Ward alderman is less resistant to the Mid-South plan because of her previous institutional affiliation with the organization. However, she is more resistant to the NHA effort for the same reason as her predecessor, despite her background as a community organizer and preservationist.

Besides the intraward politics between aldermen and CBOs, the multiward nature of the preservation initiatives caused aldermen to withhold their support. Because they had different policy agendas, it was hard for the four aldermen to unite behind the idea of recreating Bronzeville as a Black Metropolis. Furthermore, if the preservation plans were successfully implemented, community organizations or agencies surpassing the ward boundaries would have been created or empowered to mobilize resources, allocate funds, and manage the heritage area as a whole. It would have undermined the aldermen's autonomy within their wards.

The aldermen's resistance to the preservation initiatives in Bronzeville is well demonstrated in a statement by the 4th Ward alderman. Despite her good reputation for urban preservation, the alderman does not show much sympathy for the preservation initiatives in Bronzeville. Moreover, she questions the legitimacy of Bronzeville as a standard community area (C0516):

> Bronzeville? I don't know about Bronzeville. I only know what's in my ward. Bronzeville is sort of a state of mind, not a standard community area. Chicago has designated 77 community areas that go back to the 1920s. The sociologists at the University of Chicago identified the communities for the City of Chicago and named them. These 77 community areas have persisted for the last 85 years. Bronzeville is not one of them.... Bronzeville includes North and South Kenwood, Oakland, Douglas, and Grand Boulevard. Those four community areas are what they call Bronzeville. I represent Kenwood and Oakland, and part of Douglas and part

of Grand Boulevard....The difficulty in Bronzeville is there are
different aldermen with different priorities. I made a point to be
very supportive to preservation, but not every alderman thinks it is
important....In my ward, as long as community members propose
the landmark designations, in every case, I support them. I support
all preservation efforts *in my ward*. (emphasis added)

This statement reveals the conflict of boundaries between the culturally
and historically defined Bronzeville community and the politically defined
wards. As a unitary black community created in the segregation era, today's Bronzeville is divided by ward boundaries. Although the aldermen
care about certain segments of Bronzeville within their wards, they do not
have strong interests in the entire community.

In contrast to their reluctance to support policy initiatives across wards,
the aldermen are eager to develop the areas within their political control.
When making decisions about land use and urban development, they
"focused on areas closest to their own offices and constituents, without
consideration of the potential benefits of clustering activity" (Grams 2005,
9). Some of them even manipulate the policymaking process in order to
maximize the economic return for themselves and their allies. In the 3rd
Ward, for instance, the community proposed to designate 43rd Street
as a Blues District. As one of the main hubs of Chicago Blues since the
1940s, the street contains rich cultural legacies, including the Checker-
board Lounge, one of the most famous Chicago Blues clubs, and the home
of Muddy Waters, "the Father of Chicago Blues." The former alderman
supported the designation of a Blues District, but she moved its location
from 43rd Street to 47th Street, where her office and some business owners
allied with her are located (Grams 2005, 2010). The example reveals the
extraordinary power of aldermen. The decision benefits business owners
on 47th Street by bringing them financial support from the municipality
and private companies, but it perverts history and leaves the real heritage
sites to deteriorate (Figure 23).The political monopoly of each alderman
within his or her ward jeopardizes the economic and social wellbeing of
the whole community. A community leader (C0501) complains,

They [aldermen] should represent the entire community, not
just their own fiefdoms and act like a lord over the people. But
what can we do? It is in the aldermen's interest to have areas
within their political control developed. It's hard to get individual
aldermen to see the whole picture of community preservation and
development.

FIGURE 23. Dilapidation and vacancy on 43rd Street, one of the main cultural heritage sites of Chicago Blues.

This quote reveals the conflict of interest between community members and aldermen. Whereas the former attempt to preserve the entire Bronzeville and recreate the Black Metropolis, the latter concern themselves mainly with political and economic power on their own turfs. The divided monopolies of aldermen have prevented development of the entire area and thwarted preservation initiatives. For years, the Mid-South plan has largely stayed on paper and the NHA campaign remained fruitless, although it usually takes similar areas one year to obtain the NHA status.

Compared with Pilsen, Bronzeville has more bleak areas and suffers more from unbalanced development. In the words of a Bronzeville resident, "There's new development on one block, and you go across the street and there's a burned-out building." Municipal and federal officials highlight unbalanced development as the main obstacle to Bronzeville's landmark designation (C0506, C0512). The weakness of the argument is that it downplays the role of political institutions in shaping the physical conditions and development profiles of local communities. Although the unbalanced development in Bronzeville reflects disinvestment in the community that began in the 1960s, it is reinforced and institutionalized by political fragmentation along ward boundaries. Solving the problem of unbalanced development requires comprehensive land use planning, but it is extremely difficult to achieve under the fragmented monopoly of the aldermen.

The most recent urban preservation battle in Bronzeville took place at the Michael Reese Hospital campus. A major symbol of medical care on Chicago's South Side, the hospital was created at the turn of the twentieth century and grew during postwar expansion. The design of the hospital campus was deeply influenced by German architect Walter Gropius, founder of the famed Bauhaus architecture school. The modernism pioneer not only made the master plan for the campus but also designed eight of the twenty-nine buildings, which are the only Gropius-designed buildings in Illinois and make up 20 percent of his entire U.S. portfolio. Despite its significant historic and architectural value, the hospital campus was under threat after Chicago launched its bid for the 2016 Olympics. In 2009, the city purchased the hospital for $91 million and began to tear it down to make way for an Olympic Village. The plan was opposed by many preservationists and local residents, but their protests did not stop the bulldozers.

After demolition began, Chicago was among the first cities to be eliminated as a potential Olympic host. The Games went to Rio de Janeiro, and the hospital site languishes. In November 2010, the city decided to tear down the main building of the hospital, a prairie-style building erected in 1907 and one of the city's most significant early hospital designs, although it was one of the two buildings the city government promised to preserve. Preservationists proposed adaptive use of the building, but the city claimed that there was serious structural damage, and it would cost too much to fix. Preservationists criticized the city for allowing the landmark to languish after it was acquired as a city property. They argue that the mayor has no interest in preserving Michael Reese Hospital because it is "far from the power broker and the tourists." They also question the lack of public participation in the decision-making process (Kamin 2010).

In the preservation battle over Michael Reese Hospital, the reactions of the state historic preservation agency are noteworthy. When the discussion about redeveloping Michael Reese started in March 2009, the IHPA sent a letter to the Illinois Health Facilities Planning Board, which has jurisdiction over the operation of the hospital. In the letter, the IHPA requested an on-site visit at the hospital campus, and it cited an Illinois law that requires it to assess the impact on historic properties before state agencies grant funding or permission for projects. However, three months later, when the city was about to close its purchase of the hospital, the IHPA withdrew from the preservation battle. According to state officials, the sale of the hospital property was conducted by the city alone, and the state health planning board was not involved, so that they "have no hook regarding that sale" (Bergen 2009b).

After the withdrawal of the state historic preservation agency, preservationists proposed to nominate the Michael Reese Hospital to the National Register of Historic Places, in hope that the landmark status would give them at least a symbolic weapon to wield against city hall. The IHSAC agreed to hold a meeting in early September—about one month before the final voting for the host of the Olympics—to consider the nomination. However, just a few days before the meeting, IHSAC announced that it would postpone it to December because "the person preparing the nomination submitted a great deal of additional information which could not be adequately reviewed by IHPA or City of Chicago staff before this week's meeting" (Bergen 2009a). Chicago lost the Olympic bid in October, but bulldozers continued to destroy buildings at the former Michael Reese Hospital campus. Although IHSAC eventually held the meeting in December and recommended placing the hospital campus on the National Register, its nomination was rejected by the National Park Service. Federal officials particularly faulted the nomination for poorly drawn boundaries. They commented that "the district boundaries need to be reined in to eliminate areas where the buildings have been removed" (Kamin 2009). In other words, it was hard to designate the hospital campus as a landmark district because so many buildings on the site had already been torn down.

Although the hospital was rapidly razed, there is still no solid plan for redeveloping the site. After Chicago lost the Olympic bid, city officials initially intended to sell the 37-acre Reese site to developers who would build housing there. But the real estate bust has taken the air out of plans to put new housing there. The suggestion by several aldermen to build a casino there was also denied by Mayor Daley. Instead, he floated the idea of putting a technology park on the site (Spielman 2011). His successor, Rahm Emanuel, also said that he would bring a Google-like business campus to the city in his first term as mayor, possibly on the site of the Michael Reese Hospital (Chase 2011). Although political leaders consider a technology park to be a good way to bring high-paying jobs to the city and diversify the local economy, they have no plan on how to move forward. And unless the economy makes a drastic turnaround, redevelopment of the Reese site in the near future is uncertain.

Some preservationists compare the situation of the Reese site to Block 37, an entire city block at the heart of Chicago's Loop that was leveled in 1989. Fourteen of the fifteen buildings were torn down to pave the way for a new mixed-use private development. Among the buildings that were demolished, most were dated from the late nineteenth or early twentieth century, six were classified as architecturally significant, and one was an official Chicago Landmark: the McCarthy Building, built in 1871. After the demolition, the block ended up largely vacant for almost two decades until new development eventually took place. Preservationists consider the bungled redevelopment of Block 37 as a lesson to public officials not to tear down useful structures until a well-financed and well-planned redevelopment project is firmly in place. However, the uncertain future of the Reese site makes people wonder whether the lesson has been learned.

According to some longtime residents, the community change in Bronzeville has come in the form of a wrecking ball, from the collapse of Ida B. Wells housing projects, to the fall of Robert Taylor homes, to the demolition of Michael Reese Hospital. The vacant lots and tattered urban fabric of the city's South Side bear witness to the failure of postwar urban renewal programs that wiped out vibrant neighborhoods in the name of clearing slums, providing open expanses of greenery and access to light and air. As one of Chicago's largest slum clearances in recent years, the demolition of the Michael Reese Hospital lends a come-full-circle bitterness to the Bronzeville community in a new wave of urban revitalization. The politically connected wrecking companies seem to be the only winners of the game.

Conclusion

This chapter demonstrates the importance of informal submunicipal dynamics in shaping the process of urban preservation. In Chicago, the tradition of aldermanic prerogative gives aldermen substantial discretion over issues of urban preservation. Although the preservation initiatives in Pilsen and Bronzeville both provide tangible economic benefits to the local communities, the distinct boundaries of aldermanic power lead to different outcomes. Whereas Pilsen is united within one ward, Bronzeville is split between three wards. The preservation initiative in Pilsen was supported by the alderman because of its capacity to generate economic benefits within his political boundary. By contrast, the preservation initiative in Bronzeville has been largely ignored by the aldermen because it may empower CBOs and weaken their local autonomy. In other words, the structure of the local political representation defines aldermen's preferences and shapes the preservation outcomes in the two communities.

The outcomes of the two cases are not attributed exclusively to aldermanic prerogative and political fragmentation. A variety of factors, such as community-level differences, intraward power struggles, and external forces from the municipal and federal government, also affect the preservation efforts. Nonetheless, the structure of local political representation serves as an institutional constraint in the process of urban preservation. First, although urban preservation is considered a bottom-up effort initiated by local communities, any preservation proposal is impossible without local political support. Even federal preservation agencies rely on the opinions of local officials when they make decisions about local communities' preservation initiatives. Second, when a city is dominated by political fragmentation, it is difficult to process preservation initiatives covering a large geographic area. Without citywide preservation initiatives, urban preservation may show a mosaic pattern. A lack of congruence between political boundaries and community boundaries may impede the development and preservation of some communities.

Chicago is probably a special case in having maintained the ward system and aldermanic prerogative. Nevertheless, the monopoly of local political representation is not peculiar to this city. Many cities share the similar structural feature of territorial fragmentation, in which the political boundaries of submunicipal entities act as a filtering mechanism that allows some policy initiatives to get implemented and others stymied. The monopoly of local political actors demonstrates their power of agenda setting in the policy process. Although local officials might not have the authority to make decisions about the policy initiatives of local communities, without their support it is impossible for the initiatives to be processed successfully by decision makers at the upper level. The agenda-setting power of local officials constrains the bottom-up efforts of local communities in the policymaking process, and it suggests the limits of local democracy and public participation.

Urban preservation used to be the privilege of the rich. However, as this chapter demonstrates, it has been adopted by resource-poor communities as a strategy for economic growth and community revitalization. Associated with its changing functions, there are more tensions in the process of urban preservation. The tensions exist not only between preservationists and bulldozers but also between homeowners and renters, between local residents and newcomers, and between local officials and CBOs. When examining the success and failure of various preservation initiatives, it is important to be aware of the increasingly diverse interests and complex political dynamics in the process of urban preservation.

CHAPTER FOUR

Paris

Intergovernmental Competition and Joint Preservation

But if the big city is largely responsible for the invention and public extension of the museum, there is a sense in which one of its own principal functions is to serve as a museum: in its own right, the historic city retains, by reason of its amplitude and its long past, a larger and more various collection of cultural specimens than can be found elsewhere. Every variety of human function, every experiment in human association, every technological process, every mode of architecture and planning, can be found somewhere within its crowded area.
— LEWIS MUMFORD, *The City in History*

In January 2007, at the end of my research trip to Paris, I was stunned by the news that the Paris Municipal Government was sued by the French National Government in the Administrative Court of Paris. The cause of the lawsuit was an urban development plan (Plans Locaux d'Urbanisme [PLU]) made by the city in 2006, in which a total of 5,607 buildings were designated as the Municipal Heritage of Paris (Patrimoine de la Ville de Paris [PVP]). This had been the first urban development plan made by the Paris Municipality and the first landmark designation made by a local authority, instead of the national government, in the long history of urban preservation in France. However, as soon as the plan was approved by the City Council, it was denounced by the prefect of Paris, the state representative in the city, as illegal. Among a number of accusations from the national officials, the legitimacy of the 5,607 municipal heritage buildings was particularly questioned. The conflict over the urban development plan could not be reconciled, so eventually the prefect brought the case to the Administrative Court of Paris. This lawsuit became one of the most well-known political disputes in France in recent decades.

In Paris and in the rest of France, urban preservation had long been the privilege of the state. The national government invented a comprehensive legal framework of urban preservation and implements strict protection of the built environment through a group of highly specialized civil servants. The situation began to change in recent decades when decentralization reforms significantly increased the autonomy of local authorities. To exercise its discretion over the urban territory, the city government began to propose its own agenda of urban planning and urban preservation. Some of those initiatives induced severe conflicts with the state, as the beginning of the chapter shows, and reinforced the political fragmentation between tiers of government.

This chapter explores how intergovernmental fragmentation between the city and the state shapes the policy process of urban preservation in Paris. It begins with a discussion of the history of urban transformation and urban preservation in Paris. I then provide a historical overview of intergovernmental fragmentation in France, followed by an investigation of the political institution of urban preservation in Paris. In order to elaborate the impact of intergovernmental fragmentation on urban preservation, the chapter examines in detail three major preservation projects initiated by the city in recent years. They demonstrate that although the state still plays an important role in major urban projects, its presence is no longer ubiquitous because it has adopted more indirect intervention approaches. It is evident from the cases that intergovernmental fragmentation in France has increasingly caused a mix of conflict, compromise, and cooperation across levels of government. Accordingly, urban preservation in Paris is gradually transformed from the monopoly of the state to a joint venture between the city and the state.

Haussmann's Great Urban Transformation

Paris is considered by many to be the cultural capital of the nineteenth century and one of the most beautiful cities in the world. Like Beijing, the urban landscape of Paris was created by a centralized national authority, but they were fashioned in very different ways. Beijing was designed to be a cohesive artistic statement under a complex set of Chinese design philosophies when the Ming emperor Yongle launched the construction in the early fifteenth century. By contrast, Paris developed over several centuries.

It grew from a medieval town to the cultural and political center of Europe in the Age of Enlightenment and, finally, in the era of industrialization, a city of tree-lined boulevards, unified streetscapes, and magnificent vistas illuminated by thousands of elegant streetlamps. Whereas much of the splendor of Beijing was preconceived, the splendor of Paris evolved and accumulated (Sutcliffe 1993; Tung 2001).

The cityscape of Paris achieved artistic completion in the nineteenth century under the great urban transformation led by Georges-Eugene Haussmann. Appointed by Napoleon III as the prefect of the Seine, Haussmann implemented comprehensive urban reorganization in Paris from 1852 to 1869 (Jordan 1996; Van Zanten 1994). Haussmann's plan was direct, rational, and audacious in its scope. In order to eliminate filth in the city and improve the quality of life, he paved 400 miles of streets, built more than 260 miles of sewers, and improved the water supply and delivery system. He expanded the public parks from 47 acres to 4,000 acres and doubled the number of trees adorning the city's roadways. He built bridges, markets, theaters, schools, churches, synagogues, and public meeting halls and created thousands of streetlamps to illuminate the urban vista, turning Paris into the City of Light. But most of all, he carved grand boulevards through the medieval quarters and brought Cartesian order to the urban space. Haussmann mandated that the architecture of the new boulevards be unified so that each façade aligned with the street wall and combined with its neighbors to make continuous elevational composition. Like the Renaissance piazzas of the kings, every boulevard became an integrated public space in addition to offering a long urban perspective. When major historic buildings did not exist at the junction of avenues, new monuments were created in association with traffic rounds, to provide a dramatic architectural culmination to each urban vista.

Haussmann's transformation not only modernized the urban infrastructure of Paris but also gave the city artistic unity. Haussmann comprehended the historic classical legacy of the city—in which public squares, streets, and architecture had been woven into unified ensembles—and applied this model to the entire built environment. He created a spatial order that binds together geographically separated monuments and harmonizes the modern context with the character of existing landmarks (Figure 24). As one of the greatest urban transformations of the nineteenth century, Haussmann's vision for Paris influenced urban design in cities around the world, from Buenos Aires and Bucharest to Chicago. As Sir Peter Hall in *Cities in Civilization* (1998, 706) observed in regard to Haussmann's achievements, "No one in the entire history of urbanism, neither Pericles

FIGURE 24. Haussmannian Paris, postcard.

nor the Roman emperors nor the Renaissance popes, ever transformed a city so profoundly during such a short space of time."

Despite the achievement in urban artistry, Haussmann's urban transformation of Paris remains controversial largely because of the massive demolition of the medieval urban texture. The destruction of old neighborhoods, although often rationalized as a necessity for making or widening roadways, was also part of a policy of slum clearance. It has significant impact on both the historic architectural profile and the social dimension of the city. Several of the oldest historic quarters of Paris were among the most crime-ridden and dilapidated and were therefore erased. No provision was made for those displaced, and the poor were forced to move out to the city's perimeter, replaced by the middle class in new, higher-priced, upgraded, market-driven housing (Jordan 1996). The most blatant example of slum clearance and one of the city's most significant historic losses occurred on the Île de la Cité, where the medieval fabric surrounding two of the city's most significant Gothic monuments—the Cathedral of Notre Dame and the Sainte-Chapelle—was largely demolished (Tung 2001).

Aside from the discussion of its impact on the historic architectural profile of Paris, it is important to note that Haussmann's urban renovation was not only for the sake of aesthetics or the betterment of urban infrastructure but also served the political purposes of the national authority. It was intended to fortify Paris against working-class uprisings after the revolution of 1848 by discouraging the construction of barricades and displacing the proletarian population in the city center. Because the streets were much wider after the urban transformation, rebels had to build longer barricades, which would cost them more time and weaken their forces by spreading them out. Meanwhile, the widened streets allowed more troops to respond to any menace with the assistance of artillery squadrons, enabling them to efficiently destroy any barricade (Jordan 1996; Van Zanten 1994). Therefore, as one of the most remarkable urban transformations in human history, Haussmann's urban renovation significantly changed the spatial and social dimensions of Paris and reinforced the political control of the French central authority over its capital city.

Fighting the Modernism Attack: Nationalization of the Urban Landscape

After Haussmann's urban transformation, the cityscape of Paris was reshaped again in the post–World War II era. At the end of the two world wars and a global depression, Paris entered Trente Glorieuses (Thirty-Year Glories), a thirty-year period of rapid economic growth from the late 1940s to the mid-1970s. Although the Thirty-Year Glories led to rapid urban development in Paris, it also put the historic city under the attack from those wishing to modernize the city (Savitch 1988). Paul Delouvrier, the prefect of Paris under President Charles de Gaulle, is one of the main planners for the postwar transformation of Paris. In order to accommodate automobiles, hundreds of miles of new freeways were constructed in the city, including one along the Seine and another that traced the footprint of the city's old defensive wall, now Boulevard Périphérique. Dozens of old wood-frame and plaster houses of the working-class neighborhoods in eastern Paris were bulldozed to make room for generic apartment blocks. High-rise towers were built in the urban core to create the image of a modern city, and in 1972 La Tour Maine-Montparnasse was erected not far from the Luxembourg Gardens. The largest skyscraper in Europe at the time, the 210-meter modern high-rise was about six times taller than the general height allowed in Paris. It caused a national uproar and forever changed the historic milieu of Paris.

Facing the destruction of the historic city, the national government began to control development by lowering allowable building heights to historic norms. All high-rises were banned from the city center five years later, after the construction of Tower Montparnasse. And in some areas, such as Montmartre, permissible heights were even lower than historic standards, successfully discouraging new developments in existing urban quarters (Tung 2001). As a way of accommodating new developments,

FIGURE 25. La Défense, the new central business district outside Old Paris. Photograph by Keven Law.

a central business district was created in La Défense outside the old city (Figure 25). Although contemporary buildings have been added to the city periodically since the 1970s, the essential urban fabric remains largely intact. The freeway of Périphérique became a dividing line, isolating the city of Haussmann from the growing modern sprawl in the banlieues that surrounded it.

Besides applying zoning regulations to new developments, the national government has implemented a comprehensive set of policies to designate and preserve the historic architectural profile of Paris. Approximately 1,900 buildings have been designated as national monuments and two urban areas designated as preservation districts. In France, architectural legacies are considered a source of national cultural identity, meaning that the power to designate and administrate monument buildings and historic districts does not belong to local authorities. Rather, this power has long been firmly controlled by the national government (Choay 2001). On behalf of the national authority, a group of highly specialized national civil servants monitor and supervise demolition and construction in most parts of Paris. Constrained by such a strict legal system, urban preservation in Paris has become a matter of saving not just important individual structures but the special character of the whole urban profile. It is a tool for the national government to lead the direction of urban development and bolster French national pride.

In recent years, the comprehensive protection of the cityscape in Paris has caused concerns about the future of the historic city. The municipal government has long argued that the current approach of urban preservation puts Paris at risk of *muséification,* a process that strangles growth and freezes the historic city into a museum. To challenge the monopoly of the national government in urban preservation, the city has proposed a new agenda of urban preservation. Its goal is to incorporate urban preservation into the citywide planning process and use urban preservation as a tool for more sustainable urban development. The different goals of the national government and the city generate two conflicting discourses of urban preservation, which are entangled with and reinforce the power struggles between the two tiers of government, thus making the policy process of urban preservation increasingly complex. The following section discusses in detail the institutional history of intergovernmental fragmentation in France.

Dismantling the Jacobin State: Intergovernmental Fragmentation in France

The French political system has traditionally been characterized by state centralism. The state exercises its control through a unified civil service with offices of external services *(services extérieurs)* set up at the local level (Suleiman 1974, 1978). State initiatives are considered the key components of almost every major urban project, from the preservation of historic monuments to the construction of commercial complexes, cultural and sporting facilities, and public transit systems (Savitch and Kantor 2002). In the centralized system, the most important interactions are supposed to take place within the public sector, whereas an assemblage of social and private actors work under the initiative of a unified technocratic elite (Savitch 1988).

Despite the powerful role of the national government, the tension between the center and the periphery has become one of the most persistent and intractable problems facing the French state (Tarrow 1977; Ashford 1982; Levy 1999; Smyrl 2004). The complex network of intergovernmental relations dates back to the contest between the Jacobins and the Girondins during the French Revolution. Whereas the former were strong advocates of centralized state control, the latter were more in favor of local autonomy (Doyle 2003). The traditional view of France as a haven of Jacobin centralization has been under serious attack since the 1970s (Wright 1974; Schmidt 1990; Le Galès 2006). It is the traditional stifling of local autonomy and the increased demand for power at the local level that incited Kesselman (1970, 31) to comment, "To describe France merely as centralized is to ignore the extensive localistic influences that persist in French politics even in the Fifth Republic."

France has a three-tier local government system *(collectivités locales)* consisting of 22 *régions* (regions), 96 *départements* (departments), and some 36,600 *communes* (municipalities). Departments and municipalities were created in 1789, and regions were introduced as a third local government level in the 1982 decentralization reform. The multitude of small municipalities generates an unusually high degree of territorial fragmentation in the French local government system. The number of French municipalities accounts for nearly one-fourth of all the municipal-level governments in Europe (Ashford 1982; Agence Nationale pour l'Amelioration de l'Habitat [ANAH] 2003). Municipal councils vary from nine members for municipalities under a population of 100 people to forty-nine members for municipalities over 300,000. This makes a total of about 460,000 municipal councilors (Ashford 1982). The huge cumulative total of municipal councilors creates a large web of local power to balance the power of the national government. Municipal leaders have successfully resisted attempts from the center to reorganize the territorial system and downsize the municipal councils, including those of two strong national leaders, de Gaulle and Pompidou, in 1964, 1969, and 1971 (Ashford 1982; Levy 1999).

What further complicates the intergovernmental relations is the tradition of *cumul des mandats,* or accumulation of positions. It allows elected officials to hold more than one office at the same time, so that many mayors also hold seats in the national legislature or in the central ministries. Such an arrangement creates overlapping, center–local networks of power (Ashford 1982; Le Galès 2006). After the 1975 Senate elections, 161 of the 264 senators were mayors, and 247 of the 470 deputies were mayors (Ashford 1982). In 2007, almost 95 percent of the senators also had local political duties (P0720). The overlapping offices are a double-edged sword. Although they have increased democratic representation of the periphery and reinforced political solidarity nationwide, they have also blurred the jurisdictional boundaries between the center and the local. Since 1985 the *cumul des mandats* has been curtailed,[1] but the overlapping networks of power still exist. It is particularly the Senate *(Sénat)* and its mayoral members *(maire-sénateurs)* who have proven staunch advocates of local interests and defenders of the institutional status quo (Wollmann 2010).

The power of local authorities has been formally increased by the decentralization reforms (Schmidt 1990; Levy 1999; Smyrl 2004; Le Galès 2006). After the preliminary reform during the Third Republic, the Socialists of the Fifth Republic significantly increased the power of local entities as a political strategy to limit the Right's central control. From 1981 to 1986, President François Mitterrand (1981–1995) gave extensive new powers to territorial authorities through a series of more than forty laws and nearly three hundred decrees (Schmidt 1990). Those documents transferred the prefects' executive powers to the presidents of the departments and regions, turned over state administrative functions and financial resources to the localities, and proposed to reform the territorial civil service (Schmidt 1990; Le Galès 2006).

Following the epochal decentralization of 1982, Prime Minister Jean-Pierre Raffarin (2002–2005) pushed forward a constitutional amendment, Act II, in 2003. The goal of the act is to reduce the financial burden of the central government and to comply with the decentralization agenda of the European Union. Specifically, the act transferred 150,000 civil servants to the local level and legitimized the formation of policy based on local agendas (Smyrl 2004; Le Galès 2006). It is through the decentralization decrees and policies that centralist France has been transformed into a decentralized republic *(republique d'organisation décentralisée)* (Wollmann 2010).

With the increase of local autonomy, decentralization generates a by-product of intergovernmental fragmentation. A common criticism of decentralization reforms is that they failed to divide the power and responsibility between levels of the government. Although the jurisdictions of local authorities are enlarged, the state has not shrunk the boundaries of its power. Therefore, overlapping and conflicting jurisdictions between the center and the local materialize. The jurisdictional conflict also exists between territorial authorities. According to the general legal principle of decentralization, all units of the territorial government are equal (Smyrl 2004; Le Galès 2006). In other words, commune, department, and region can each freely manage the affairs pertaining to their areas of jurisdiction, none of which has precedence, or is permitted to exercise control, over any of the others. Without a clear division of responsibility, the equal legal status only intensifies the turf wars between territorial entities.

In the situation of intergovernmental fragmentation, the policy process is fraught with conflicts, struggles, and intermingling. Political actors at different levels compete with one another for preferred tasks and attempt to leave the undesirable ones to others. This situation is described by French urban economist Vincent Renard as *mistigri,* a popular French card game in which every player tries to pass the bad cards to others (P0605). Meanwhile, political actors make deals across government levels in order to maximize the benefit to their own agencies. For example, a city may choose to ally with the state against the region or ally with the region against the state, all depending on the specific issues and the agendas of the local authority (P0643).

Despite the drawbacks of intergovernmental fragmentation, decentralization is not a zero-sum game. First, although the French national government decentralized its power, it has not vanished from city hall. The state still pays for more than 40 percent of local budgets and continues to have a substantial impact on major urban projects (Savitch and Kantor 2002). As state representatives at the local level, prefects have changed their role from power holders to power brokers. Although they no longer exercise *la tutelle*, or guidance, over local officials, they continue to monitor local authorities, ensuring consistency in the application of national rules at the local level (Savitch and Kantor 2002).

Second, the struggles between the center and the local are often tempered by the need to achieve shared policy goals, by interlocking political positions, and by a mutual respect for the state. Politicians at different levels usually make compromises and take collective actions in order to fulfill policy goals. The linkages between levels of government are reinforced through a variety of intergovernmental agencies, including planning agencies *(agencies d'urbanisme)*, semipublic development corporations *(sociétés d'économie mixte)*, and the network of financial institutions linked to the Caisse des Dépôts[2] (Ashford 1982; Sadran 2004). The French policy process is described as a marble cake, a pattern characterized by the overlapping, shared, or contested control over individual issues and projects by a mix of central and local political actors (Webman 1981).

Intergovernmental relations in France provide a background for understanding the relationship between the French state and its capital city. Unlike most cities in the world, Paris did not have a mayor until 1977. Except for brief interludes between 1789 and 1871, the city was ruled by the state and its appointed prefect of the Seine along with the city council.[3] The long absence of the mayor in Paris is largely due to the central authority's mistrust and fear of the Parisian populace. Throughout French history, from the ancient regime to the Revolutionary era, Parisians were always the leading force of uprisings (Harsin 2002). In more recent decades, the demonstrations of 1968 showed again that disorder on the streets of Paris can directly threaten the stability of the national government (Alexander 2007). The response of the state is to eliminate the position of mayor and rule the capital through state representatives, so Paris was tightly kept within the clutches of the state.

The political dynamics in Paris was substantially changed when Jacques Chirac was elected the first modern mayor of Paris in 1977 (Chevalier 1977; Ashford 1982; Schmidt 1990). Chirac ruled Paris for eighteen years, resigning only after he was elected president of France in 1995. As a Gaullist loyalist, Chirac enjoyed party cohesion and a strong Gaullist majority on the city council. He governed the city like an old-fashioned city boss, efficiently, authoritatively, and with unquestioned popular support. The political popularity of Chirac went beyond Paris and expanded to the rest of the country.

At the base of Chirac's regime was the Parisian city council, most of whose 163 representatives were members of Chirac's Gaullist party. Besides the majority support in the city council, Chirac extended his influence to the local districts. Paris is divided into twenty *arrondissements* (municipal administrative districts), and each has its own mayor and local city hall. All arrondissement mayors are voting representatives on the city council. Nevertheless, unlike in Chicago, arrondissement mayors in Paris have limited local autonomy, so there is little evidence of territorial fragmentation in Paris. On one hand, having little control over budget matters or resources, arrondissement mayors had to rely on municipal benefits such as community development funds, assistance to the needy, and programs to modernize housing. It is through the allocation of those favors that Chirac made his weight felt in almost every arrondissement. On the other hand, arrondissement mayors also served as deputy mayors in the municipality so that they became an integral part of Chirac's political coalition and extended his legislative influence.

Chirac's political capacity was further increased through the *cumul des mandats*. At one time, Chirac held offices simultaneously as mayor, prime minister, member of the national assembly, and head of his party. These positions allowed him to work across government lines and to coordinate efforts by municipal, regional, and national governments. His allies on the city council also exercised the *cumul des mandats*: four municipal councilors served as ministers in the national government, six served as senators, nineteen held office in the national assembly, and twenty-one sat on the regional council. The extent of overlapping offices was astounding, and it amounted to the substantial power and resources obtained by the municipality (Savitch and Kantor 2002).

While the state continued to show a remarkable presence in Paris through public administrators and civil servants of the external services, the autonomy of the municipality significantly increased, and the mayor began to promote his own lines of urban policies (Ashford 1982; Alexander 2007). Soon after his inauguration, Chirac traded favors with President Giscard d'Estaing and obtained the power to redevelop Les Halles, the site of a large marketplace in the center of Paris that had remained vacant for nearly ten years after the demolition of the market. This was the first time that the city took over a major urban project from the hands of the state. In 1983, Chirac opposed the national government's plan to host the 1989 World's Fair in Paris, claiming that it would disrupt life in his city and cause unreasonable tax increases, even though President Mitterrand and his socialist allies hoped the fair would be a bicentennial celebration of the French Revolution.[4]

The discords over specific urban projects do not necessarily mean that the city and the state are in antagonism. Instead, Chirac highlighted the role of the national government during his first mayoral campaign (Haegel 1994, 75):

> Paris needs a mayor who can study and treat its problems. It also needs national intervention if Parisians are to stop the incursion of cement onto the streets of Les Halles, halt the destruction of the quays on the Left Bank, and stop the developers from putting up towers.

Critics might counter that the statements were campaign rhetoric, but they were consonant with the Gaullist regard for a strong state. More importantly, Chirac worked closely with national leaders in matters of urban development, regardless of political stripe (Savitch 1988).

Chirac resigned from city hall after he was elected president of France in 1995. His strong ally and former first deputy mayor, Jean Tiberi, succeeded him as the mayor of Paris. However, the Socialists began to pose a real challenge to Tiberi from the early days of his mayoralty. While Paris remained in the Gaullist hands under the mayoralty of Tiberi, its arrondissements were gradually drifting toward the left. In 2001, the Socialists took over twelve of the twenty arrondissements, and the leftist coalition won ninety-two seats in the city council against seventy-one seats for the right. In the same year, Socialist Party spokesman and senator Bertrand Delanoë was elected the first Socialist mayor of Paris. With huge popular support, Delanoë won the reelection in 2008.

Intergovernmental relations in Paris have become more complicated after a left-wing coalition came to power in the city for the first time. Although the capital city is governed by a leftist mayor, the central government is under the command of the rightists. Nicolas Sarkozy, the successor to Chirac's presidency, and Prime Minister François Fillon are both from Union pour un Mouvement Populaire (Union for a Popular Movement), a central-right party that has an absolute majority in the National Assembly. The ideological cleavage between the left and the right has intertwined with the intergovernmental power struggles between the city and

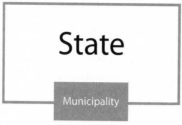

Before decentralization reform

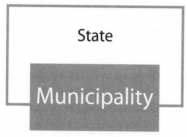

After decentralization reform

FIGURE 26. Intergovernmental fragmentation in Paris.

the state, thus intensifying the extent of political fragmentation in Paris.

Alongside the rise of the Paris municipality, the region of Île-de-France has gained more weight since the 1982 decentralization reform. Presided over by an elected council that selects its chief executive, Île-de-France is able to fund infrastructure, undertake strategic planning, and coordinate common policies. The waters of Paris are further roiled with the involvement of the region in some urban projects. However, because of the still limited power and resources of the region, the tension between the city and the state is the main discord in Parisian politics. As Figure 26 shows, when the city has expanded its boundary of power, the state does not withdraw; hence, the overlapping jurisdiction between the center and the local is enlarged, and the potential for intergovernmental conflict is increased.

Urban Preservation in Paris: From State Monopoly to Joint Venture

Urban preservation is one of the best issue areas for examining intergovernmental fragmentation in Paris. Because historic monuments are considered an important source of French cultural identity and national pride, urban preservation has long been the privilege of the national government.

In Paris, the state has implemented strict protection of the architectural heritage through a series of legal documents and a group of highly specialized civil servants. Although the centralized preservation system has resulted in effective protection of the architectural heritage, it has placed constraints on the autonomy of local authority and thus become one of the focal points of intergovernmental conflicts. This section discusses how the policy process of urban preservation in Paris is reshaped by intergovernmental fragmentation and increasingly transformed from a monopoly of the state to a joint venture between the central and local authorities.

The effort of the French central authority to preserve historic structures began during the French Revolution, when Abbé Gregoire called in 1794 for the preservation of monuments as national heritage. A Commission of Historic Monuments was established in 1830 by Louis Philippe to survey historic monuments nationwide and recognize their national status (Choay 2001; Boyer 1994). The early preservation initiatives allowed the French emperors to convert historic monuments into a symbol of tradition and norm, on which moral, political, and social foundations could stand. The return to history most often occurs in moments of crisis, when the goal is not only to appreciate the historic or aesthetic value of the monuments but also to stabilize and legitimize the current regimes. It is important to note that the politicization of historic monuments is not unique to France but existed in a number of European countries at the time, including Britain, Italy, and Germany (Boyer 1994; Lowenthal 1985).

The French national government created a legal framework of urban preservation in the early twentieth century. As the first modern preservation statute, the 1913 act identifies two categories of historic monuments: Monuments Historiques (Listed Monuments) and Inventaire Supplémentaire des Monuments Historiques (Registered in the Additional Inventory of Historic Monuments).[5] A supplement to the 1913 act was passed in 1930, which extends the protection from single buildings to historic sites. Finally, the 1943 act extends the protection of both historic monuments and sites to their surrounding environment within a radius of 500 meters. The act places historic buildings in their urban context and enables the preservation of historic monuments, sites, and their environment as a whole.

The postwar urban renewal made the state realize the vulnerability of inner-city neighborhoods, so that it began to make new laws to protect the urban texture. Under the promotion of André Malraux, the first minister of culture in France, an act was passed in 1962 to legalize the designation of historic neighborhoods as Secteurs Sauvegardés (Safeguarded Sectors) under state protection. According to the Malraux Act, named after the minister, once an area is designated as a Safeguarded Sector, it cannot be

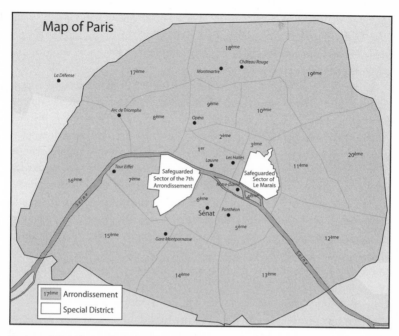

FIGURE 27. Safeguarded Sectors in Paris.

FIGURE 28. Le Marais: the first Safeguarded Sector in France.

included in any local development plan. The Safeguard and Development Plan (Sauvegardé et de Mise en Valeur [PSMV]), made by the state, provides precise rules to prescribe any demolition, construction, or planning activities in the designated area.

Under the centralized legal framework of urban preservation, a large number of buildings, sites, and areas in Paris are designated as cultural heritage. A total of 1,900 buildings in the city are designated as historic monuments[6] (ANAH 2003). Two historic areas are designated as Safeguarded Sectors (Figure 27). One is Le Marais, a historic neighborhood at the right bank of the Seine, designated in 1964 as the first Safeguarded Sector in France (Figure 28). The other one is part of the 7th Arrondissement, designated in 1972, which is adjacent to the Hôtel des Invalides and contains a large number of national institutions. Combining the two Safeguarded Sectors, 1,900 historic monuments—as well as the surroundings within a radius of 500 meters of each monument, in essence the center of Paris—were made into a vast historic district covering about 80 percent of the entire city (ANAH 2003). This may well be the largest single continuous preservation area in any city in the world.

The power to oversee and manage historic monuments and preservation districts does not belong to any local authority but is in the hands of a group of highly specialized civil servants, National Heritage Architects (Architectes des Bâtiments de France [ABF]). As architects specialized in historic preservation, the profession of ABFs has a long history that traces back to 1897. Today an architect has to go through rigorous, specialized training and pass competitive examinations in order to be recruited by the Ministry of Culture as an ABF. This group of cultural elites is authorized by the state as the only people qualified to supervise works relating to historic monuments and Safeguarded Sectors. To better reinforce preservation decrees at the local level, the Ministry of Culture establishes the office for external service (Service Départemental de l'Architecture et du Patrimoine) in each department and sends the ABFs to those local offices. There are eight ABFs in Paris, and each is in charge of two or three arrondissements (P0610). Any private or public work inside or outside the protected buildings, even a proposal made by the mayor, has to be submitted to the ABFs for approval.

The centralized control of the state in urban preservation has largely prevented the problems of bureaucratic segmentation and local parochialism that are prevalent in Beijing and Chicago. Meanwhile, the involvement of the ABFs reinforces the role of expertise and professional norms in urban preservation. However, the professionalism of the ABFs cannot eliminate the complex politics of urban preservation. Despite the fact that most of their decisions are well grounded and based on technical concerns, the involvement of the ABFs represents the absolute power of the state in local affairs and therefore is considered by the Paris Municipality as a threat to its autonomy. Given that 80 percent of the city's land is under state supervision, the issue of who has the authority to make decisions about urban preservation became extremely critical when the city began to propose its own urban agenda.

Paris began to challenge the state monopoly on urban preservation after the inauguration of its first mayor. For example, the city has repeatedly defeated the state's proposal to designate a third Safeguarded Sector in Paris since the late 1970s (P0621, P0630, P0708, P0602, P0614). Meanwhile, a number of municipal-level agencies such as Atelier Plan d'Urbanisme de Paris (Urban Planning Workshop of Paris), Direction du Patrimoine et de l'Architecture (Department of Heritage and Architecture), and Commission du Vieux Paris (Commission of Old Paris) began to serve the ambition of the mayor in urban policy by conducting research and laying out strategies for planning and preservation (Savitch and Kantor 2002). The efforts of the city demonstrate that the conflict between the city and the state on preservation issues is a power struggle between the two levels of government about who should control the territory of Paris. Urban preservation in Paris is no longer a technical issue exclusively controlled by unified technocratic elite but a political matter shaped by intergovernmental fragmentation.

In an interview with *Paris Projet* (1983), a leading professional journal on planning and preservation issues in Paris, Chirac discusses the tension between the center and the local in urban preservation. He contends that although legislation gives the state "quasi-kingly" *(quasi régalien)* power over the cultural heritage *(patrimoine),* the local authorities have gradually increased their competence in decentralization and asked to share some of the state's power in urban preservation. The situation generates jurisdictional conflict between the two levels. However, he emphasizes the importance of empowering the local authorities in urban preservation, because the state is "too far away" from the cultural heritage, and much can be lost in lengthy administrative and bureaucratic procedures controlled by the center. Finally, Chirac maintains that it is critical to create a "delicate equilibrium" between the state and the municipality, and between preserving the cultural heritage of Paris and enriching its architectural diversity through urban development and innovation. Chirac clearly laid out his vision for urban preservation in Paris and highlighted the importance for intergovernmental cooperation. Although he could not fulfill all the goals during his tenure as the mayor of Paris, some of his ideas materialized in the preservation practices of Paris in later years.

Decentralization reforms have largely increased the power of local authorities in urban planning and preservation. The creation of Zones de Protection du Patrimoine Architectural, Urbain et Paysager (protected zones for architectural, urban, and landscape heritage) in 1993 allows cities to make their own urban development plans. The Loi Solidarité et Renouvellement Urbains (SRU) (law of urban solidarity and renewal), passed in 2000, further expands the power of cities by enabling them to make urban preservation policies. It also allows mayors to negotiate with ABFs and adjust the 500-meter protected areas surrounding historic monuments (Le Galès 2006; Institute de la Décentralisation 2004).

Empowered by the decentralization decrees, Paris made its urban development plan (PLU) in 2006. As the first urban development plan made by the municipality in the history of Paris, PLU pays special attention to urban preservation. Particularly concerned with the *muséification* of Paris, the danger of turning the historic city into a museum, PLU laid out the notion of incorporating urban preservation as a coherent part of the agenda of urban development. It proposes to give historic buildings a new life through renovation and adaptive reuse. In order to keep Paris a lively city, it maintains the importance of allowing space for innovative architectural design instead of reproducing pastiche in a neo-Haussmannian style.[7]

PLU presents a serious challenge to the PSMV. It made clear the city's opinion that the PSMV for the two protected areas is out of date and runs counter to a variety of economic and social goals pursued by the municipality, so a new version of the PSMV is needed (P0630, P0602, P0614). After lengthy negotiations, the state agreed to work with the city and make a new PSMV for the two protected areas. Described by a municipal official as a "compromise between the city and the state" (P0708), the new PSMV will remain under the supervision of the ABFs but will take into account the demands of the city on issues such as social housing, commercial facilities, and parking space in Safeguarded Sectors (P0708, P0711).

After the agreement was reached between the city and the state on making the new PSMV, an official from the Ministry of Culture commented on the intergovernmental relations as follows (P0711):

> The SRU law says the preservation of those Safeguarded Sectors is the responsibility of both the city and the state, so the state cannot have a decision if the city doesn't agree. This is very new. The decentralization is on its way, so the state is no longer the only power holder. It cannot decide just on its own. This is the case for everything, not just for heritage.

This quote illustrates how decentralization has increased the autonomy of local authorities and intensified the struggles between the city and the state. The notion of local authorities as new power holders shaking the monopoly of the state challenges the traditional view of statism in France. However, decentralization is not a zero-sum game. The agreement between the city and the state on the new PSMV shows a balance of power between the two political actors. Such a balance is favored in the French political culture.

The following sections investigate three preservation projects initiated by the city. The projects address various aspects of urban preservation and demonstrate different extents of state intervention. The designation of the 5,607 PVPs challenges the authority of the state in defining and protecting cultural heritage, so it was strongly opposed by the state and brought the two levels of government to the administrative court. In the redevelopment of Les Halles, although the state seems absent from the implementation of the project, it uses invisible hands to shape the direction of the project through a state-owned transportation company. Such a strategy helps the state reduce its financial burden but remain on board. Finally, the renovation of Château Rouge is an effort by the city to strengthen its control over a predominantly ethnic community at the edge of the city. The project is carried out primarily under the discretion of the city, whereas the role of the state is limited to setting general principles.

Inventing the Municipal Heritage

Following the urban preservation initiatives laid out in PLU, the city designated 5,607 buildings as the Municipal Heritage of Paris (PVP). Because the designation of historic monuments is a privilege of the national government, this proactive step by the city is a huge challenge to state authority. However, the city maintains that, because there are more than 1,000,000 buildings in Paris and only 1,900 of them are designated as national monuments, the state's protection of cultural heritage is limited. Therefore, the designation of the PVPs is considered by the city as an important supplement to the national heritage system, which will increase the cultural integrity of Paris and promote development of the tourism economy (P0602, P0630, P0708).

The PVPs and national monuments have different designation processes. National monuments are designated by the minister of culture based on the advice of Commission Supérieure des Monuments Historiques (Higher Historic Monuments Committee), which consists of renowned architectural historians and architects. The designation is dominated by the knowledge and preferences of a small number of cultural elites, and the general public is excluded (ANAH 2003). By contrast, PVPs are designated through more democratic procedures. The municipality holds public hearings in every arrondissement of Paris, which give municipal officials a chance to know what citizens want to preserve. More than 10,000 designation requests were collected from residents, local associations, and historic societies at the hearings. After conducting research on the sites, the municipality designated 5,607 buildings as municipal heritage (P0602, P0614).

The different designation processes give different meanings to the term *cultural heritage*. A municipal official explains the difference (P0708):

> The Ministry [of Culture] only protects those big monuments designed by famous architects, such as the Opéra and Notre Dame. But we may preserve an ordinary working-class residential building that is important to the local community and represents a certain period of local urban history. The Ministry has too many things to protect, so they don't have the sense for the local history. We know the local situation better than the state, and we care more about the will of the local communities. Actually, this is a new way of thinking about heritage, a more democratic way. It's emerging in not only France but also the whole Europe.

It is evident from the quote that the designation of the PVPs creates a new dimension of cultural heritage, which is associated with ordinary urban dwellings and the history of local communities (Figure 29). With the shift in focus from historic monuments to urban fabric, the designation of the PVPs demonstrates a democratization of urban preservation: the designation of cultural heritage is no longer the privilege of a small group of cultural elites but a component of urban life that can be practiced by ordinary citizens.

Regardless of the merits of the PVPs laid out by municipal officials, the designation generates heated debates between the city and the state. The Ministry of Culture has serious concerns about the motives of the municipality in designating PVPs. An official from the ministry put it in this way (P0708):

> The city designated those buildings just because it wants to increase its power, but it doesn't have the competence to protect them. PLU wanted to protect more than it really can. It is true there are *Architectes Voyers*[8] in the city, but they are not trained

FIGURE 29. Residential buildings designated as the Municipal Heritage of Paris.

> to protect heritage. The only people qualified to protect cultural
> heritage are ABFs. As technocrats of the state, ABFs can make
> objective judgment and provide constant protection to the
> heritage.... PLU is new and it might be subject to changes during
> the mayoral elections and other political occasions, so it cannot
> provide constant protection to the buildings. As a matter of fact,
> urban preservation can be manipulated by local politicians as
> a boutique window to show off their policies and achieve their
> political goals.

To the Ministry of Culture, the designation of the PVPs is a dangerous sign
of the politicization of cultural heritage. Without the involvement of professionally trained ABFs, it worries that the city does not have the capacity
to protect historic buildings. Therefore, urban preservation would be manipulated by local officials as a tool to fulfill their own parochial interests.

Besides the concern about the politicization of culture heritage, the
state opposes the designation of the PVPs also for financial reasons. According to the preservation laws, the state should provide tax deductions
and subsidies to owners of the landmark buildings to encourage them to
maintain and renovate historic buildings. However, as an official from
the Ministry of Finance points out, the state is not willing to grant fiscal
exemptions to such large numbers of PVP buildings because the commit-
ment will place too great a financial burden on the shoulders of the state.

Although municipal officials held public hearings and conducted research on historic buildings, ABFs criticize the designation of the PVPs as "lacking scientific ground." In their words, "It is not clear why some of the buildings are worth preserving" (P0723). Furthermore, they complain that the designation of the PVPs undermines their authority and complicates the policy process of urban preservation in Paris (P0632, P0710). An ABF explains the problems as follows (P0710):

> Eighty percent of Paris is under state protection inspected by ABFs. When there is no PVP, we can just make judgment on individual buildings in the protected areas, based on their values. But now, when there is PVP, an owner could come to us and propose the demolition of his building by claiming that it is not a PVP. If we want to protect the building from demolition, he would ask, "If the building is so important, why is it not listed as PVP?" Then we cannot answer it. Also, citizens don't understand why there are two institutions. The situation becomes very complicated after the city designates those PVPs.

The ABF is apparently anxious to defend his authority. The designation of the PVPs weakens the authority of the ABFs by providing property owners another set of criteria to examine their buildings. Property owners can even use PVP status as a weapon to challenge the decisions of the ABFs. Thus, the conflicting jurisdictions between the city and the state are clearly demonstrated.

At the other side of the debate, municipal officials use the decentralization decrees to justify their preservation initiatives (P0708):

> When we start to think about the designation of PVP in 2002, we got all the critiques from the Ministry [of Culture], "You are nothing; you are working in a city; you don't know what heritage is, blah, blah, blah." But we have the legitimacy to do it, because the law SRU gives us the power to make preservation policies at the local level. So no matter what the Ministry says, we just keep it going in our way.

Besides holding on to the laws of decentralization, municipal officials highlight the democratic nature of the designation procedures for the PVPs. Because the designations are based primarily on the demands of residents, an official criticizes the state's attack on the PVPs as an attempt to stomp out local democracy (P0614):

> The attack on the heritage policy is very silly. The heritage policy in PLU is based on local public hearings. If the Prefect disagrees with it, he is against the will of the people.

To municipal officials, the designation of the PVPs is not only important for protecting cultural heritage in Paris but also essential for promoting more open, democratic procedures of urban planning and preservation. As an alternative to the elitist approach of urban preservation adopted by the state, public participation in the designation process provided the municipality a weapon to defend the legitimacy of the PVPs.

Despite the democratic elements in the designation process, it is important to note the limits of the public hearings in Paris. As a new form of public participation, the public hearings are not well attended. Several municipal officials point out that although attendance at the public hearings varies between arrondissements, it is not very high in general. Most of attendees are well-educated upper- or middle-class people (P0614, P0709, P0720, P0702). The problems of low attendance and the narrow range of the attendees also appear in public hearings held for other urban projects in Paris. Although public participation is articulated by the Socialist mayor as a new goal for local government, there is a long way to go in order to achieve better democratic representation in the policy process.

Party cleavage exacerbates the battle between the city and the state over the designation of the PVPs. An official from the Ministry of Culture expressed his distrust of the left in preserving cultural heritage by arguing that the Socialists consider the construction of social housing more important than the protection of historic buildings, because such social policies can help them attract votes (P0621). In other words, although the municipal government has designated the PVPs, it is not serious about preserving them. Municipal officials fight back by claiming that the Ministry of Culture opposes the designation just because the mayor and the president are from different political parties (P0614, P0708). To them, the accusation has nothing to do with the social or cultural policies adopted by the Socialists; instead, it is driven by the parochial party interest of the right. It is evident from their arguments that party cleavage provides politicians at the two levels with weapons to attack each other. Although party identity may no longer be the determining factor in French politics, it sometimes still shapes the discourse of intergovernmental relations.

Despite the opposition of the Ministry of Culture, the City Council approved the PLU and the designation of the 5,607 PVPs in June 2006. The documents were forwarded to the prefect for final approval; however, the prefect pronounced them illegal. After several rounds of negotiations, the mayor refused to give up, so the prefect brought the case to the Administrative Court of Paris in January 2007. The prefect's action was criticized by the mayor as "an unprecedented political operation." The case was pending in the court for almost half a year and went through numerous debates. In July 2007, one year after the PLU was first approved by the City Council, the judge finally recognized the legitimacy of the PLU and the 5,607 PVPs (P0709).

The debate on the legitimacy of the PVPs is a power struggle between the city and the state on who should control the territory of Paris. The successful designation of PVPs demonstrates that the power of the local authority is increased, but it does not indicate the retreat of the state in urban preservation. Municipal officials emphasize that they will continue to work with ABFs in the daily practice of urban preservation (P0708, P0709). Furthermore, the city needs to negotiate and cooperate with the state and other national agencies[9] in order to provide tax deductions or subsidies for housing renovation to the owners of the PVP buildings (P0709). In a word, compromise and collaboration between the center and the local are increasingly important for urban preservation in Paris.

As one of the most aggressive steps the city has taken in urban preservation, the designation of the PVPs shows that cultural heritage has gained new meanings in the changing political world. It is no longer exclusively defined by the professional knowledge of a small number of national civil servants but also reflects the local history and community life that local residents cherish. Despite the limits of public hearings and other opportunities for public participation launched by the city, a process of democratization is under way in the field of urban preservation in France, a field that used to be the privilege of the national authority exclusively managed by a handful of cultural elites.

The case of designating PVPs can also lead to interesting discussions about the role of political parties in French politics. Obviously, different party identities of the mayor and the president have increased the hurdles between the two levels of government in the battle over urban preservation. However, the same party identity does not guarantee cooperative intergovernmental relations. For example, although the president of the Île-de-France region, Jean-Paul Huchon, is from the same faction of the Socialist Party as Mayor Delanoë, he is against Delanoë's initiative of creating a Great Paris. Huchon considers the mayor's ambition of expanding the city into a real metropolis by connecting Paris and its surrounding suburbs a threat to his authority (Sabbah 2008). The divergence between the two territorial leaders gives President Nicolas Sarkozy a chance to break the leftist alliance and "play them one against the other" (Sabbah 2008). Claiming that the squabbles between local authorities have slowed down the creation of the Great Paris, Sarkozy has legitimate reasons to step in and take over the project from Delanoë. In 2008, Sarkozy appointed a new secretary of state in charge of development of the capital region. Later the same year, he invited ten architectural teams to draw the blueprint for the Great Paris (Ramnoux 2008). Although the creation of the Great Paris is still in progress, it is clear that the state has reinforced its control over the capital region through the struggles between local authorities.

Party identity is still important in French politics, but it is not a decisive factor when political actors make their decisions by coercion or coalition. The division between the left and the right, as Vincent Renard points out, is not very clear in French politics today and varies "subject by subject" (P0605). His comment is supported by the statement of a municipal official. When asked to describe the relations between the city, the region, and the state, she answers, "It is hard to say. Sometimes we work with the region against the state; sometimes we work with the state against the region. It just depends on the project" (P0708). When decentralization has empowered local authorities, their local interests are likely to play a more important role than party lines in intergovernmental relations. Under such circumstances, party identity might become a discourse of intergovernmental power struggles, which offers politicians a convenient weapon to attack their opponents at other levels of the government.

The Redevelopment of Les Halles

Les Halles is an unavoidable topic when one is talking about urban preservation in Paris. Located between the Louvre, the Palais Royal, and the Hôtel de Ville, the Les Halles quarter was historically one of the central quarters of Paris. The area has served as the marketplace for Paris since the twelfth century. Because of its centrality and visibility, Les Halles has been under constant pressure to showcase the ability of the political authority to manage the circulation of products and population. The history of the area is characterized by creative destructions and reconstructions. Every time, the redevelopment process was fraught with political battles, diverse conflicting interests, and compromises between preservationists and modernists. A problem constantly facing policymakers is how to maintain spatial continuity between new construction and the historic urban landscape of central Paris.

The groundbreaking development of Les Halles took place in the nineteenth century. Under the imperative of Napoleon III, Victor Baltard

FIGURE 30. Les Halles, ca. 1867. Photograph by Charles Marville, Library of Congress, Prints and Photographs Division (LC-DIG-ppmsca-33514).

designed twelve market pavilions in 1853 to host the commercial life of the area (Figure 30). Made of metal and glass instead of the conventional building materials of the day, the Baltard Pavilions became the new landmark of Paris. From the outside, the pavilions looked like shiny rectangular blocks with a giant iron awning sitting atop each of them. From the inside, they resembled an ornate railroad station with embroidered archways delineating each subsection. Dubbed by Émile Zola as the "stomach of Paris," Les Halles is not simply a place where food was bought and sold but also a node of communication between Paris and its surrounding territory. A vibrant neighborhood of more than 21,000 inhabitants, consisting primarily of a working-class and transient population, had also grown around the marketplace (Wakeman 2007).

Les Halles outgrew itself and became a dirty, crowded, and unhealthy area. The de Gaulle government decided by 1959 to demolish the pavilions and move the marketplace to the Parisian suburb of Rungis. The plan was part of a broad slum clearance program that would redevelop central Paris to accommodate businesses and the middle class. It was promoted by the postwar economic revitalization and the modernist urban planning agenda, which aims to transform Paris into a modern metropolis (Baud-ouin and Collin 2007; Savitch 1988).

The demolition of Les Halles was opposed by many Parisians. They called the demolition a crime against Paris that would eventually destroy the historic capital at the hands of modernism. The preservation campaign launched by Parisians was supported by architects, the intellectual left, and Communists and was energized by the student revolts in May and the summer of 1968. Unfortunately, mass opposition failed to save Les Halles, and the pavilions were torn down in 1971. The demolition of the Baltard Pavilions is considered one of the great tragedies in the city's history—the equivalent, for Parisians, of the demolition of New York's Pennsylvania Station. Although the demolition was justified by the construction of the underground Regional Express Railway station, it was emblematic of the absolute power of the state. With the eradication of the pavilions, the surrounding neighborhood was razed, and more than 1,400 households, approximately 3,000 to 5,000 people, were displaced (Baudouin and Collin 2007; TenHoor 2007).

Although preservationists lost the battle to the absolute power of the state, there are positive legacies for urban preservation. First, the outcry over the destruction of the Baltard Pavilions and the modernist plans for redevelopment succeeded in limiting the height of all buildings in the center of Paris to 25 meters (Savitch 1988). Second, the loss of Les Halles motivated the state and French intellectuals to take a new interest in nineteenth-century architecture, whose value was previously underestimated (TenHoor 2007). A good example of this interest is the creation of Musée d'Orsay, a nineteenth-century railway station preserved and renovated into an art museum by the national government in the 1980s.

After the destruction of Les Halles, what should replace Baltard's pavilions remained controversial. Under the promotion of President Georges Pompidou, the Centre Pompidou was constructed on the nearby site of Beaubourg and opened in 1977 as a hub for modern arts. However, Les Halles itself was left a vast cavern, used as a parking lot and surrounded by an abandoned neighborhood for some ten years. Despite the fact that both Georges Pompidou and Valéry Giscard d'Estaing made plans for the area and attempted to lead the construction during their presidencies, endless political and design squabbles substantially slowed down the implementation of their plans (Savitch 1988).

The redevelopment of Les Halles was completed by Jacques Chirac, the first mayor of Paris (Figure 31). To have complete discretion in designing Les Halles, Chirac arranged a trade with Giscard d'Estaing by offering him a large site in northeastern Paris, La Villette, which d'Estaing later converted into the Cité des Sciences et de l'Industrie. After the deal was made with the president, Chirac triumphantly told a journalist (Savitch 1988), "L'architecte en chef des Halles, c'est moi!" ("The chief architect of Les Halles is me!"). He rejected the architectural design chosen by d'Estaing, even though part of the construction had already started, and completed the construction in 1979 based on a new design that he chose. The new structures have received numerous criticisms. Although it is low in height, the design is criticized as ugly and dated, with incongruous spatial arrangements between the streets and the buildings (TenHoor 2007). However, as the first major urban project the city has taken over from the hands of the state, the redevelopment shows the rising power of the municipal government.

Today, Les Halles is the center of gravity for the Île-de-France region of more than 11 million people. It has the largest underground rail station in Europe, which each day floods with some 800,000 travelers surging onto five subway lines and three Regional Express Lines (Réseau Express Régional). Above the transportation hub is a Forum containing underground facilities for shopping. The largest shopping mall in France, the Forum is a sunken concrete-and-glass structure, ziggurat in shape, and reaches four stories down (Figure 32). It is visited by more than 40 million people every year, the majority of whom are young adults from the Parisian suburbs. The neighborhood immediately around the gardens and the Forum has about 9,000 inhabitants. The majority of the residents are young adults and young families, more often professional and well educated than working class (Wakeman 2007).

Overwhelmed by the tsunami of daily visitors, Les Halles is aging and deteriorating. Delanoë made the redevelopment of Les Halles one of his major campaign promises in the 2001 mayoral election and eventually launched the project in 2003. The project is intended to solve various problems, including the conundrum of congestion and circulation in the underground rail station, the increasingly transgressive street life, and the disconnection between the underground complex and the street-level space. The mayor maintains that the project will not only improve the security and quality of the architectural landscape of Les Halles but also strengthen the connection between the city and the suburbs. In his words, it will "reinsert the heart of Paris in its body and restore the link between Paris and its surrounding territories" (Edelmann 2009). By rebuilding the link between Paris and its suburbs, he believes the project will bring more people from the suburbs to the city, creating more jobs in Les Halles

FIGURE 31. Redevelopment of Les Halles in the late 1970s. Photograph by Keith Munro.

and the surrounding areas and promoting the local economy of Paris.

The project also has political significance. It gives the Socialist mayor an opportunity to claim his authority and challenge the supremacy of the former mayor, Jacques Chirac, who, coming from the Rightist Party, was the president of the republic at that time. An article in *Le Monde* puts it in this way: "For Bertrand Delanoë, the stake is sizable. Here, he is attacking the symbol of Jacques Chirac's Paris, since it is Chirac who had called himself 'the chief architect of Les Halles' in the 1970s" (De Chenay 2004).

The redevelopment of Les Halles is very complicated, not only because of its location in the heart of Paris and the large scale and huge cost[10] of the operation but also because diverse interests are involved in the policy process. The city is the main initiator and funder of the project, but it implements the redevelopment plan through a partnership with various actors. The main partners include the Paris regional transit authority (Syndicat des Transports d'Île-de-France [STIF]); the Autonomous Operator of Parisian Transports (Régie Autonome des Transports Parisiens [RATP]), which manages the rail station on behalf of STIF; and the owner of the commercial space in Forum des Halles, Unibail. Meanwhile, the city needs to take into account the opinions of local associations and the mayor of the 1st Arrondissement, where Les Halles is located. The public–private

FIGURE 32. Les Halles today.

entity *(société d'économie mixte)*, SemPariSeine, coordinates with various actors and manages the project on behalf of the city.

It seems that the state is absent from the project, but in fact it plays an invisible role through the RATP. Both STIF and RATP were created as state-owned agencies. Whereas STIF was transferred to the region in 2005, its operator, RATP, remains under state control. Whereas the chairman of RATP is directly appointed by the state, the governing body of RATP, Établissement Public à Caractère Industriel et Commercial (the Industrial and Commercial Public Establishment), consists of public administrators of the state. The arrangement generates an odd situation between the two agencies: as the operator of STIF, RATP should be under the administration of STIF; however, the status of RATP as a state agency gives it more political privilege than STIF. The twisted interrelations create many conflicts and disputes between the two agencies. Nonetheless, it allows the state to keep a close watch on the region and to continue to have a prominent presence in local affairs.

A municipal official, who served as chief of the Les Halles Mission for the Municipality of Paris, explains the strategy of the state (P1001):

> In the redevelopment of Les Halles, the city wants the state to
> pay for part of the bill, but it does not want the state to control
> the project. So the state decides not to directly participate in the
> project, but only to be indirectly involved through RATP. This is
> very clever of the state, because in this way it can still influence the
> direction of the project without paying for the bill.

This quote shows that the state has adopted new governance approaches in the context of decentralization. Whereas the state used to be the visible, dominant force in initiating and supervising major urban projects, nowadays it uses invisible hands to influence local decisions. The indirect involvement helps the state reduce its financial burden but still places constraints on local authorities. Because STIF relies on RATP in the management and renovation of the railway systems of Les Halles, the region plays a limited role in the project. It is primarily the interactions between the city and RATP that shape the policy process of Les Halles.

Making public participation a new goal of the municipality, Delanoë announced that the redevelopment of Les Halles would be undertaken with Parisians, especially local associations. Unfortunately, the project has been rejected by a number of local associations, such as Accomplir and Paris des Halles. Their opposition was backed by Jean-François Legaret, the conservative mayor of the 1st Arrondissement, who called the project "an enormous fraud" (Sasportas 2010). The chief of the Les Halles Mission for the Municipality of Paris notes that although the locals were against the redevelopment of Les Halles in the 1970s and today, their positions have fundamentally changed. The campaign in the 1970s aimed to stop the demolition of the pavilions and save the center of Paris from the destruction of modernism, whereas today's opposition is due to the local associations' reluctance to open up their neighborhood to "outsiders" (P1001).

The majority of visitors to Les Halles are young adults from the Parisian suburbs, many of whom are of North African origin. The mall and public space in Les Halles provide them a channel to engage in the urban life of Paris. However, locals consider the presence of suburbanites and the amenities catering to their interests an interruption to their life. The locals are concerned that the redevelopment will make the area more crowded and noisy by encouraging more suburbanites to come to the city. The resistance of the local associations demonstrates the tension between the central city and the suburbs. It not only complicates the redevelopment of Les Halles but also generates obstacles to the creation of the Great Paris.

Despite various squabbles and challenges, the city held an international competition in 2004 to select the architectural design for revitalization of the area. Four architectural firms were selected as finalists from the twenty-eight submissions. The city organized an exhibition of the four proposals at the Forum des Halles and invited visitors to cast ballots for their favorite project. The ballots were not official votes, but they were supposed to act as an opinion poll on the public's preferences, even though the results of the ballots were not disclosed by the municipality. On December 15, 2004, the mayor announced that French architect David Mangin had won the competition and complimented his design as "realistic and sustainable" (Edelmann 2004).

The mayor's decision is the result of his compromise with diverse interests. As an official from RATP reveals, the most important actor that influences the mayor's decision is Unibail, owner of the commercial space in Forum des Halles and one of the city's partners in redevelopment. He points out that Mangin was favored by Unibail because he has close personal connections with the business group, and his design brings the least disruption to the underground business activities (P0732). By contrast, although celebrity Dutch architect Rem Koolhaas's design was initially favored by the mayor, it was opposed by Unibail because of its disruption of business. The design would take more time to complete and requires closing much of the Forum during the construction. More importantly, it allows commuters to exit directly from the underground transportation center without going through the shopping mall, which is detrimental to the underground business (Baudouin and Collin 2007).

Although newspaper and magazine articles damned Mangin's design as dull and retrograde, local associations showed their support for the design after the mayor announced his decision. This is because the design maintains the separation between the underground complex and the street-level space, maximizing the number of visitors from the underground world to the neighborhood (Baudouin and Collin 2007). However, the design can hardly fulfill the mayor's wish to reintegrate the underground and the street-level space and strengthen the connection between the city and the suburbs. It is likely that the segmentation between Paris and its surrounding territories will continue to exist. The experience for many suburban visitors would continue even after the redevelopment of Les Halles: they would take the Regional Express Lines to Les Halles, shop in the underground mall, and leave Paris without going above ground.

Although public hearings were held in the neighborhood to allow citizens to express their opinions, most people were only informed of the progress of the project instead of being empowered to influence the decisions of the municipality. Furthermore, the public hearings included mainly the wealthier inhabits of the city center, and the hundreds of thousands of users of Les Halles throughout the Île-de-France region were excluded from the policy process (Diméglio and Zetlaoui-Léger 2007; TenHoor 2007; Baudouin and Collin 2007).

Implementation of the redevelopment has been delayed. Although Delanoë made the Les Halles project one of his major campaign promises in 2001 and launched the project in 2003, he slowed down the project in the following years so that it did not jeopardize his reelection in 2008 (Diméglio and Zetlaoui-Léger 2007). Even after the mayor won reelection, the city announced that construction would not begin until 2013 (P1001). Political and design squabbles are the main reasons for the delay, and the most important dispute is between the city and RATP over the renovation of the underground railway station (P1001). To successfully carry out the project, the mayor and his team must align the often contradictory interests of their partners and the receivers of this operation, but this is not an easy task. As a megaproject located in the urban core of Paris, the redevelopment of Les Halles has significant impacts on the spatial organization of the historic city. Although it is still too early to know how the project will proceed, it is likely that the diverse interests and constant power struggles will keep shaping the policy process of redevelopment.

Landscape Preservation in Château Rouge

The city initiated a new approach to urban preservation in recent years, called *preservation du paysage,* or landscape preservation. The idea is to demolish dilapidated buildings and replace them with new ones. Although the new buildings might have different styles from the old ones, they share the same height and density, so that the scale of the historic streetscape can be maintained. This approach is different from the market-driven housing renewal prevalent in Western cities in the postwar era or in today's China. In those cases the old buildings are usually substituted by high-rises in order to intensify land use and maximize economic return from urban land, and the streetscape is fundamentally altered. In an effort to improve housing quality while maintaining the urban scale, the approach of landscape preservation has been applied to several old quarters in Paris, such as la Butte-aux-Cailles and Château Rouge.

Located in the northern part of the city, Château Rouge is adjacent to Montmartre, which is one of the most popular tourist attractions in Paris and a hotspot for artists and bobos.[11] At the summit of Montmartre is Basilique du Sacré-Coeur, a white-domed Roman Catholic Church that is a French national historic monument and the highest point in Paris. Climbing down Montmartre and walking several streets east, you will enter Château Rouge, a historic neighborhood with dilapidated buildings and a unique ethnic culture.

The area is historically a *faubourg,* or suburb, outside the city walls of Paris. During Haussmann's urban transformation, many ancient faubourgs were incorporated into the boundaries of the city, and the old buildings were erased. It was also during that period of time that the word *faubourg* was replaced by *banlieue,* a new term coined in the nineteenth century to describe the outskirts of the city. Château Rouge is one of a few faubourgs that escaped the demolition. Most buildings in the neighborhood were built in the 1830s. Although it is not an area of historic monuments, the pre-Haussmannian architectural style and street view give the neighborhood unique characters.

Château Rouge has long been the home of a transient population in Paris. It has absorbed migrants from other provinces of France since the nineteenth century, and it has become the main immigrant enclave in Paris in the past three decades (Figure 33). The foreign population makes up 15.6 percent of the city of Paris and 20.6 percent of the 18th Arrondissement, where Château Rouge is located (Bouly 1999). But the proportion is as high as 41.4 percent in Château Rouge. The majority of the immigrants in Château Rouge are from Sub-Saharan African. Because almost

FIGURE 33. Streetscape and ethnic activities in Château Rouge.

70 percent of all Sub-Saharan African activities in Paris are concentrated in this area, it is also known as the African Center of Paris (Bouly 1999). The open market in Château Rouge is the largest ethnic market in the city that not only carries diverse ethnic food and supplies but also is a gathering place for the locals.

As one of the largest ethnic neighborhoods in Paris, Château Rouge contributes to the cultural diversity of the city. However, the high volume of immigrants generates social and economic problems in the area. Because of the low socioeconomic status of the immigrants, poverty is concentrated in the neighborhood. Many buildings are not being maintained and have suffered from dilapidation for a long time (Alexander 2007). Crime, prostitution, and drug abuse are plaguing the local community and threatening public safety in the area.

The city launched the renovation of Château Rouge in 2002. Its proximity to Montmartre and the unique streetscape motivated the city to implement *preservation du paysage,* or landscape preservation, in order to maintain the urban scale of the area. According to municipal officials, the project reflects a double agenda (P0622, P0624). The explicit objective is to improve the housing conditions of the neighborhood. A municipal research report shows that nearly 60 percent of the buildings in the

Figure 34. Demolition of old buildings in Château Rouge.

neighborhood are deteriorating and overcrowded, necessitating different degrees of renovation. Thirty-one buildings are too dilapidated to be renovated, so they will be demolished and replaced by new ones (Figure 34). To maintain the historic streetscape, new buildings will be similar to old ones in terms of height and density.

The more implicit agenda of the municipality is to change the social equilibrium of the neighborhood by bringing in a more mixed population. In an urban planner's words, the intention of the municipality is to "break the 'walls' of the ghetto" (P0622). As the largest immigrant enclave, the neighborhood is considered by municipal officials to be segregated from the rest of the city. In fact, this is also the impression visitors normally have when they walk into the area: they would wonder whether they are in Paris or not. To municipal officials, the ethnic enclave has the potential to become a hub of social unrest and threaten the political stability of the city. After riots broke out in deprived immigrant communities at the outskirts of Paris in 2006, municipal officials considered it an urgent matter to prevent such riots from happening again so that the redevelopment of Château Rouge became politically important.

To reduce the density of the immigrant population in Château Rouge, residents are not allowed to move back into their homes where buildings are undergoing renovations. Instead, they will be relocated to other parts of the 18th Arrondissement or other arrondissements nearby. The ground floors of most buildings will be adopted for commercial, artisan, or service use. Nonethnic shops, supermarkets, and restaurants will open in the neighborhood, in an effort to generate more comprehensive changes in urban life (P0622). Some buildings in the area were already demolished and replaced by new ones, whose design was supposed to be suitable for the historic streetscape (Figure 35). But the entire project will not be completed until 2015, with an estimated cost of 150 million euros.

The project's location in the 18th Arrondissement placed it within the bailiwick of Daniel Vaillant, an ally of Delanoë who held posts as arrondissement mayor, deputy mayor, municipal councilor, and deputy of the National Assembly. Containing a population of more than 180,000, the 18th Arrondissement is one of the most populous districts in Paris. The large population makes it a critical area for the mayoral election. Meanwhile, common party affiliation and shared interest between Delanoë and Vaillant increase the weight of the 18th Arrondissement. The conservative mayor of the 7th Arrondissement explains the decisions of the mayor as follows (P0709):

> The mayor wants to put money where he could get more votes, such as the 18th. In the last election, his party got 60 percent of the votes in the 18th, but only 14 percent of the votes in my district, so he doesn't want to put money in our arrondissement. We also made lots of propositions for urban projects in our arrondissement, such as building day-care centers, social housing, and underground parking, but the mayor doesn't want to support us. The mayor and I are from different political parties and we have different approaches.

Because of the importance of the 18th Arrondissement in mayoral election, the project can help the mayor increase his popularity and control votes. By bringing pork to his ally, the project increases the political capacity of the Socialist Party and strengthens its internal solidarity. Thus, the renovation of Château Rouge is not only a preservation project intended to change the physical form and social structure of the neighborhood but also an investment by the mayor to increase his electoral base and strengthen his political coalition.

Different from the redevelopment of Les Halles, where the state indirectly influences the operation through RATP, the renovation of Château Rouge is primarily under the control of the mayor. Although the state

FIGURE 35. A new apartment building in Château Rouge.

signed a convention with the city on general principles of building renovation, titled the Control of Urban and Social Work, it leaves the particulars
of the project to the discretion of the city. One of the mayor's special assistants, who is in charge of the project on behalf of the mayor, describes
the policy process (P0624):

> Château Rouge is not a very big project, so it is easy for everyone
> to reach an agreement. But if there is a dispute, the mayor has
> the power to make the final decision. In this project, the state is
> "nothing"—it is not the manager of the project, so it does not play
> an important role. You have to understand it in the background
> of decentralization. The state can no longer be the manager of
> everything, so it makes decisions on bigger principles, and the local
> authorities decide on the specifics. We are in the same situation as
> other French cities.

This quote shows that decentralization not only increases the autonomy
of local authorities but also generates a pattern of divided control between
the center and the local. Although the state makes decisions on general
principles, it allows local authorities to manage specific issues. Nonetheless, it is important to note the conditions under which the state is willing
to share its power with local authorities. As the assistant to the mayor
points out, the share of power usually happens when the project has a
smaller scale and does not relate to historic monuments.

Under the command of the municipality, the project is carried out by
a public–private entity, Société d'Économie Mixte d'Aménagement de la
Ville de Paris (SEMAVIP). Created by the municipality in 1985, SEMAVIP
is one of the five major public–private entities (*sociétés d'économie mixte*
[SEMs]) in Paris. Although the SEMs are organized like private companies,
they have majority public ownership, so they are considered the "municipal public sector" (Lorrain 1991). For example, 51 percent of SEMAVIP's
capital and 85 percent of its employees' salaries are from the city (P0624).
The SEMs help the city manage major urban projects with different geographic focuses (Caillosse, Le Galès, and Loncle-Moriceau 1997). Different
from a private company whose goal is to maximize profit, the economic
goal of a SEM is to break even. The operation of SEMs is under strict supervision of the municipal government and Cour des Comptes (Court of
Audit), to make sure that the projects are not manipulated by the leaders
of the entities for their own benefit (P0622).

SEMAVIP manages the renovation of buildings through three major steps
(P0622, P0624). First, it obtains *déclarations d'utilité publique* (declaration

of public utility) from the city in order to declare the public nature of the project and purchase the buildings from the owners. The public nature of the project allows SEMAVIP to evict owners who refuse to sell their property. Second, SEMAVIP conducts research on the buildings and evaluates their qualities. This is an important step for urban preservation, because it distinguishes which buildings should be maintained and which should be demolished. Finally, SEMAVIP holds competitions for architecture firms and construction companies in order for the city to select appropriate ones to conduct the redevelopment project. It is important to note the limited role of the private sector in urban development. Private companies were invited to submit competitive bids for development rights only after the public sector laid out the scale and specified particulars of the project. Once contracts were awarded, the private companies were still governed by a series of standards supervised by the public sector.

Besides building renovation, another major task of SEMAVIP is the relocation of residents. It makes decisions about residents' relocation and financial compensation based on two legal documents, Code de l'Urbanisme (Code of Urban Planning) and Code de la Construction et de l'Habitation (Code of Construction and Housing). If a resident is not satisfied with the decisions of SEMAVIP, he or she can appeal to the judge of expropriation *(juge de l'expropriation)* and go to court, where he or she will be offered three relocation choices. He or she must choose between the three offers and move out of the apartment or be evicted under the order of the judge. About 20 percent of the residents in the area have decided to go to court (P0623, P0622, P0624). Nonetheless, the laws and legal procedures of relocation do not apply to undocumented immigrants. In other words, undocumented immigrants will lose their residence and eventually be evacuated from the neighborhood in the process of redevelopment.

The renovation of Château Rouge is considered by the municipality as a great innovation in urban preservation. In contrast to conventional preservation practice, the project combines the goals of improving housing quality, maintaining the historic streetscape, and revitalizing the local economy. A municipal official describes the merits of the project (P0614):

> The project shows a more intelligent way of urban preservation, because it cares about not only historic monuments, but also the character of the place. We also include urban renewal in the new scheme of urban preservation, because we don't want to maintain the city like a museum. Otherwise the city would die; it would become a place only for tourists.

The danger of turning the lively city into a museum is an inherent tension in the practice of urban preservation that challenges many historic cities. The quote shows that municipal officials are striving to find creative ways to handle the problem, and the renovation of Château Rouge is one of their efforts. However, with the demolition of the historic faubourgs and the removal of the ethnic community, it is doubtful that the character of the place can be saved. A number of preservationists have expressed concern that when demolition and reconstruction are incorporated into the scheme of urban preservation, it is unclear where to draw the boundary between preservation and redevelopment (P0703).

The project is also problematic because of its exclusive operational process and its negative impact on social equity. Although the city holds public hearings in Château Rouge to inform people about the progress of the project and to solicit public opinion, most attendees are middle-class residents or small business owners who intend to move into the area. More than 40 percent of the residents living in the neighborhood are ethnic minorities or foreign born, but their large number does not grant them a voice. The majority of immigrants, even with legal status, are excluded from the public hearings, and the reason for their absence seems quite simple: they do not speak French (P0628, P0703). The language issue can be easily solved if the city provides translators during the public hearings, but little has been done by the city to encourage the participation of minorities.

The situation echoes Bird's (2004, 14) comments on the underrepresentation of minorities in France: "It would be an understatement to suggest that ethnic minorities in France tend to be politically marginalized. There is likely no greater democratic state in the world where ethnic minorities are excluded . . . to a greater extent than they are in France." Although the project intends to increase social cohesion and political stability in the ethnic neighborhood, the people whose lives are most directly influenced by the project are largely excluded from the policy process. The exclusive nature of the project undermines the interests of the minorities, a group of people who are already worse off in French society. By reinforcing socioeconomic inequality in the urban population, the project might not fulfill the goal of increasing political stability but might generate more uncertainty for Paris in terms of class and racial relations.

Conclusion

Urban preservation in Paris must be understood in the context of intergovernmental fragmentation. Although urban preservation has long been the privilege of the state, the city has increased its control over the urban territory through decentralization reforms. The designation of the PVPs is the first time in the history of Paris that the city defined its own cultural heritage, which challenges the elitist tradition of urban preservation in France. The two rounds of redevelopment of Les Halles under the leadership of Chirac and Delanoë demonstrate the discretion of the mayor over megaprojects. The renovation of Château Rouge shows the desire of the municipality to balance between urban preservation and redevelopment and to prevent the historic city from being turned into a museum.

When the discretion of local authorities has been increased but the national government has not withdrawn, there are jurisdictional conflicts between the center and the local. The three cases demonstrate different degrees of conflicting jurisdictions between the national government and the Paris Municipality. The designation of the PVPs challenged the privilege of the state over cultural heritage, so it was strongly opposed by the state and had to be settled in administrative court. By contrast, the redevelopment of Les Halles and the renovation of Château Rouge did not involve cultural heritage, so the state did not contest the autonomy of the city in the two projects. In the redevelopment of Les Halles, however, the central location and the large scale of the project make it impossible for the state to take its hands off. To relieve itself of the financial burden but remain on board, the state indirectly involves itself in the project through the state-owned transportation company RATP. As a much smaller project, the renovation of Château Rouge is the effort of the city to strengthen its control over a predominantly ethnic community at the edge of the city. Thus, the state is only symbolically involved in the project, setting up the general principles of renovation and leaving the specifics to the city's discretion.

Urban preservation and urban development in Paris are no longer exclusively governed by the state through a group of unified technocratic elites. Intergovernmental fragmentation generates a mix of conflict, compromise, and cooperation between tiers of government. Centralism is still valid, but the state selectively gets involved in local projects that are at the core of national value and interest instead of dictating every local initiative. To do so more efficiently, it has developed new intervention approaches, such as relying on state-owned agencies and manipulating the discord between territorial authorities. Although decentralization intensifies intergovernmental fragmentation, which sometimes leads to stalemates and blocks the policy process, political actors often choose to compromise because of the need to achieve, the interlocking political positions, and the mutual respect for the state. Therefore, urban preservation in Paris has gradually changed from a monopoly of the state to a joint venture between the city and the state.

Under the traditional centralism model, the most important interactions in the French system take place in the public sector. Today, although bargaining between political elites remains crucial, intergovernmental fragmentation increases the chances for a variety of social and private actors to be involved in the policy process. For example, local associations are part of almost every urban project in Paris. The owner of the commercial space in Forum des Halles, Unibail, is one of the city's key partners in the redevelopment of Les Halles. Those actors are allowed to influence policy dynamics because they provide local authorities with resources, help them share costs, and increase the democratic base of their decisions. Actors from different spheres do not have the same weight, nor do their opinions necessarily influence the decisions of the municipality; sometimes their presence is only a strategy by public officials to justify their policy choices. However, the involvement of various social and private actors brings in diverse interests and makes the policy process more complicated. It urges us to revisit the political and policy realities in France so as to draw more accurate conclusions.

Political Boundaries and Beyond

The real meaning of this word [*city*] has been almost wholly lost in modern times; most people mistake a town for a city, and a townsman for a citizen. They do not know that houses make a town, but citizens [make] a city.

—JEAN-JACQUES ROUSSEAU, *The Social Contract*

Urban preservation is fraught with paradox and controversy. Despite the original goals of urban preservation to protect the architectural integrity and social sustainability of cities, the practice of urban preservation in modern cities is motivated by different political and economic concerns. In Beijing, urban preservation is a tool for the local government to promote economic growth and to create a better image for the city. Preservation projects do not stop the destruction of the historic city but smooth out the function of the growth machine and facilitate the commodification of cultural heritage. In Chicago, urban preservation has evolved into the equivalent of tax benefits. No longer exclusively belonging to white neighborhoods, it began to be used in diverse ethnic communities to increase property values and promote community revitalization while being entangled with the issues of gentrification and racial inequality. In Paris, the urban preservation narrative is defined quite differently by the state and the municipality. The former considers urban preservation as its own privilege exercised to protect French cultural integrity and national pride, whereas the latter conceives it as part of the agenda for more balanced citywide urban development.

Whereas the content of preservation initiatives is shaped by the interests and values of different actors, the policy process of implementing their initiatives is constrained by the fragmented power structure in cities. The analysis of the evidence in the previous pages reveals that a preservation initiative is more likely to be implemented if it is within the boundaries of single jurisdictions and less likely so if it crosses multiple jurisdictions. This is observed in the three major types of political fragmentation: functional, territorial, and intergovernmental. Different types of political fragmentation are associated with predictable patterns of policy processes and settlements regarding cross-boundary issues, in turn generating different patterns of urban preservation.

Beijing, Paris, and Chicago each demonstrate one of the three major types of political fragmentation. Although Beijing is the capital city of a centralized one-party state, the political structure of urban preservation in Beijing is characterized by the functional segmentation among various municipal agencies. In Chicago, despite the dominant role of the mayor in downtown development and citywide issues, the real power of landmark designation and zoning is controlled by aldermen and is territorially fragmented along ward boundaries. In contrast to the functional fragmentation in Beijing and the territorial fragmentation in Chicago, urban preservation in Paris was long the privilege of the national government, but decentralization reforms have reinforced the central–local conflicts so that urban preservation is increasingly subject to the intergovernmental fragmentation between the national government and the Paris municipality.

The three different types of political fragmentation suggest a general rule in processing preservation initiatives. They tend to facilitate the processing of preservation initiatives within jurisdictional boundaries, yet they inhibit the processing of those across jurisdictional boundaries. Historic monuments are under a unified administrative structure in Beijing, thus their renovation and restoration are carried out more smoothly than preservation projects in historic districts. Urban areas within a single ward of Chicago are more likely to be designated as landmark districts than those across multiple wards. And preservation projects are more easily implemented in Paris if they are within the domain of either the state or the municipality and less easily if they are within the overlapping jurisdictions of the two actors. In a word, the fragmented political structure operates like a filter, facilitating or inhibiting the government's processing of preservation initiatives, depending on whether the initiatives are situated within or across jurisdictional boundaries.

For cross-boundary issues, different types of political fragmentation are associated with predictable patterns of policy processes and settlements, thus creating different patterns of urban preservation. In Beijing, bureaucratic segmentation at the municipal level leaves the protection of urban texture unattended and devolves power to district governments. Combining the restoration of monument buildings and the marginalization of historic neighborhoods, urban preservation becomes increasingly symbolic. In Chicago, preservation initiatives across ward boundaries are largely ignored or opposed by local aldermen. Without a citywide preservation agenda, urban preservation shows a mosaic pattern confined within individual wards. In Paris, both the city and the state tend to solve their conflict over heritage buildings through compromise and negotiation, so urban preservation gradually changes from a state monopoly to a joint venture between the city and the state.

Political fragmentation does not dictate the policy process. Rather, it creates a tendency for blockage that can be overcome by effective coordination. Comparison of the policy processes of urban preservation in the three cities shows different probabilities of overcoming the hurdles of fragmentation. Generally speaking, political actors in a system of intergovernmental fragmentation have the highest degree of interdependence. Therefore, they are most likely to overcome the hurdles of fragmentation and solve cross-boundary issues through modest compromise, negotiation, and collaboration. In contrast, actors in both functional fragmentation and territorial fragmentation have lower degrees of interdependence and are more likely to leave those cross-boundary issues alone. To be sure, it takes time for different parties in a system of intergovernmental fragmentation to overcome structural constraints and reach a common ground. Furthermore, their compromise and collaboration might produce a lowest-common-denominator policy instead of a perfect solution (Pierson 1995). Nevertheless, such a settlement could mitigate the negative effects that stalemate or policy drift has on the decision-making process. Consequently, intergovernmental fragmentation tends to have less severe negative effects on urban preservation than the other two types of political fragmentation. Meanwhile, the possibility of overcoming the hurdles of political fragmentation alerts us to pay attention to not only the formal structures but also the informal political relations in a fragmented urban polity.

My findings resonate with prior scholarship on historical institutionalism by demonstrating how institutions define the rules of the political game, shape the preferences of actors, and condition their interactions with one another. However, the theory of political fragmentation advances us a great deal in revealing the association between types of political fragmentation and policy processes of urban preservation. It demonstrates that what matters is not only whether the system is fragmented but how it is fragmented. Besides investigating the content of any given policy initiative, we must carefully examine the fragmented power structure by which the initiative is implemented, if we want to better understand and further improve the policy process.

In this book, the theory of political fragmentation is examined through the policy process of urban preservation. Testing the explanatory power of the theory in other issue areas requires fuller examinations than I can provide here. However, the impact of political fragmentation is emphasized in a number of scholarly works covering a wide variety of issues, such as health insurance, pensions, school districts, environmental pollution control, and public transportation (Immergut 1992; Banting 1985; Meyer, Scott, and Strang 1987; Sayre and Kaufman 1960). These studies provide evidence on the applicability of the theory of political fragmentation in issue areas beyond urban preservation. Their findings, as well as the present book, offer the foundation for further research to understand the ways in which different types of political fragmentation shape the policy process in various issue areas.

Urban Preservation in a Fragmented Political World

Political fragmentation is by no means exclusive to Beijing, Chicago, or Paris. It exists in cities around the globe despite the differences between those localities in terms of history, culture, regime type, and economic conditions. Therefore, the theory of political fragmentation can be applied to different urban settings beyond the three major cases of this book and advance our understanding of their policy processes of urban preservation. In this section, I use the examples of urban preservation in several other world cities to demonstrate the generalizability of my theory.

Like Chicago, the political structure of urban preservation in New York is characterized by territorial fragmentation. A municipal-level preservation agency, the Landmarks Preservation Commission, was created in New York in 1965. Although the commission was given comprehensive authority to designate and regulate individual landmarks, historic districts, interiors, and parklands, the real autonomy of the commission was constrained by the territorial authority of elected officials (Tung 2001). In particular, the fate of buildings in the outer boroughs was considered a parochial matter by borough presidents, who would rarely vote for confirmation in opposition to another borough president. This tacit understanding among the borough presidents gave each a veto over preservation procedures in his or her part of the city. Very rarely would the Landmarks Commission go against the will of the borough presidents, primarily because the members of the commission were appointed for fixed terms of three years, and their reappointment had to be confirmed by the mayor and city council members. For the same reason, the Landmarks Commission would not typically advance the designation of a structure in the face of mayoral objections.

Despite the existence of a centralized municipal preservation agency, the privilege of borough presidents over their electoral districts tends to generate a pattern of territorial fragmentation. Such fragmentation prohibits the implementation of citywide preservation initiatives and has introduced the possibility of public office holders wielding their authority for the benefit of private interests. To maintain their right to alter, enlarge, or demolish historic structures, many property owners vigorously opposed landmark designation of their own properties by bribing local officials. In 1988, an investigation by the New York State Commission on Government Integrity substantiated that all important elected municipal officials received contributions to their campaigns from major developers, landowners, and businesses in the city (Tung 2001). Although landmark designation began to receive more public support in New York in the 1990s, the authority of preservation professionals is still largely constrained by political decisions.

One of the oldest and most well-preserved cities in Europe, Prague in the postcommunist era is similar to Paris in terms of the impact of intergovernmental fragmentation on urban preservation. Throughout the country's communist era, urban preservation was considered a priority by the Czech Communist Party because it showed the cultural superiority of socialism over pragmatic and brutal capitalism. The political structure of urban preservation under the communist regime was highly centralized (Horak 2007). A professional body associated with the city's Department of Culture, named the Prague Center of State Monument Preservation and Nature Protection (PSSPPOP), emerged as the de facto dominant force in the 1960s. Made up of a cohesive group of senior bureaucrats, the PSSPPOP was able to make long-range, continuous policies and implement systematic protection of the entire historic core. This centralized administrative apparatus of urban preservation ended after the Velvet Revolution. In 1990, the PSSPPOP was changed from a municipal agency to a state administration, renamed the Prague Institute for Monument Preservation (PUPP). Because the PUPP refused to ease its constraints on new development, the city created a Department of Historic Preservation (OPP) to manage preservation and development issues. Whereas the PUPP is preservation oriented, the OPP is development friendly. The institutional change has generated intergovernmental fragmentation in the preservation administration and weakened the overall power of the PUPP.

Intergovernmental fragmentation between the PUPP and the OPP prohibits the making and implementation of consistent preservation guidelines for the historic core of Prague. The lack of concrete, systematic regulation on real estate development provides opportunities for public officials to take bribes from investors and adopt a progrowth agenda (Horak 2007).

Under strong pressure for development, the historic core has undergone rapid commercialization, with almost all vacant land in the historic core filled with offices, hotels, or high-end retail establishments by the end of the 1990s. Some historic buildings went through substantial alterations to meet the demands of commercial use, and a few of them were torn down to make way for new ones. A large number of long-time residents were driven out of the historic center by the high rent, and Prague soon became a city of tourists (Hoffman and Musil 1999). Although Prague's record of urban preservation was praised by UNESCO in 1992 when the city's core was added to the list of World Heritage Sites, by 1995 the city received damning assessments from various international organizations because of inappropriate development in the historic core (Horak 2007).

A capital as ancient as Beijing, Rome is another good case in point to demonstrate how functional fragmentation shapes the policy process of urban preservation. Although preservation has a long history in Rome, the modern political institution of urban preservation in the city is characterized by a complex overlay of legislative structures and uncoordinated agencies (Tung 2001). The legal basis for urban preservation in Rome was established by two national preservation statutes enacted in 1939. The power to enforce those statutes is not centralized in any government agency but is divided between three superintending offices *(sovrintendente)* of the national Ministry for Cultural Properties, depending on the construction time of the historic structures. What adds to the bureaucratic complexity is the involvement of the municipal government. Responsibility for municipally owned properties of cultural value, including city monuments, walls, gateways, gardens, villas, and fountains, is administered by the municipal Superintending Office of Fine Arts (Sovrintendenza delle Belle Arti of the Comune di Roma). In addition to the regulation on individual historic structures, planning bureaus at both the national and the municipal levels implement zoning and building code controls on the area within the Aurelian walls (Choay 2001).

The functional complexity of preservation agencies is a double-edged sword. On one hand, it increases the difficulty of tearing down a major or minor structure of the historic city or building a new one. On the other hand, it causes segmentation and inefficiency and makes it almost impossible for many property owners and institutions to know with certainty their exact rights and responsibilities. The widespread laxity of the Italian bureaucracies exacerbates this complexity (Tung 2001). When the giant administrative machine becomes an obstacle to the functioning of daily life, people attempt to escape the rules. Thus, the overcomplication of government rules and agencies creates a culture of illegality and space for unregulated transformation of the physical environment. The complexity of the bureaucratic machine also makes it easy to hide all sorts of illegal and quasi-illegal infractions (Tung 2001). As a result, Rome is deemed by the public as one of the most overprotected historic cities in the world, but it is extraordinarily prone to unregulated violations of its law in all the places that the public cannot see. This contradiction prompts preservationists to claim that extended illegal modernization of Rome is occurring behind its historic façades (Appleyard 1979).

Although detailed empirical studies of the influence of political fragmentation on urban preservation in other cities are scarce, evidence can still be found in the limited information available. In Cairo, for example, the massive, ineffective bureaucracy creates functional fragmentation and causes an illicit use of as much as 50 percent of the Egyptian government's annual budget. Meanwhile, a magnificent medieval Muslim cityscape is suffering from decades of deterioration because of a lack of maintenance funds (Palmer, Leila, and Yassin 1989; Bacharach 1995). In Berlin, the segmentation between the East and the West still exists even though the wall that physically divided the city during the Cold War was dismantled long ago. The legacy of territorial fragmentation hinders the making and implementation of comprehensive, citywide policies on urban preservation and development (Cooper and Mele 2002; Albers 2006). In Kyoto, the intergovernmental fragmentation between the state and the municipality generates hurdles for scaling down new construction around the historic core of the city. The combined effect of Kyoto's speculative real estate market and various preservation laws creates a mixed landscape, where the precincts of major monuments stand out as islands of green amid the labyrinth of modern high-rises (Mimura 1989).

Nevertheless, none of the three ideal types of political fragmentation alone can fully capture the entire institutional features of a city. In many big cities, such as London, Moscow, Mumbai, and Mexico City, two or three different types of political fragmentation mix together and generate a more complex picture of power allocation (Tung 2001). We can still identify the dominant type of political fragmentation in those cities regarding specific cases or issue areas, but their overall institutional structures demonstrate a hybrid type. By contrast, some small urban polities provide examples of low fragmentation. In Singapore, a small city-state of 3 million people, a highly unified administration system was created under the leadership of the People's Action Party. The unified administration system and efficient bureaucracy enabled the city to quickly stop urban demolition and enact a preservation agenda in the late 1980s and early 1990s as an effort to promote tourism (Yeoh 2003). A similar case is Macau, where the unified political structure gives the city leverage when handling challenges from the real estate market and thus results in a largely intact historic urban center (Porter 1999).

Besides the diversity of the urban political institution, many other factors influence the decisions of policymakers and affect the patterns of urban preservation, including municipal finance, technical skills, and local culture. It is not the stance of the theory of political fragmentation to overlook other institutional features of the political system or to deny the inputs of other factors. Instead, the theory of political fragmentation puts different elements in context, showing how they relate to one another by drawing attention to the way political situations are structured. Through an emphasis on the structural constraints on the policy process of urban preservation, the theory of political fragmentation offers a useful analytical framework for cross-national comparative urban studies.

Urban Preservation and Human Conditions in Cities

Urban preservation is about protecting the physical form of historic structures. However, there is a significant social dimension in preservation practice when it expands from rarefied individual landmarks to historic neighborhoods. As a response to urban renewal and its devastating social effects, the preservation of residential blocks in cities aims to stabilize local communities and improve quality of life for residents. As Jane Jacobs (1961) maintains, old buildings are an indispensable component of healthy, vibrant urban life because they provide space for mixed residents and diverse business. Despite its initial goal of improving the livelihood of citizens, urban preservation seems to go in a different direction and cause new problems for city residents. This section discusses the impacts of urban preservation on three aspects of human conditions: the quality of housing, the affordability of housing, and the livability of historic neighborhoods.

The first aspect is housing quality in historic districts. In many cities, some of the oldest neighborhoods are a unique urban texture that determines in great part the aesthetic character of the city; however, buildings in those areas are usually physically or technically obsolete because of their old age. Maintaining the original architectural profile requires minimum changes to the structure; therefore, the pursuit of architectural authenticity is sometimes in conflict with the goal of upgrading historic buildings. For example, in Prague during the communist era, the city limited investment in the historic core to control development and therefore demonstrate the superiority of the communist regime over capitalism in cultural heritage protection. Although the policy largely maintained the authenticity of the urban fabric, it resulted in a chronic lack of money for restoration and generated wretched living conditions for residents. Many buildings in the city core suffered from dilapidation and were often converted from residences and offices into low-end storage space (Horak 2007).

Unlike Prague, which attempted to maintain architectural authenticity despite prevailing urban decay, other cities made a different choice when facing the same challenge. They considered old districts as a symbol of misery and cleared the slums to make way for new and more sanitary housing. In Vienna after World War II, an effort to provide better housing to people of all classes resulted in four decades of destruction of late-nineteenth-century architecture (Tung 2001). This is a decision in favor of social equity at the price of aesthetic continuity. The drastically different choices made by the two cities under the similar pressure of urban decay make us wonder: were preservation and better housing truly at odds?

The second aspect is the affordability of housing in historic districts. Some cities launched preservation projects that encourage property owners to renovate their historic houses with subsidies or tax benefits provided by the government. However, the indigenous residents in old urban quarters are usually working-class or low-income people who lack resources to invest in their homes. Therefore, preservation projects are more likely to benefit middle-class newcomers who are interested in older, more architecturally interesting neighborhoods and who often possess the necessary financial means for housing renovation. With the inflow of wealthier newcomers and the renovation of their houses, property values and rents in the preservation districts often increase beyond the capacity of many long-time residents, and thus gentrification takes place (Fitch 1982; Zukin 1987; Frank 2002; Brown-Saracino 2007). There is a growing awareness among preservationists that some preservation programs might become a real-estate gimmick, which helps people who are financially better off exert control and achieve a homogeneous neighborhood at the cost of the less affluent (Frank 2002).

To ameliorate the negative social impacts of urban preservation, European cities commonly offer rent subsidies to preserve the mix of social classes and economic uses in historic districts. In Amsterdam, to reduce the financial burden on homeowners for renovating and maintaining their historic houses, the government gives eligible owners as much as 70 percent of the costs of restoration (Paulen 1997). This policy helps cities reach a balance between protection of the physical form of buildings and protection of the general benefits of residents. Although the policy is actively implemented in some European cities, it remains rare in other parts of the world. Without a genuine concern for the human conditions of the urban population, preservation policies may continue to reinforce the entrenched social inequality in cities.

The third aspect is the livability of the urban environment. Globalization and transnational cultural consumption serve as new incentives for urban preservation. In many cities, historic districts are preserved and repackaged into cultural commodities to meet the demands of tourists (Judd and Fainstein 1999; Trasforini 2002; Kwok and Low 2002). Although the strategy has saved old quarters from the wrecking ball and promoted the vitality of local economies, it leads to rapid commercialization of historic districts, undermines the authenticity of local culture, and has negative impacts on the daily life of the locals. From Xintiandi in Shanghai, Asakusa in Tokyo, to Bercy in Paris, numerous historic districts are undergoing a process of Disneyfication, in which they are remolded into theme parks in the service of the global consumerist elite (Strom 2002; While 2006; Ren 2011). Local residents generally receive little benefit from the new development. However, they have to suffer from various misfortunes, including the privatization of public space, the loss of public facilities, the noise and congestion caused by tourist crowds, and the demise of community life.

The physical condition of housing, the affordability of housing, and the livability of neighborhoods are three criteria for evaluating the quality of life. In places where some people have to suffer from dilapidated housing conditions, housing prices that are way beyond their financial capacity, a lack of public facilities, or the demise of community life, their quality of life is undermined and social equity is at risk. Although the history of inequality is as long as that of human society, increased disparities in the quality of life among urban dwellers raise fundamental questions of social justice in cities. In her book on modern planning and development practice, Susan Fainstein (2010) argues that urban planners and policymakers often prioritize economic growth over other social concerns so that cities become increasingly unjust places. A similar argument can be made about the policy process of urban preservation. The initial goal of protecting the urban environment is to reduce the harm of urban renewal on the human society and maintain a good quality of life for the residents. However, the practice of urban preservation seems to go in the opposite direction. More often than not, the protection of historic structures is rationalized by their potential to raise property values and attract tourists rather than improve the quality of peripheral neighborhoods or to support those already worse off. These policies generate outcomes against the initial goal of urban preservation and undermine the human conditions in cities.

There are two possible ways to improve human conditions in the process of urban preservation. The first is to let the government play a more active role in regulating the market. Although the market is increasingly important in today's housing development and tourism industry, market actors' decisions are constrained by their pursuit of economic competitiveness. Generous public subsidies and government intervention can mitigate the negative impacts of the market and better address questions of social justice. The second way is to encourage democratic participation and make the decision-making process more inclusive so as to achieve better representation of the people who are most directly and adversely affected by preservation decisions. The existing population should not be the sole arbiter of the future of an area; citywide considerations must also apply. But policymakers should pay particular attention to the voice of the targeted population and integrate their voice with professional opinions.

It should be noted that the protection of historic structures is not inherently in conflict with the betterment of residents' quality of life. However, they do appear to be in conflict with one another when the concern for social equity is lost in the policy arena. It is critical for policymakers to increase their concern about the human condition in relation to urban preservation, because such concern can prevent urban regimes from displacing residents involuntarily, destroying communities, and increasing poverty. More positively, it can make local decision making more transparent and open, generating more benefits for citizens and producing a more lively, diverse, and accessible public sphere.

At the time of this writing, the urban world is experiencing substantial challenges. Whereas a significant wave of globalization in the past few decades has greatly transformed the economic and social makeup of urban areas, the global economic downturn of 2008–2009 has brought hardships to cities, characterized by the collapse of credit markets, soaring unemployment, and budgetary crises for local governments. With the economic foundations of cities now becoming highly problematic, the conflicts and the uncertainties regarding urban policies for the future have naturally increased. Still, the preservation of the urban environment must remain a top priority for urban policymakers, indeed for all of us. It is this environment, but especially its buildings as well as its neighborhoods, that we must constantly try to understand and hope to enhance. For it is these material elements of the urban landscape that represent the true human and cultural legacy of cities, a legacy that we can and should bequeath more or less intact to the generations of urban dwellers that follow in our footsteps.

Introduction

1. For example, Fitch (1982) notes the different impacts of the centralized and federalist political structures on the legal systems of urban preservation. Frank (2002) emphasizes the role of local authorities in managing the built environment in urban America. Tung (2001) discusses how local politics influences the decisions of preservation or demolition in eighteen major world cities.

2. http://whc.unesco.org/en/list/.

2. Beijing

1. The Outer City was added in 1553, more than a century after the construction of the rest of the city. For more information on the urban history of Beijing, see Naquin (2000).

2. The four inner-city districts—Dongcheng, Xicheng, Chongwen, and Xuanwu—were merged into two districts in 2010. Dongcheng and Chongwen became one named Dongcheng, and Xicheng and Xuanwu became one named Xicheng. Because the research took place beforehand, the older district names are used in this book.

3. These mega projects are called the New Oriental Plaza (Dongcheng District), Financial Street (Xicheng District), New World Shopping Center (Chongwen District), and SOGO Plaza (Xuanwu District).

4. The interview codes in this book take the form "B/P/CYYXX," in which B, P, and C refer to Beijing, Paris, and Chicago, respectively; YY is the year the interview was conducted; and XX is the number of the interview in that year.

5. http://www.china.com.cn/chinese/CU-c/521549.htm.

6. http://news.xinhuanet.com/zhengfu/2003-08/28/content_1048844.htm.

7. New Oriental Plaza is a high-end complex of shopping malls, office buildings, and hotels in the heart of the old city.

8. http://www.china.com.cn/chinese/CU-c/521549.htm.

9. The forced demolition has been widely reported in Chinese newspapers and other media. For example, see http://www.chinadaily.com.cn/opinion/2010-04/19/content_9746595.htm.

10. In 1998, the EU launched a program named Asia Urbs to facilitate cooperation between local governments of EU member states and Asian countries. The main areas of cooperation are urban preservation and sustainable urban development. For more information, see http://www.asiaurbschn5-08.org.

3. Chicago

1. One of the largest U.S. disasters of the nineteenth century, the Great Chicago Fire of 1871 destroyed more than 73 miles (120 kilometers) of roads, 120 miles (190 kilometers) of sidewalk, 2,000 lampposts, 17,500 buildings, and $222 million in property—about a third of the city's valuation. Of the 300,000 inhabitants, 90,000 were left homeless. To this day, the exact cause and origin of the fire remain uncertain. However, rebuilding began almost immediately after the fire, and it spurred Chicago's development into one of the most populous and economically important American cities. For more information about the fire and its impact, see Sawislak (1995).

2. Aldermanic seats in Chicago are determined by election, but when someone dies or leaves office during his or her term, the mayor appoints the replacement, who must then run in the next election. See Gosnell (1937) and Simpson (2001).

3. http://www.chicagobungalow.org/.

4. http://webapps.cityofchicago.org/landmarksweb/web/home.htm.

5. http://www.state.il.us/hpa/ps/; http://www.nps.gov/history/heritageareas/REP/criteria.pdf.

6. http://www.illinoishistory.gov/PS/taxfreeze.htm.

7. http://www.thepilsenalliance.org/.

8. In 1998, nine buildings in Bronzeville were designated by the municipality as Chicago Landmarks. These buildings were major business or cultural institutions for the African American community or were designed by black architects, and they highlight the prosperity of the community in the first half of the twentieth century. Nevertheless, the landmark designation of individual buildings has had little impact on the general community. Worse, many of the landmark buildings are abandoned or dilapidated, because of their owners' lack of money. For more information on the nine landmark buildings in Bronzeville, see http://webapps.cityofchicago.org/landmarksweb/web/districtdetails.htm?disId=6&counter=28.

4. Paris

1. Since 1985 the *cumul des mandats* has been reduced to just two offices, and further restrictions were placed on the ability of big-city mayors to hold seats in the National Assembly or Senate. See Savitch and Kantor (2002).

2. The Caisse des Dépôts et Consignations (Deposits and Consignments Fund) is a French financial institution created in 1816 under the control of the national government. See http://www.caissedesdepots.fr/.

3. Historically, Paris has two prefects *(préfets)*: prefect of the Seine and prefect of police. Whereas the prefect of the Seine is in charge of general planning and development issues in Paris, the prefect of police takes care of police and security issues. Prefects in other parts of France are appointed by the Council of Ministers on the recommendation of the minister of the interior, but the prefect of the Seine is appointed directly by the president. Meanwhile, Paris is the only place in France that has a prefect of police. After the election of the first mayor of Paris in 1977, the position of prefect of the Seine was terminated. The prefect of police remains in Paris, representing the state in the urban governance in Paris. See Ashford (1982) and Schmidt (1990).

4. http://news.google.com/newspapers?nid=1320&dat=19830704&id=ecYx AAAAIBAJ&sjid=i-kDAAAAIBAJ&pg=1490,1624980.

5. Both categories are under the centralized supervision and management of the state, yet the first involves more strict protection. See ANAH (2003).

6. One-third of the buildings are Listed Monuments, and two-thirds are registered in the Additional Inventory of Historic Monuments. See ANAH (2003).

7. The neo-Haussmannian style is the building style that imitates the one invented by Haussmann in the nineteenth century. Neo-Haussmannian buildings usually have five to seven floors, covered by an iconic black roof with a 45-degree incline (P0630).

8. These are a group of architects working for the City of Paris who specialize in urban projects, such as road construction and housing renovation.

9. One of the key national agencies that work with the city on housing renovation is ANAH. ANAH is a public body under the control of the Ministry of Housing. The role of ANAH is to allocate nonreimbursable grants to owners who carry out renovation work on their properties. Grants are distributed on the condition that the housing is more than fifteen years old and that the housing is currently rented out or is vacant (ANAH 2003).

10. The entire budget of the project is approximately 760 million euros. The STIF covers one-third of the cost, whereas the city is responsible for the other two-thirds, approximately 500 million euros. See Edelmann (2009).

11. *Bobo* refers to Bohemian-Bourgeois, that is, middle-class people choosing a bohemian lifestyle.

Abbott, Andrew. 1988. *The System of Professions: An Essay on the Division of Expert Labor*. Chicago: University of Chicago Press.

Abu-Lughod, Janet L. 1999. *New York, Chicago, Los Angeles: America's Global Cities*. Minneapolis: University of Minnesota Press.

Agence Nationale pour l'Amelioration de l'Habitat (ANAH). 2003. *Rehabilitation in France*. Paris: ANAH.

Albers, Gerd. 2006. "Urban Development, Maintenance and Conservation: Planning in Germany—Values in Transition." *Planning Perspectives* 21:45–65.

Alexander, Michael. 2007. *Cities and Labour Immigration: Comparing Policy Responses in Amsterdam, Paris, Rome and Tel Aviv*. Aldershot, England: Ashgate.

Appleyard, Donald. 1979. *The Conservation of European Cities*. Cambridge, Mass.: MIT Press.

Argentati, Angela. 2009. "The Bronze Age: Harold Lucas Fights to Preserve Bronzeville's Historic Heritage." *Chicago Weekly*, March 5. http://chicagoweekly.net/2009/03/05/the-bronze-age-harold-lucas-fights-to-preserve-bronzevilles-historic-heritage/.

Ashford, Douglas. 1982. *British Dogmatism and French Pragmatism: Central–Local Policymaking in the Welfare State*. London: George Allen & Unwin.

Azrael, Jeremy. 1970. "The Internal Dynamics of the CPSU." In *Authoritarian Politic in Modern Society: The Dynamics of Established One-Party Systems*, ed. Samuel Huntington and Clement Moore, 261–83. New York: Basic Books.

Bacharach, Jere L. 1995. *The Restoration and Conservation of Islamic Monuments in Egypt*. Cairo: American University in Cairo Press.

Bacon, Edmund. 1967. *Design of Cities*. New York: Viking Press.

Banfield, Edward C. [1961] 1964. *Political Influence*. New York: The Free Press of Glencoe.

Banting, Keith. 1985. "Institutional Conservatism: Federalism and Pension Reform." In *Canadian Social Welfare Policy: Federal and Provincial Dimensions*, ed. Jacqueline S. Ismael, 48–74. Montreal: McGill-Queens.

Bardhan, Pranab, and Dilip Mookherjee. 2006. *Decentralization and Local Governance in Developing Countries: A Comparative Perspective*. Cambridge, Mass.: MIT Press.

Barnett, A. Doak. 1967. *Cadres, Bureaucracy and Political Power in Communist China*. New York: Columbia University Press.

Barthel, Diane. 1996. *Historic Preservation: Collective Memory and Historical Identity*. New Brunswick, N.J.: Rutgers University Press.

Baudouin, Thierry, and Michèle Collin. 2007. "L'enjeu metropolitain des Halles." *French Politics, Culture & Society* 25, no. 2: 93–114.

Baumgartner, Frank R., and Bryan D. Jones. 1993. *Agendas and Instability in American Politics*. Chicago: University of Chicago Press.

Beijing Municipal Commission of Urban Planning (BMCUP). 2002. *Conservation Planning of 25 Historic Areas in Beijing Old City*. Beijing: Yanshan Publishing House.

Beijing Municipal Policy Research Bureau (BMPRB). 2004. *The Study on Housing Renovation in Historic Preservation Districts in the Old City of Beijing*. Beijing: Beijing Municipality.

Bergen, Kathy. 2009a. "State Hearing on Michael Reese Campus Moved from Sept. 11 to Dec. 4." *Chicago Tribune,* September 8. http://featuresblogs.chicagotribune.com/theskyline/2009/09/state-hearing-on-michael-reese-moved-from-sept-11-to-dec-4-.html.

———. 2009b. "State Historic Preservation Officials Withdraw from Battle to Save Reese Buildings." *Chicago Tribune,* June 29. http://featuresblogs.chicagotribune.com/theskyline/2009/06/state-historic-preservation-officials-withdraw-from-battle-to-save-reese-buildings-.html.

Betancur, John. 2002. "The Politics of Gentrification: The Case of West Town in Chicago." *Urban Affairs Review* 37, no. 6: 780–814.

———. 2005. "Gentrification Before Gentrification? The Plight of Pilsen in Chicago." White paper at Nathalie P. Voorhees Center for Neighborhood and Community Improvement, College of Urban Planning and Public Affairs, University of Illinois at Chicago.

Bigott, Joseph. 2001. *From Cottage to Bungalow: Houses and the Working Class in Metropolitan Chicago, 1869–1929*. Chicago: University of Chicago Press.

Biles, Roger. 1995. *Richard J. Daley: Politics, Race, and the Governing of Chicago*. DeKalb: Northern Illinois University Press.

Bird, Karen. 2004. "Unequal Gains: Patterns of Ethnic Minority Representation in the Political Systems of France, Denmark and Canada." Paper presented to the International Political Science Association RC 14 "Ethnicity and Politics" Meeting, Ottawa, Canada, October.

Blatter, Joachim. 2004. "From 'Spaces of Place' to 'Spaces of Flows'? Territorial and Functional Governance in Cross-Border Regions in Europe and North America." *International Journal of Urban and Regional Research* 28, no. 3: 530–48.

Bluestone, Daniel. 1993. *Constructing Chicago*. New Haven, Conn.: Yale University Press.

————. 1994. "Preservation and Renewal in Post–World War II Chicago." *Journal of Architectural Education* 47, no. 4: 210–23.

Bouly, Sophie de Lesdain. 1999. "Château Rouge, une centralité Africaine à Paris." *Ethnologie Française* 29, no. 1: 86–99.

Boyd, Michelle R. 2008. *Jim Crow Nostalgia: Reconstructing Race in Bronzeville.* Minneapolis: University of Minnesota Press.

Boyer, M. Christine. 1994. *The City of Collective Memory: Its Historical Imagery and Architectural Entertainments.* Cambridge, Mass.: MIT Press.

Brown-Saracino, Japonica. 2007. "Virtuous Marginality: Social Preservationists and the Selection of the Old-Timer." *Theory and Society* 6, no. 5: 437–68.

Bruegmann, Robert. 1997. *The Architects and the City.* Chicago: University of Chicago Press.

Brunn, Stanley. 1974. *Geography and Politics in America.* New York: Harper & Row.

Bullock, Charles S., III. 2010. *Redistricting: The Most Political Activity in America.* Lanham, Md.: Rowman & Littlefield.

Cahan, Richard. 1994. *They All Fall Down: Richard Nickel's Struggle to Save America's Architecture.* Washington, D.C.: Preservation Press.

Caillosse, Jacques, Patrick Le Galès, and Patricia Loncle-Moriceau. 1997. "Les sociétés d'économie mixte locales: outils de quelle action publique?" In *Le Gouvernement des Villes: Territoire et Pouvoir,* ed. Francis Godard, 23–96. Paris: Éditions Descartes et Cie.

Campanella, Thomas J. 2008. *The Concrete Dragon: China's Urban Revolution and What It Means for the World.* New York: Princeton Architectural Press.

Caro, Robert. 1984. *The Power Broker: Robert Moses and the Fall of New York.* New York: Alfred A. Knopf.

Chase, John. 2011. "Emanuel Offers Budget Thoughts, but Leaves Questions." *Chicago Tribune,* February 8. http://newsblogs.chicagotribune.com/clout_st/2011/02/emanuel-offers-budget-thoughts-but-leaves-questions.html.

Chevalier, Louis. 1977. *L'Assassinat de Paris.* Paris: Calmann-Levy.

Chicago Tribune. 2009. "City's Striking Take on Aldermanic Privilege." *Chicago Tribune,* July 27. http://articles.chicagotribune.com/2009-07-27/news/0907260248_1_alderman-congress-plaza-hotel-sidewalk-cafe.

Choay, Francoise. 2001. *The Invention of the Historic Monument.* New York: Cambridge University Press.

Clark, Terry N. 2003. *The City as an Entertainment Machine.* Oxford: Elsevier.

Clifford, Thomas P. 1975. *The Political Machine: An American Institution.* New York: Vantage Press.

Collier, David, ed. 1979. *The New Authoritarianism in Latin America.* Princeton, N.J.: Princeton University Press.

Cooper, Cindy T., and Christopher Mele. 2002. "Urban Redevelopment as Contingent Process: Implicating Everyday Practice in Berlin's Renewal." *City & Community* 1, no. 3: 291–311.

Curran, Winifred, and Euan Hague. 2006. "The Pilsen Building Inventory Project."

Research report by the Department of Geography, DePaul University, Chicago.

Dahl, Robert. 1961. *Who Governs? Democracy and Power in an American City.* New Haven, Conn.: Yale University Press.

Danielson, Michael. 1976. *The Politics of Exclusion.* New York: Columbia University Press.

Datel, Robin E., and Dennis J. Dingemans. 1988. "Why Places are Preserved: Historic Districts in American and European Cities." *Urban Geography* 9, no. 1: 37–52.

De Chenay, Christophe. 2004. "Le 'ventre' de Paris va être de nouveau remodelé." *Le Monde,* February 23.

Deng, Qi. 2003. "Renovation of Old and Dilapidated Houses: Tianqiao Xiejie, Ju'er Hutong and Others." *Beijing City Planning & Construction Review* 91:58–59.

Diméglio, Pierre, and Jodelle Zetlaoui-Léger. 2007. "Les rapports ambigus entre politiques et citoyens: le cas du réaménagement du Quartier des Halles à Paris." *French Politics, Culture & Society* 25, no. 2: 115–40.

Domhoff, William. 1967. *Who Rules America?* Englewood Cliffs, N.J.: Prentice Hall.

Doyle, William. 2003. *The Oxford History of the French Revolution.* New York: Oxford University Press.

Drake, St. Clair, and Horace R. Cayton. [1945] 1993. *Black Metropolis: A Study of Negro Life in a Northern City.* Chicago: University of Chicago Press.

Duckett, Jane. 1998. *The Entrepreneurial State in China: Real Estate and Commerce Departments in Reform Era Tianjin.* London: Routledge.

Edelmann, Frédéric. 2004. "Les Halles à l'heure du choix." *Le Monde,* December 16.

———. 2009. "Le gigantesque projet du Forum des Halles est voté." *Le Monde,* April 12.

Einhorn, Robin L. 1991. *Property Rules: Political Economy in Chicago, 1833–1872.* Chicago: University of Chicago Press.

Fainstein, Susan S. 2010. *The Just City.* Ithaca, N.Y.: Cornell University Press.

Fang, Ke. 2000. *Contemporary Redevelopment in the Inner City of Beijing: Survey, Analysis and Investigation.* Beijing: Architecture and Industry Publishing House.

Feiock, Richard C., ed. 2004. *Metropolitan Governance: Conflict, Competition, and Cooperation.* Washington, D.C.: Georgetown University Press.

———. 2007. "Rational Choice and Regional Governance." *Journal of Urban Affairs* 29, no. 1: 47–63.

Ferman, Barbara. 1996. *Challenging the Growth Machine.* Lawrence: University Press of Kansas.

Fischer, Frank, and John Forester. 1993. *The Argumentative Turn in Policy Analysis and Planning.* Durham, N.C.: Duke University Press.

Fitch, James Marston. 1982. *Historic Preservation: Curatorial Management of the Built World.* New York: McGraw-Hill.

Frank, Karolin. 2002. *Historic Preservation in the USA.* Berlin: Springer.

Freeman, Lance. 2006. *There Goes the 'Hood: Views of Gentrification from the Ground Up.* Philadelphia, Pa.: Temple University Press.

Fremon, David K. 1988. *Chicago Politics Ward by Ward.* Bloomington: Indiana University Press.

Friedberg, Aaron L. 2000. *In the Shadow of the Garrison State.* Princeton, N.J.: Princeton University Press.

Fuchs, Ester R. 1992. *Mayors and Money: Fiscal Policy in New York and Chicago.* Chicago: University of Chicago Press.

Gao, Baoyi. 2003. "Experts' Comment on the Reconstruction of Yongdingmen Gatetower." *Beijing City Planning & Construction Review* 90:54–55.

Gaubatz, Piper. 1999. "China's Urban Transformation: Patterns and Process of Morphological Change in Beijing, Shanghai and Guangzhou." *Urban Studies* 36:1495–521.

Gilboa, Itzhak. 2010. *Rational Choice.* Cambridge, Mass.: MIT Press.

Gosnell, Harold F. 1937. *Machine Politics: Chicago Model.* Chicago: University of Chicago Press.

Gourevitch, Peter. 1978. "Reforming the Napoleonic State: The Creation of Regional Governments in France and Italy." In *Territorial Politics in Industrial Nations,* ed. Sidney Tarrow, Peter J. Katzenstein, and Luigi Graziano, 28–63. New York: Praeger.

Grams, Diane. 2005. "Territorial Markers: A Case Study of the Public Art of Bronzeville." Working paper, Cultural Policy Center at the University of Chicago.

Grams, Diane. 2010. *Producing Local Color: Art Networks in Ethnic Chicago.* Chicago: University of Chicago Press.

Grimshaw, William. 1992. *Bitter Fruit: Black Politics and the Chicago Machine, 1931–1991.* Chicago: University of Chicago Press.

Grodzins, Morton. 1966. *The American System: A New View of Government in the United States.* Chicago: Rand McNally.

Guterbock, Thomas M. 1980. *Machine Politics in Transition: Party and Community in Chicago.* Chicago: University of Chicago Press.

Hadoulis, John. 2004. "Greek Antiquities in the Doldrums." *Athens News,* March 26. http://www.athensnews.gr/old_issue/13059/11077.

Haegel, Florence. 1994. *Un Maire à Paris: Mise en scène d'un nouveau rôle politique.* Paris: Presses de la Fondation Nationale des Sciences Politiques.

Hall, Peter. 1998. *Cities in Civilization.* New York: Pantheon.

Hall, Peter A. 1986. *Governing the Economy: The Politics of State Intervention in Britain and France.* New York: Oxford University Press.

Halliday, Terence C., and Bruce G. Carruthers. 2007. "The Recursivity of Law: Global Norm-Making and National Law-Making in the Globalization of Corporate Insolvency Regimes." *American Journal of Sociology* 111:1135–202.

Harding, Harry. 1981. *Organizing China: The Problem of Bureaucracy 1949–1976.* Stanford, Calif.: Stanford University Press.

Harrop, Martin, and William Miller. 1987. *Elections and Voters.* Basingstoke, Hampshire: Macmillan Education.

Harsin, Jill. 2002. *Barricades: The War of the Streets in Revolutionary Paris 1830–1848*. New York: Palgrave.

Hild, Theodore. 2001. "The Chicago Heritage Committee and the New Preservation." *Journal of Illinois History* 4, no. 3: 1–22.

Hirsch, Arnold R. [1983] 1988. *Making the Second Ghetto: Race and Housing in Chicago 1940–1960*. Chicago: University of Chicago Press.

Hoffman, Lily M., and Jiri Musil. 1999. "Culture Meets Commerce: Tourism in Postcommunist Prague." In *The Tourist City*, ed. Dennis R. Judd and Susan S. Fainstei, 179–97. New Haven, Conn.: Yale University Press.

Holmes, MacDonald. 1944. *The Geographical Basis of Government*. Sydney: Angus and Robertson.

Hooghe, Liesbet, and Gary Marks. 2003. "Unraveling the Central State, but How? Types of Multi-Level Governance." *The American Political Science Review* 97, no. 2: 233–43.

Horak, Martin. 2007. *Governing the Post-communist City: Institutions and Democratic Development in Prague*. Toronto: University of Toronto Press.

Huang, Yasheng. 1996. *Inflation and Investment Controls in China: The Political Economy of Central–Local Relations during the Reform Era*. New York: Cambridge University Press.

Hunter, Floyd. 1953. *Community Power Structure*. Chapel Hill: University of North Carolina Press.

Hyra, Derek. 2006. "Racial Uplift? Intra-racial Class Conflict and the Economic Revitalization of Harlem and Bronzeville." *City & Community* 5, no. 1: 71–92.

———. 2008. *The New Urban Renewal: The Economic Transformation of Harlem and Bronzeville*. Chicago: University of Chicago Press.

Ikenberry, G. John. 1988. "Conclusion: An Institutional Approach to American Foreign Economic Policy." In *The State and American Foreign Economic Policy*, ed. G. John Ikenberry, David A. Lake, and Michael Mastanduno, 219–43. Ithaca, N.Y.: Cornell University Press.

Immergut, Ellen M. 1992. "The Rules of the Game: The Logic of Health Policy-making in France, Switzerland, and Sweden." In *Structuring Politics: Historical Institutionalism in Comparative Analysis*, ed. Sven Steinmo, Kathleen Thelen, and Frank Longstreth, 57–89. Cambridge: Cambridge University Press.

Innes, Judith E., David E. Booher, and Sarah Di Vittorio. 2011. "Strategies for Megaregion Governance." *Journal of the American Planning Association* 77, no. 1: 55–67.

Institute de la Décentralisation. 2004. *Pouvoirs Locaux*, no. 63.

Jacobs, Jane. 1961. *The Death and Life of Great American Cities*. New York: Vintage Books.

Jordan, David. 1996. *Transforming Paris: The Life and Labors of Baron Haussmann*. Chicago: University of Chicago Press.

Jowitt, Kenneth. 1971. *Revolutionary Breakthroughs and National Development: The Case of Romania, 1944–1965.* Berkeley: University of California Press.

Judd, Dennis R., and Susan S. Fainstein. 1999. *The Tourist City.* New Haven, Conn.: Yale University Press.

Kamin, Blair. 2009. "Michael Reese Hospital Preservation: Preservationists Stumble in Bid to Protect Campus." *Chicago Tribune,* December 20. http://articles.chicagotribune.com/2009-12-20/news/0912190210_1_preservationists-campus-historic-places.

———. 2010. "Daley Reneges on Plan to Save Prairie Style Landmark." *Chicago Tribune,* November 4. http://articles.chicagotribune.com/2010-11-04/news/ct-met-kamin-michael-reese-1105-20101104_1_michael-reese-hospital-campus-chicago-architects-schmidt-building.

Kaufman, Ned. 2009. *Place, Race, and Story: Essays on the Past and Future of Historic Preservation.* London: Routledge.

Keating, Michael. 2003. "The Invention of Regions: Political Restructuring and Territorial Governance in Western Europe." In *State/Space: A Reader,* ed. Neil Brenner, Bob Jessop, Martin Jones, and Gordon Macleod, 256–77. Oxford: Blackwell.

Kesselman, M. 1970. "Over-institutionalisation and Political Constraint: The Case of France." *Comparative Politics* (October): 21–44.

King, David. 1997. *Turf Wars: How Congressional Committees Claim Jurisdiction.* Chicago: University of Chicago Press.

Kleppner, Paul. 1985. *Chicago Divided: The Making of a Black Mayor.* DeKalb: Northern Illinois University Press.

Knox, Douglas. 2005. "Ward System." In *The Encyclopedia of Chicago,* ed. Janice L. Reiff, Ann Durkin Keating, and James R. Grossman. http://www.encyclopedia.chicagohistory.org/pages/1316.html.

Kohli, Atul. 2004. *State-Directed Development: Political Power and Industrialization in the Global Periphery.* Cambridge: Cambridge University Press.

Kong, Fanzhi. 2001. "Exploring and Restoring the Site of the Eastern Imperial Wall and the Protection of the Whole Imperial City." *Beijing Cultural Relics and Museum* 26:5–15.

———. 2002. "The Construction of the City Walls Site Parks and the Preservation of the Old City Walls of Beijing." *Beijing Cultural Relics and Museum* 28: 5–17.

Koval, John P., Larry Bennett, Michael I. J. Bennett, Fassil Demissie, Roberta Garner, and Kiljoong Kim, eds. 2006. *The New Chicago: A Social and Cultural Analysis.* Philadelphia: Temple University Press.

Kwok, Kian Woon, and Kee Hong Low. 2002. "Cultural Policy and the City-State: Singapore and the New Asian Renaissance." In *Global Culture: Media, Arts, Policy, and Globalization,* ed. Diana Crane, Nobuko Kawashima, and Ken'ichi Kawasaki, 149–68. London: Routledge.

Lamont, Michèle, and Virág Molnár. 2002. "The Study of Boundaries in the Social Sciences." *Annual Review of Sociology* 28:167–95.

Le Galès, Patrick. 2006. "The Ongoing March of Decentralization within the Post-Jacobin State." In *Changing France: The Politics That Markets Make,* ed. Pepper D. Culpepper, Peter A. Hall, and Bruno Palier, 219–43. New York: Palgrave Macmillan.

Leibfried, Stephan, and Paul Pierson, eds. 1995. *European Social Policy: Between Fragmentation and Integration.* Washington, D.C.: Brookings Institute.

Levy, Jonah D. 1999. *Tocqueville's Revenge: State, Society, and Economy in Contemporary France.* Cambridge, Mass.: Harvard University Press.

Lieberman, Evan. 2003. *Race and Regionalism in the Politics of Taxation in Brazil and South Africa.* Cambridge: Cambridge University Press.

———. 2009. *Boundaries of Contagion: How Ethnic Politics Have Shaped Government Responses to AIDS.* Princeton, N.J.: Princeton University Press.

Lieberthal, Kenneth G., and David M. Lampton, eds. 1992. *Bureaucracy, Politics, and Decision Making in Post-Mao China.* Los Angeles: University of California Press.

Lieberthal, Kenneth G., and Michel Oksenberg. 1988. *Policy Making in China: Leaders, Structures, and Processes.* Princeton, N.J.: Princeton University Press.

Logan, John, and Harvey Molotch. 1987. *Urban Fortunes: The Political Economy of Place.* Berkeley: University of California Press.

Logelin, Edward C. 1957. "This Is Chicago Dynamic." *Inland Architect* 1:9–10.

Long, Xinmin. 2003. "Enhance Understanding and Fix Responsibility to Raise Cultural Relics Undertaking to a New Level." *Beijing Cultural Relics and Museums* 31:5–12.

Lorrain, Dominique. 1991. "Public Goods and Private Operation in France." In *Local Government in Europe: Trends and Developments,* ed. Richard Batley and Gerry Stoker, 89–109. London: Macmillan.

Lowe, David. 2000. *Lost Chicago.* New York: Watson-Guptill.

Lowenthal, David. 1985. *The Past Is a Foreign Country.* Cambridge: Cambridge University Press.

Lowi, Theodore J. 1967. "Machine Politics—Old and New." *The Public Interest* 9:84–92.

———. [1969] 1979. *The End of Liberalism: The Second Republic of the United States.* New York: W. W. Norton.

Lowry, William R. 2003. *Dam Politics: Restoring America's Rivers.* Washington, D.C.: Georgetown University Press.

Ma, Laurence J. C., and Fulong Wu. 2005. "Restructuring the Chinese City: Diverse Process and Reconstituted Space." In *Restructuring the Chinese City: Changing Society, Economy and Space,* ed. Laurence J. C. Ma and Fulong Wu, 1–20. London: Routledge.

MacPherson, C. B. 1977. *The Life and Times of Liberal Democracy.* Oxford: Oxford University Press.

Maidenberg, Micah. 2010. "Weekend Reading: Alderman Solis." *Chicago Journal,* March 16. http://chicagojournal.com/Blogs/Near-Loop-Wire/04-16-2010/Weekend_reading:_Alderman_Solis.

McCubbins, Matthew, Roger Noll, and Barry Weingast. 1989. "Structure and Process, Politics and Policy: Administrative Arrangements and the Political Control of Agencies." *Virginia Law Review* 75, no. 2, Symposium on the Law and Economics of Bargaining (Mar. 1989): 431–82.

Mertha, Andrew. 2005a. "China's 'Soft' Centralization: Shifting *Tiao/Kuai* Authority Relations." *The China Quarterly* 184:791–810.

———. 2005b. *The Politics of Piracy: Intellectual Property in Contemporary China.* Ithaca, N.Y.: Cornell University Press.

Meyer, John, and W. Richard Scott. 1983. *Organizational Environments: Ritual and Rationality.* Beverly Hills, Calif.: Sage.

Meyer, John, W. Richard Scott, and David Strang. 1987. "Centralization, Fragmentation, and School District Complexity." *Administrative Science Quarterly* 32, no. 2: 186–201.

Mihalopoulos, Dan. 2008. "Unwritten Rule Is Out for Kid's Museum: Alderman Can't Kill Deal Simply Because the Site Falls within His Ward." *Chicago Tribune,* June 5: 1.

Mihalopoulos, Dan, and Noreen S. Ahmed-Ullah. 2008. "Children's Museum Clears 2nd Hurdle: City Council Zoning Panel Backs Grant Park Move, but Foes File Suit." *Chicago Tribune,* June 6: 1.

Mihalopoulos, Dan, Robert Becker, and Darnell Little. 2008. "Tribune Investigation: Neighborhoods for Sale." *Chicago Tribune,* January 27–29.

Miller, Donald L. 1996. *City of the Century: The Epic of Chicago and the Making of America.* New York: Simon & Schuster.

Miller, Gary. 1981. *Cities by Contract: The Politics of Incorporation.* Cambridge: Massachusetts Institute of Technology Press.

Mills, C. Wright. 1956. *The Power Elite.* New York: Oxford University Press.

Mimura, Hiroshi. 1989. *Development and Conservation of the Traditional Inner City of Kyoto and Its Wooden Houses.* Kyoto: Kyoto University Department of Architecture.

Morgan, David, and Patrice Mareschal. 1999. "Central-City/Suburban Inequality and Metropolitan Political Fragmentation." *Urban Affairs Review* 34, no. 4: 578–95.

Mufson, Steven. 1997. "Beijing's Newest Invaders: City That Defied Conquering Hordes Being Leveled by Developers." *The Washington Post,* August 26: A1.

Mumford, Lewis. 1961. *The City in History: Its Origins, Its Transformations, and Its Prospects.* San Diego, Calif.: Harcourt.

Murtagh, William J. 2006. *Keeping Time: The History and Theory of Preservation in America.* Hoboken, N.J.: Wiley.

Naquin, Susan. 2000. *Peking: Temples and City Life, 1400–1900.* Berkeley: University of California Press.

Newman, Harvey K. 2001. "Historic Preservation Policy and Regime Politics in Atlanta." *Journal of Urban Affairs* 23, no. 1: 71–86.

Oksenberg, Michel, and James Tong. 1991. "The Evolution of Central-Provincial Fiscal Relations in China, 1971–1984: The Formal System." *China Quarterly* 125: 1–32.

Olson, Mancur. 1971. *The Logic of Collective Action*. Cambridge, Mass.: Harvard University Press.

Orfield, Gary. 1974–75. "Federal Policy, Local Power, and Metropolitan Segregation." *Political Science Quarterly* 89, no. 4: 777–802.

Ostrom, Vincent, Charles M. Tiebout, and Robert Warren. 1961. "The Organization of Government in Metropolitan Areas: A Theoretical Inquiry." *American Political Science Review* 55:831–42.

Paddison, Ronan. 1983. *The Fragmented State: The Political Geography of Power*. New York: St. Martin's Press.

Page, Max, and Randall Mason, eds. 2004. *Giving Preservation a History: Histories of Historic Preservation in the United States*. London: Routledge.

Palmer, Monte, Ali Leila, and El Sayed Yassin. 1989. *The Egyptian Bureaucracy*. Cairo: American University in Cairo Press.

Paris Projet. 1983. "Questions au Maire de Paris, M. Jacques Chirac." *Numéro* 23–24: 8–15.

Park, Robert E., and Ernest W. Burgess. 1925. *The City: Suggestions for Investigation of Human Behavior in the Urban Environment*. Chicago: University of Chicago Press.

Pateman, Carole. 1970. *Participation and Democratic Theory*. Cambridge: Cambridge University Press.

Pattillo, Mary E. 2007. *Black on the Block: The Politics of Race and Class in the City*. Chicago: University of Chicago Press.

Paulen, Francoise. 1997. *The Amsterdam Social Housing Atlas*. Amsterdam: Architecture & Nature.

Pierson, Paul. 1995. "Fragmented Welfare States: Federal Institutions and the Development of Social Policy." *Governance: An International Journal of Policy and Administration* 8, no. 4: 449–78.

Polsby, Nelson. 1963. *Community Power and Political Theory*. New Haven, Conn.: Yale University Press.

Porter, Jonathan. 1999. *Macau: The Imaginary City*. Boulder, Colo.: Westview Press.

Pryor, Frederic L. 1973. *Property and Industrial Organization in Communist and Capitalist Nations*. Bloomington: Indiana University Press.

Putnam, Robert D. 1993. *Making Democracy Work: Civic Traditions in Modern Italy*. Princeton, N.J.: Princeton University Press.

Ramnoux, Sébastien. 2008. "Delanoë se rappelle au Grand Paris de Sarkozy." *Le Parisien*, December 8.

Rast, Joel. 1999. *Remaking Chicago: The Political Origins of Urban Industrial Change*. DeKalb: Northern Illinois University Press.

Reichl, Alexander J. 1997. "Historic Preservation and Progrowth Politics in U.S. Cities." *Urban Affairs Review* 32, no. 4: 513–35.

Ren, Xuefei. 2011. *Building Globalization: Transnational Architecture Production in Urban China.* Chicago: University of Chicago Press.

Riegl, Alois. [1903] 1982. "The Modern Cult of Monuments: Its Character and Its Origin." *Oppositions* 25:21–51.

Riker, William H. 1964. *Federalism: Origin, Operation and Significance.* Boston: Little, Brown.

Rochefort, David A., and Roger W. Cobb. 1994. *The Politics of Problem Definition: Shaping the Policy Arena.* Lawrence: University Press of Kansas.

Rodden, Jonathan. 2004. "Comparative Federalism and Decentralization: On Meaning and Measurement." *Comparative Politics* 36, no. 4: 481–500.

Royko, Mike. 1970. "There's Gold in Zoning Laws." *Chicago Daily News,* January 14.

Ruble, Blair A. 2001. *Second Metropolis: Pragmatic Pluralism in Gilded Age Chicago, Silver Age Moscow, and Meiji Osaka.* Cambridge: Cambridge University Press and Woodrow Wilson Center Press.

Sabbah, Catherine. 2008. "Le Grand Paris à la recherché d'une nouvelle gouvernance." *Les Echos,* November 27.

Sadran, Pierre. 2004. "Public–Private Partnership in France: A Polymorphous and Unacknowledged Category of Public Policy." *International Review of Administrative Science* 70, no. 2: 233–51.

Saito, Leland T. 2009a. "From 'Blighted' to 'Historic': Race, Economic Development, and Historic Preservation in San Diego, California." *Urban Affairs Review* 45, no. 2: 166–87.

———. 2009b. *The Politics of Exclusion: The Failure of Race-Neutral Policies in Urban America.* Stanford, Calif.: Stanford University Press.

Sasportas, Valérie. 2010. "Paris prêt à lancer les grands travaux au Forum des Halles." *Le Figaro,* March 26.

Sassen, Saskia. 1994. *Cities in a World Economy.* Thousand Oaks, Calif.: Pine Forge Press.

———. 2001. *The Global City: New York, London, Tokyo.* Princeton, N.J.: Princeton University Press.

Savitch, H. V. 1988. *Post-Industrial Cities: Politics and Planning in New York, Paris, and London.* Princeton, N.J.: Princeton University Press.

Savitch, H. V., and Paul Kantor. 2002. *Cities in the International Marketplace: The Political Economy of Urban Development in North America and Western Europe.* Princeton, N.J.: Princeton University Press.

Savitch, H. V., and Ronald K. Vogel. 2000. "Metropolitan Consolidation versus Metropolitan Governance in Louisville." *State and Local Government Review* 32, no. 3: 198–212.

Sawislak, Karen. 1995. *Smoldering City: Chicagoans and the Great Fire, 1871–1874.* Chicago: University of Chicago Press.

Sayre, Wallace, and Herbert Kaufman. 1960. *Governing New York City: Politics in the Metropolis.* New York: Russell Sage Foundation.

Schattschneider, E. E. 1960. *The Semisovereign People: A Realist's View of Democracy in America.* New York: Holt, Rinehart and Winston.

Schmidt, Vivien A. 1990. *Democratizing France: The Political and Administrative History of Decentralization.* Cambridge, England: Cambridge University Press.

Schurmann, Franz. 1966. *Ideology and Organization in Communist China.* Berkeley: University of California Press.

Schwieterman, Joseph P., and Dana M. Caspall. 2006. *The Politics of Place: A History of Zoning in Chicago.* Chicago: Lake Claremont Press.

Seligman, Amanda. 2005. *Block by Block: Neighborhoods and Public Policy on Chicago's West Side.* Chicago: University of Chicago Press.

Shapiro, Ian, Stephen Skowronek, and Daniel Galvin, eds. 2006. *Rethinking Political Institutions: The Art of the State.* New York: New York University Press.

Shen, Yurong. 2002. "The Whole Story of Demolishing Beijing City Wall." *Beijing City Planning & Construction Review* 86:61–64.

Shirk, Susan. 1993. *The Political Logic of Economic Reform in China.* Berkeley: University of California Press.

Simpson, Dick. 2001. *Rogues, Rebels, and Rubber Stamps: The Politics of the Chicago City Council from 1863 to the Present.* Boulder, Colo.: Westview Press.

Smith, Hedrick. 1989. *The Power Game: How Washington Works.* New York: Ballantine Books.

Smith, Neil. 1996. *The New Urban Frontier: Gentrification and the Revanchist City.* London: Routledge.

Smyrl, Marc. 2004. "France: Challenging the Unitary State." In *Federalism and Territorial Cleavages,* ed. Ugo M. Amoretti and Nancy Bermeo, 201–26. Baltimore, Md.: Johns Hopkins University Press.

Spielman, Fran. 2011. "Daley Wants Old Michael Reese Site Turned into Technology Park." *Chicago Sun-Times,* May 11. http://www.suntimes.com/5321948-417/daley-wants-old-michael-reese-site-turned-into-technology-park.html.

Steinmo, Sven. 2001. "Institutionalism." In *International Encyclopedia of the Social and Behavior Sciences 11,* ed. Neil J. Smelser and Paul B. Baltes, 7554–58. Oxford: Elsevier.

Steinmo, Sven, Kathleen Thelen, and Frank Longstreth. 1992. *Structuring Politics: Historical Institutionalism in Comparative Analysis.* Cambridge: Cambridge University Press.

Stevenson, Angela. 1996. "Lost Treasures of Bronzeville." *Chicago Sun-Times,* May 28.

Stone, Deborah. 2002. *Policy Paradox: The Art of Political Decision Making.* New York: W. W. Norton.

Strom, Elizabeth. 2002. "Converting Pork into Porcelain: Cultural Institutions and Downtown Development." *Urban Affairs Review* 38, no. 1: 3–32.

Suleiman, Ezra. 1974. *Politics, Power, and Bureaucracy in France*. Princeton, N.J.: Princeton University Press.

———. 1978. *Elites in French Society: The Politics of Survival*. Princeton, N.J.: Princeton University Press.

———. 1987. *Private Power and Centralization in France: The Notaires and the State*. Princeton, N.J.: Princeton University Press.

Sutcliffe, Anthony. 1993. *Paris: An Architectural History*. New Haven, Conn.: Yale University Press.

Suttles, Gerald D. 1972. *The Social Construction of Communities*. Chicago: University of Chicago Press.

———. 1990. *The Man-Made City: The Land-Use Confidence Game in Chicago*. Chicago: University of Chicago Press.

Tarrow, Sidney. 1977. *Between Center and Periphery: Grassroots Politicians in Italy and France*. New Haven, Conn.: Yale University Press.

Teaford, John C. 1979. *City and Suburbs: The Political Fragmentation of Metropolitan America, 1850–1970*. Baltimore, Md.: Johns Hopkins University Press.

TenHoor, Meredith. 2007. "Architecture and Biopolitics at Les Halles." *French Politics, Culture & Society* 25, no. 2: 73–92.

Thale, Christopher. 2005. "Aldermanic Privilege." In *The Encyclopedia of Chicago*, ed. Janice L. Reiff, Ann Durkin Keating, and James R. Grossman. http://www.encyclopedia.chicagohistory.org/pages/2197.html.

Tiebout, Charles M. 1956. "A Pure Theory of Local Expenditures." *Journal of Political Economy* 64, no. 5: 416–24.

Townsend, James. 1974. *Politics in China*. Boston: Little, Brown.

Trasforini, Maria Antonietta. 2002. "The Immaterial City: Ferrara, a Case Study of Urban Culture in Italy." In *Global Culture: Media, Arts, Policy, and Globalization,* ed. Diana Crane, Nobuko Kawashima, and Ken'ichi Kawasaki, 169–90. London: Routledge.

Travis, Dempsey J. 2005. "Bronzeville." In *The Encyclopedia of Chicago*, ed. Janice L. Reiff, Ann Durkin Keating, and James R. Grossman. http://www.encyclopedia.chicagohistory.org/pages/171.html.

Truman, David B. 1960. *The Governmental Process*. New York: Knopf.

Tsebelis, George. 1995. "Decision Making in Political Systems: Veto Players in Presidentialism, Parliamentarism, Multicameralism and Multipartyism." *British Journal of Political Science* 25, no. 3: 289–325.

Tung, Anthony M. 2001. *Preserving the World's Great Cities: The Destruction and Renewal of the Historic Metropolis*. New York: Clarkson Potter.

Van Zanten, David. 1994. *Building Paris: Architectural Institutions and the Transformation of the French Capital, 1830–1870*. New York: Cambridge University Press.

Vicino, Thomas J. 2008. "The Quest to Confront Suburban Decline: Political Realities and Lessons." *Urban Affairs Review* 43, no. 4: 553–81.

Wakeman, Rosemary. 2007. "Fascinating Les Halles." *French Politics, Culture & Society* 25, no. 2: 46–72.

Walzer, Michael. 1981. "Totalitarianism vs. Authoritarianism." *Dissent* 18:400–403.

Wang, Ju. 2003. *Cheng Ji.* Beijing: Sanlian Bookstore.

Wang, Yin, et al. 2003. "Research on Planning and Design of Yongdingmen and Some Areas Along South Central-Axis Road." *Beijing City Planning & Construction Review* 90: 44–48.

Washburn, Gary. 2008. "Daley Defends System of Aldermanic Zoning Decisions." *Chicago Tribune,* January 29.

Weber, Max. 1978. *Economy and Society: An Outline of Interpretive Sociology.* Ed. Guenther Roth and Claus Wittich. Berkeley: University of California Press.

Webman, Jerry A. 1981. "Centralization and Implementation: Urban Renewal in Great Britain and France." *Comparative Politics* 13, no. 2: 127–48.

Weiher, Gregory. 1991. *The Fractured Metropolis: Political Fragmentation and Metropolitan Segregation.* Albany: State University of New York Press.

While, Aidan. 2006. "Modernism vs. Urban Renaissance: Negotiating Post-war Heritage in English City Centers." *Urban Studies* 43:2399–419.

Whyte, Martin King, and William L. Parish. 1984. *Urban Life in Contemporary China.* Chicago: University of Chicago Press.

Wilson, William Julius. 1990. *The Truly Disadvantaged.* Chicago: University of Chicago Press.

Wollmann, Hellmut. 2010. "Comparing Two Logics of Interlocal Cooperation: The Cases of France and Germany." *Urban Affairs Review* 46, no. 2: 263–92.

Wong, Paul. 1976. *China's Higher Leadership in the Socialist Transition.* New York: The Free Press.

Wright, Vincent. 1974. "Politics and Administration under the French Fifth Republic." *Political Studies* 22, no. 1: 44–65.

Wu, Hung. 2005. *Remaking Beijing: Tiananmen Square and the Creation of a Political Space.* Chicago: University of Chicago Press.

Wu, Liangyong. 1999. *Rehabilitating the Old City of Beijing: A Project in the Ju'er Hutong Neighborhood.* Vancouver: UBC Press.

Xie, Qingshu, A. R. Ghanbari Parsa, and Barry Redding. 2002. "The Emergence of the Urban Land Market in China: Evolution, Structure, Constraints and Perspectives." *Urban Studies* 39:1375–98.

Yang, Dali L. 1997. *Beyond Beijing: Liberalization and the Regions in China.* London: Routledge.

———. 2004. *Remaking the Chinese Leviathan: Market Transition and the Politics of Governance in China.* Stanford, Calif.: Stanford University Press.

Yeoh, Brenda S. A. 2003. *Contesting Space in Colonial Singapore: Power Relations and the Urban Built Environment.* Singapore: Singapore University Press.

Zheng, Bo. 2003. "Dare Not Talk Irresponsibly About the City Walls of the Ming Dynasty." *Beijing City Planning & Construction Review* 91:146–49.

Zukin, Sharon. 1987. "Gentrification: Culture and Capital in the Urban Core." *Annual Review of Sociology* 13:129–47.

———. 1993. *Landscapes of Power: From Detroit to Disney World.* Berkeley: University of California Press.

———. 1996. *The Cultures of Cities.* Cambridge, Mass.: Blackwell.

———. 2010. *The Naked City: The Death and Life of Authentic Urban Places.* New York: Oxford University Press.

Zukowsky, John, ed. 1987. *Chicago Architecture, 1872–1922: Birth of a Metropolis.* Munich: Prestel-Verlag.

(continued from page ii)

Yue Zhang is assistant professor of political science at the University of Illinois at Chicago.